The Siege that Changed the World

The Siege that Changed the World

Paris, 1870–1871

N.S. 'Tank' Nash

Pen & Sword
MILITARY

First published in Great Britain in 2021 by
PEN & SWORD MILITARY
an imprint of
Pen & Sword Books Ltd
47 Church Street
Barnsley
South Yorkshire
S70 2AS

ISBN 978-1-52679-029-3

Typeset by Concept, Huddersfield HD4 5JL
Printed and bound in the UK by CPI Group (UK) Ltd, Croydon CR0 4YY

Pen & Sword Books Limited incorporates the imprints of Atlas, Archaeology,
Aviation, Discovery, Family History, Fiction, History, Maritime, Military,
Military Classics, Politics, Select, Transport, True Crime, Air World,
Frontline Publishing, Leo Cooper, Remember When, Seaforth Publishing,
The Praetorian Press, Wharncliffe Local History, Wharncliffe Transport,
Wharncliffe True Crime and White Owl.

For a complete list of Pen & Sword titles please contact
PEN & SWORD BOOKS LIMITED
47 Church Street, Barnsley, South Yorkshire, S70 2AS, England
E-mail: enquiries@pen-and-sword.co.uk
Website: www.pen-and-sword.co.uk

Contents

List of Maps vii

Acknowledgements viii

Abbreviations used in chapter notes ix

  1. On Sieges 1

  2. The Background: Hubris and the Great Exposition 5

  3. The Protagonists – The French 13

  4. The Protagonists – The Prussians 24

  5. … and So, To War 30

  6. Wissembourg, Spicheren and Frœschwiller, 4–6 August 1870 39

  7. Prussia Invades, Metz Invested 48

  8. Beaumont and Sédan: 29 August–27 October 59

  9. Sédan: The Aftermath 73

10. September: Investment of Paris and the Fall of Strasbourg 92

11. October: Civil Disorder and the Fall of Metz 108

12. November: Coulmiers and *La Grande Sortie* 133

13. December: Belfort, Amiens, Orléans 155

14. January: A New German Empire 171

15. January: Bombardment – Ethics and Practicality 178

16. January: Chanzy, Faidherbe, Bourbaki and Armistice 188

17. February: Election, Peace and Reparations – The Gathering Storm 206

18. March: Rise of the Commune 215

19. March: Thirteen Important Days 233

20. April: Civil War 240

21. May: Rossel and the Fall of Fort Issy 254

22. May: Bloody Week 260

23. Retribution 274

24. Did the Siege of Paris Change the World? 278

Bibliography 283

Index 287

List of Maps

Prussia and all the German states   3

The disposition of forces on the French/German border, 1 August 1870   34

The site of the Battle of Frœschwiller   43

The juxtaposition of Saarbrücken and Spicheren   46

The area of France eventually occupied by Prussia   49

The significance of Metz as a communication centre   52

Deployments around Metz, 14–15 August   54

Country over which much of the Franco-Prussian war was waged   61

Sédan and the area of the battle   65

The encirclement of Sédan, 1 September 1870   67

Paris and outlying villages   90

The siege lines around Paris   94

Strasbourg and area 100

La Grande Sortie – disposition of forces, 30 November 1870 148

The area over which *La Grande Sortie* was fought 150

Plan of Fort Issy 182

Battle of Buzenval 195

The demise of the French Army of the East 203

Paris – North-west 1 218

Paris – North-west 2 250

Paris – South-west 266

Acknowledgements

The Franco-Prussian war has attracted the attention of many historians and, predictably, the majority are French or German. This book quotes, wherever possible, from those contemporary sources. Initial research was largely the work of the pre-eminent British military historian of the twentieth century, Professor Sir Michael Howard. He wrote the definitive and masterly work in 1961. In 1965 Alistair Horne wrote on the same topic, but his focus was on the social/political aspects of the war and the civil war that followed.

This book seeks to navigate a line between those distinguished historians. In the interests of brevity, it avoids detailed accounts of battles, other than to place events in their chronological context. Where possible, I have acknowledged the copyright of maps, photographs and illustrations, but there are many cases where I cannot. The maps from Stephen Badsey's work are, demonstrably, first class and their use is gratefully acknowledged.

Robert Tombs, Professor Emeritus of French History at Cambridge University and expert in this topic, was kind enough to offer his advice on my conclusions in Chapter 24. Lieutenant Colonel W.W.T. Gowans considered my draft text, as he has in my previous books. I am grateful to him, yet again, for his unstinting support and shrewd appraisal that contributes to my work. John Woody researched the *Illustrated London News* on my behalf and provided me with source material, evidenced by the wonderful map of Paris on page 90.

Linne Matthews has been my forensically effective text editor and working with her was, as always, a great pleasure. She excised my egregious errors, and polished and enhanced the text. Her oft-expressed view that 'we are on the same side' is why I habitually seek her services. Finally, Pen & Sword have produced, as is their wont, a first-rate book, and I applaud the production and design skills of Matt Jones and Noel Sadler, who have combined to make a silk purse from the pig's ear of legend.

I hope that, in these pages, I have managed to show that indeed the Siege of Paris *did* change the world. However, I leave the reader to be the judge.

Tank Nash
Malmesbury, Wiltshire
September 2021

Abbreviations used in notes

DT   *Enquête parlementaire sur les Actes du Gouvernement de la Défense: Depositions des Témoins* (Versailles, 1873).

Guerre   *La Guerre de 1870–71, Publiée par la Revue d'Histoire, rédigée à la Section historique de l'Etat- Major de l' Armée* (Paris, 1901–1913).

GGS   German General Staff, *The Franco German War 1870–71*, 5 vols.

HHSA   Haus-Hof-und Staatsarchiv (Vienna).

MMK   Moltke, H.C.B., von Graf, *Militärische Korrespondenz: Aus den Dienstschriften des Krieges 1870–71* (Berlin, 1897).

PRO   Public Record Office, Foreign Office files (Kew).

SHAT   Service Historique de l'Armée de Terre (Vincennes).

ILN   *Illustrated London News.*

Chapter One

On Sieges

Sieges have been a feature of warfare since man first took up arms. A perusal of the internet reveals that there had been 2,075 sieges, worldwide, from the birth of Christ until 1900. (*I counted them*! Author's note.) The bulk of these occurred in the period 1500–1899.

Most sieges are long forgotten, but some are dimly remembered long after the event; Badajoz, Petersburg, Metz, Mafeking and Kut are examples. All of these had a major impact in a campaign, but their significance was restricted to the theatre in which they were located.

Rarely does a general willingly allow himself to be besieged because, by doing so, he cedes the initiative to his adversary. However, a siege situation is never an isolated event because it is invariably the consequence of earlier battlefield reverses and, in every case, it is the cutting of the logistic chain that completes the investment. The longer the siege and the larger the size of the besieged population, the greater is the chance of starvation being a factor in the outcome. Simple human needs and their supply are invariably critical.

Most military campaigns are eventually decided by the superiority of one side over the other in supply terms. Examples of that are Napoleon in 1812 and Rommel at Second Alamein in 1942. In both cases, the defeated were at the end of vastly over-extended lines of communications and suffered the consequent supply difficulties. These are precisely the same circumstances that led to the loss of Kut in 1916. The logistic issue is why Dien Bien Phu (1954) was a siege and Khe Sanh (1968) was not.

The logistic support of an army is mundane, routine and relatively unimportant, *until it fails*. Then, within forty-eight hours it begets a crisis. Men (and horses) must be fed and watered, weapon systems must have ammunition, vehicles must have fuel and be maintained, the wounded must be cared for and the dead must be buried in marked graves.[1] The list is endless and tedious, and 'without supplies neither a general nor a soldier is good for anything'[2] – a view expressed by Clearchus well over 2,000 years ago.

There is, however, one siege that changed world history and its effects are still evident today. That is the Siege of Paris (1870–71). The siege was the central element in the Franco-Prussian War. It was the catalyst for profound social, diplomatic, political and military change, at an international level, for decades. The Siege of Paris was the second and the most important of two sieges in which the effect was cumulative. Yet the previous capture of Napoleon III by the Prussians at Sédan and the loss of an entire army led by Marshal de MacMahon led directly to the fall of the Second Empire and the formation of a republican form of French government.

The fall of Sédan hastened the investment of Paris, seventeen days later. The salvation of Paris was now vested in the army of Marshal Bazaine, which was besieged in the fortress of Metz. His was the only force that could lift the Siege of Paris, but starvation in Metz brought about its capitulation on 27 October 1870. From this point, the result of the Franco-Prussian War and the fate of Paris were never in doubt.

The Siege of Paris had three significant differences that set it apart from most other sieges. First was the enormous captive population of 2 million, all of whom had to be fed and watered daily.[3] The second was the internal domestic strife amongst those 2 million that vastly complicated the defence of the city, and third, the barbarous civil war that erupted after the French had capitulated to the Prussians.

It would be fallacious to suppose that any besieging force is at ease, comfortable and well supplied. It has to ensure that its own logistic chain functions efficiently, especially when that chain has to traverse hostile territory. That said, time is always on the side of the besieger. He can dictate the manner of the siege and does not have to expend lives in attempts to breach the defences that oppose him. Starvation takes several weeks to manifest itself and patience, and yet more patience, will usually reap rich rewards. The encirclement of the enemy position calls for constant vigilance, as a 'breakout' is always a favoured option for those incarcerated. During the Siege of Paris there were several such forays.

In examining the Siege of Paris, it would be superficial to take it in isolation because it was an integral part of a much wider military and ideological tapestry. To get the siege into its correct perspective it is necessary to trace the path to war and to compare the capacity of the two protagonists. The sieges of Metz and Paris were the inevitable by-product of French earlier military failures elsewhere.

What started as a purely military matter in 1870 was superseded in early 1871 by social and ideological issues that had far-reaching impact, well beyond the frontiers of France. The armed civil conflict that followed was fuelled by the siege and, arguably, provided the kindling for the Bolshevik revolution in 1917. Communists believe that the Siege of Paris is vastly overshadowed in importance by the Paris Commune and its suppression. Alistair Horne suggested that, to some degree, the collapse of France in 1940 can be attributed to the attitudes stemming from the Commune – formed seventy

years earlier. The Siege of Paris was a 'one-off' in several ways, as this text will
demonstrate.

*   *   *

The events chronicled in this book can be traced back to 1866 and the Austro-
Prussian War, in which the Prussian Army crushed the Austrians in just seven
weeks and inflicted 132,414 casualties killed, wounded or captured for a loss
of only 39,990.[4] This stunning success was due in large measure to the use of
the breech-loading Dreyse needle-gun. The Prussian infantry had a rate of
fire that was 6:1 faster than the Austrians'.[5] After the decisive and final Battle
of Königgrätz, Prussia climbed from the lower range of great powers to the
top, gaining 7 million subjects and 1,300 square miles (3,367km[2]) of territory.[6] The formation of the North German Confederation swallowed up the
existing thirty-nine members of the German Confederation that had been
established in 1815. As part of the expansion process Prussia annexed most

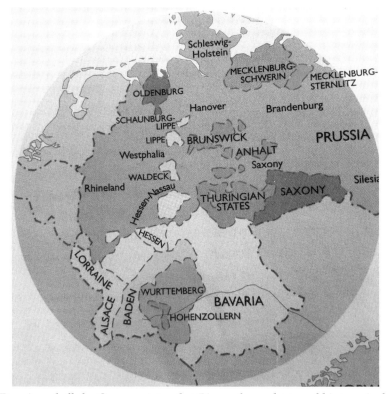

**Prussia and all the German states that Bismarck sought to weld into a single
sovereign nation.** (*Badsey*)

of the northern members, and added the cities of Hamburg, Lübeck and Bremen as well as the states of Saxony, Hesse, Darmstadt, Mecklenburg and the Thuringian duchies.

Notwithstanding the demonstrable power of the Prussian Army, the Chancellor, Bismarck, was conscious that France or Russia, or both, might intervene. In order to obviate any 'unnecessary bitterness of feeling or desire for revenge', King Wilhelm I of Prussia was encouraged by Bismarck to make peace with the Austrians. The approach was successful, and the Austrians accepted Napoleon III in the role of mediator. He fostered the Peace of Prague on 23 August 1866 and, at much the same time, with quite stunning insouciance, demanded that Prussia provide 'compensations' as a reward for France's neutrality. He got a very dusty answer from Bismarck, who recognised that, at sometime in the future, a war with France was very likely. Indeed, the triumphant Prussians, with their army mobilised and deployed, were well placed to attack an unprepared France in 1866. General Moltke urged Bismarck to do so, but without success.[7]

Prussia incorporated all the small German states north of the Main River into the North German Confederation. This made Prussia the dominant force in German affairs and was a first significant, political step towards the creation of a German Empire. However, Bismarck recognised that the advance to Empire might take decades.

Notes

1. Nash, N.S., *Logistics of the Vietnam Wars 1945–1975* (Barnsley, Pen & Sword, 2020), p. 1.
2. Clearchus, 401 BC, 'Speech to the Ten Thousand', quoted in *Xenophon Anabasis*, 1.3, *c.*360 BC (*The Persian Expedition*, tr. Rex Warner, 1949).
3. The city of Leningrad (St Petersburg) had a population of over 3 million when it was besieged for 872 days by the Germans from September 1942.
4. Clodfelter, M., *Warfare and Armed Conflicts: A Statistical Encyclopedia of Casualty and Other Figures, 1492–2015*, 4th ed. (Jefferson, N. Carolina, McFarland, 2017), pp. 183–4.
5. Howard, M., *The Franco-Prussian War* [1961] (Oxon, Routledge, 2006), p. 6.
6. Wawro, G., *The Franco-Prussian War* (Cambridge University Press, 2003), p. 17.
7. *MMK*, pp. 66–70.

Chapter Two

The Background: Hubris and the Great Exposition

The winter of 1866/67 had been wet and miserable in Paris and the adverse weather had inhibited preparations for the planned International Exposition (*Exposition universelle d'art et d'industrie de 1867*), which was due to open on 1 April. However, in late March the weather cleared, the backlog of work was tackled and, to general surprise, Emperor Napoleon III was able to preside at the opening ceremony – on time. Thereafter, the Exposition ran for seven months until 3 November.

The world and his wife came to visit Paris and to view the wonders of the age. A total of 52,000 businesses were represented in the vast principal building (erected on a site that now houses the Eiffel Tower), which measured about 1,600 by 1,300 yards. It was divided into seven regions, 'each representing a branch of human endeavour', and here forty-two countries exhibited in national pavilions.[1] The staff wore national dress and extolled the virtues and products of their homeland. Great Britain sent a highly polished steam locomotive, the USA fielded a field medical unit or 'ambulance'. That country was recovering from the deep wounds of its civil war and had some expertise in modern military medicine. However, somewhat ominously, Prussia played host to Herr Krupp's 50-ton siege gun. This weapon fired a 1,000lb shell and was without comparison. Krupp also exhibited his new steel field guns, a technical advance on the bronze construction that was the current norm. Prussia thought it appropriate to send an equestrian statue of King Wilhelm I, although many in the crowd wondered why they bothered. In contrast, and probably just as unappreciated, Louis Napoleon caused a statue symbolising 'peace' to be erected; this took the unlikely form of a naked lady reclining upon a lion.

The Prussian officers, who visited the Exposition in droves, were fascinated to be offered the chance to view the detailed plans of the comprehensive defences of Paris and the mutually supporting fortresses that ringed the city. This was an early example of French naivety – and the first of so many miscalculations.

The Exposition was proving to be a success on many fronts, although not financially, and the accounts were manipulated to conceal the deficit. Whilst

The Paris Exposition of 1867. (World's Fair *magazine, Vol. VI, No. 3, 1886*)

the Exposition was in full swing the USA completed the purchase of Alaska and Joseph Lister was discovering antiseptic surgery – probably just as well because at about the same time, Nobel was inventing dynamite. Aluminium made its debut, as did petroleum.

In 1867 Paris was *en fête* and, to many visitors, the epitome of sophistication and gracious living. Pickpockets and pimps mingled with street performers and confidence tricksters, all adding to a carnival atmosphere. There was also wholesale debauchery among the more monied residents and their foreign visitors. *Les grandes horizontales* were fully employed; they were numerous and among them was Marie Duplessis, the epitome of the virtuous courtesan. Another, Apollonie Sabatier, was famously polished and socially adept, and 'able to put men of letters at ease amidst the bawdy talk of her salon'. La Paiva, a Russian Jewess, appeared to be particularly predatory in her dealings with the men of Paris. Cora Pearl was English and 'very athletic' (make of that what you will). She had the ability 'to make bored men laugh'.[2] Little wonder she was so popular. Prostitution took off and was conducted on an industrial scale. The demand for the attention of these ladies, and their sisters in the profession, was such that their prices rose to astronomical

Herr Krupp's steel field guns, which, surprisingly, attracted little attention.
(World's Fair *magazine, Vol. VI, No. 3, 1886*)

heights. Countless balls, receptions, luncheons and dinners were held. The theatre, in all its forms, flourished and provided at least a veneer of culture. But all of this was very expensive as the sybarites held sway.

This hedonistic lifestyle was not without hazard, one of which was syphilis, a fearful disease that was rife in the city and incurable. It spread rapidly and with lethal effect. Among the better-known victims of sexual indulgence were Maupassant, Jules de Goncourt, Dumas *fils*, Baudelaire and Manet. Renoir, by happy chance, was not afflicted – he suggested that his apparent immunity was proof of his genius.[3] 'This terrible disease was symptomatic of the whole Second Empire; on the surface, all gaiety and light; and below, sombre purulence, decay and ultimately death.'[4]

Both King Wilhelm I, accompanied by his formidable Chancellor Bismarck, and Alexander III, Tsar of Russia, visited. Louis Napoleon took great pride in showing them both his city, but there was an atmosphere of underlying tension. Wilhelm was aware of the possibility, indeed likelihood, of a war with France. Napoleon, despite his unsophisticated, hubristic political view, was undaunted and made every effort to entertain his guests.

Wilhelm was less than diplomatic when he remarked, 'What marvellous things you have done since I was last here.'[5] That had been in 1815, after Waterloo, in which Prussian troops had played a part in defeating the uncle of Louis.

Bismarck struck a magnificent figure in a pristine white uniform, topped by a helmet that bore a large spread eagle. He was a centre of attention but would not be provoked, and downplayed the crushing defeat that the Prussians had inflicted on the Austrians in the previous year, asserting, 'Thanks to you [the French] no permanent cause of rivalry exists between us and the Court at Vienna.'[6] He was referring to the Peace of Prague, brokered by Napoleon the previous year.

France had suffered political humiliation, that previous year, in Mexico when its Latin-Catholic empire collapsed in disarray. French forces in the theatre, commanded by Marshal of France François Bazaine, were defeated. They were obliged to evacuate, leaving behind the French puppet 'Emperor' Maximilian, a cousin of Napoleon III, who was duly executed by Mexican nationalists. The USA had provided the Mexican nationalists with tacit support and Franco-American relations were adversely affected. France had few allies in 1866.

A year later at the Exposition, all was ostensibly sweetness and light, and the reverses suffered by Napoleon in his search for *La Gloire* had been put aside. In early June, one of the highlights was staged when 31,000 troops paraded, demonstrated and manoeuvred. Napoleon III, flanked by King Wilhelm I and Tsar Alexander II, took the salute. The colourfully uniformed parade, although impressive in size, nevertheless revealed the martial deficiencies of the French Army. The artillery on parade had been used in Crimea, and at Solferino in 1859. The brass and bronze guns looked like antiques and paled into insignificance when compared to Herr Krupp's breech-loading, rifled, steel guns. The grand finale was a mass cavalry charge of '10,000 cuirassiers, carabineers and scouts, which halted only 5 yards from the royal spectators. The cavalrymen stopped in perfect unison and saluted with their drawn sabres to tumultuous applause.[7] That moment was a palpable high.'

The visit of Tsar Alexander II had started on a positive and amiable note as Louis Napoleon made every effort to entertain his distinguished guest, seeking to obviate residual hard feeling from the Crimean War.[8] Nevertheless, although there were isolated instances of barracking as the two monarchs rode together from the parade at Longchamp on 6 June, the catcalling was nothing of consequence. At 1700 hrs, a 22-year-old Polish man called Antoni Berezowski emerged from the crowd, levelled a pistol at the Tsar and fired one round.

He missed and hit an adjacent horse minding its own business.

Young Berezowski was defended at his trial by Étienne Arago. This brought national renown to a republican, who later played a part in politics

Antoni Berezowski (1847–1916), the would-be assassin of Alexander II.

after the fall of the Empire and during the Siege of Paris. Arago was briefly mayor of Paris in late 1871.

The Tsar was monumentally unamused, and the visit ended on a very sour note. Alexander left Paris as soon as possible and three days later, so did his enormous entourage. Louis Napoleon's hopes of securing an accord with Russia were dashed. The would-be assassin spent the next thirty-nine years in prison.

Beginning in 1854, on Louis Napoleon's command, and under the direction of Georges-Eugène Haussmann (usually known as 'Baron Haussmann'), hundreds of old buildings were razed. Around 50 miles (80km) of new avenues were constructed and there was the strictest control on the buildings to be built along them. They were required to be the same height and in a similar style, and to be faced with cream-coloured stone, creating the uniform look of Paris boulevards today. It was a bold and imaginative scheme; what it lacked was any form of compassion for the inhabitants.

Haussmann rebuilt Paris over a period of seventeen years. 'On his own estimation the new boulevards and open spaces displaced 350,000 people ... By 1870, one fifth of the streets in central Paris were his creation; he had spent ... 2.5 billion francs on the city ... One in five Parisian workers was employed in the building trade.'[9]

The rebuilding swept away some of the worst slum areas and in their place created the wide boulevards that are pleasing to the eye. These sweeping boulevards were not just created for their aesthetic value – they had the object of being too wide to barricade and they also provided swift access by the Army to any part of the city. This was the Paris that visitors from around the world came to see, admire and enjoy.

The accommodation that Haussmann razed was not all replaced. The biting resentment of the dispossessed was exacerbated when they visited the Exposition and saw how the other half lived. Unwittingly, by 1871 Haussmann had built not only a city but also a revolution. A young man called Raoul Rigault was a political activist and he, among others, worked hard in the mid-1860s to feed discontent wherever he found it.

In London, an exiled German-Jewish professor had just published a work entitled *Das Kapital* and over the last 150 years, that book has taken on a biblical status in some political circles around the globe. In 1867, from across the Channel, Karl Marx was, unknowingly, articulating the unregimented views of thousands of poor Parisiennes.

Amongst the exotic sights at the Exposition was that of a tethered double-decked balloon in which the famous photographer 'Nadar' took twelve passengers at a time to view Paris from the air. Just three years later, Nadar and balloons were to play an important role in the Siege of Paris.

Baron Georges-Eugène Haussmann (1809–91), Prefect of Paris.

In the early spring of 1868 Paris had an almost inevitable atmosphere of anti-climax. The circus had moved on and now the site had to be cleared. Napoleon III was in poor health, suffering from a gallstone, but he wallowed in the approbation heaped upon the Exposition that had attracted 15 million visitors and, by extension, upon himself. November 1867 had been the high-water mark of the Second Empire but from here it was downhill all the way.

Notes

1. Horne, A., *The Fall of Paris: The Siege and Commune 1870–71* (London, Macmillan, 1965), p. 4.
2. Rounding, V., *Les Grandes Horizontales* (London, Bloomsbury, 2003).
3. Horne, *Paris*, p. 19.
4. Ibid.
5. Tsar Nicholas II to Napoleon III, June 1870.
6. Horne, p. 9.
7. Ibid., p. 11.
8. Crimean War, 1853–56.
9. Clark, T.J., *The Painting of Modern Life: Paris in the Art of Monet and his Followers* (New Jersey, Princeton University Press, 1984), p. 3.

Chapter Three

The Protagonists – The French

In 1859, France was generally perceived to be the most sophisticated, erudite and dominant power in Europe. Its influence was such that the tactics used in the American Civil War were French in origin.[1] However, shrewd observers had noted the rising military strength and prowess of Prussia, which was to be amply demonstrated in 1866. French military scholars were alerted to the need for significant change.

It is germane to consider the two adversaries in the Franco-Prussian War, especially the men who initiated the conflict, and to examine the forces under their control. The first of these is Louis-Napoleon III, a man with a degree of military know-how. He was a complex character and was described as:

> Outrageous audacity and great personal courage wrestled with timidity; astuteness with almost incredible fallibility; seductive charm with its antonym; downright reaction with progressiveness and humanity ahead of their age. Machiavelli jousted with Don Quixote and the arbiter was Hamlet.[2]

Louis-Napoleon III (1808–73), photographed in 1871 after his return from captivity and the fall of the monarchy.

The journalist Émile de Girardin summed him up by saying, 'If surnames were given to princes, he would be called Mr Well-Meaning.'[3] The Emperor was widely educated and wrote a well-received treatise on sugar beet that was gratefully acknowledged by the industry. He applied his intellect to military matters and as far back as 1835 he had authored *Manuel d'Artillerie*. In 1860 he started work on a biography of Julius Caesar. His overriding passion, however, was the French Army: its recruitment, training and organisation.

Herein lay a problem of long-standing. Every country, not least France, aimed to employ the smallest army possible and, given that it is civilian politicians who provide the military budget, they usually succeeded – just as they do today in the UK. On the other hand, soldiers of every generation see permanent, military capability comprised of men, materiel and money as a means of countering any perceived threat. It is a philosophy surprisingly difficult to 'sell' to politicians who hold the purse strings.

From 1818 to 1870, France filled the ranks of its army by means of a bizarre but curiously effective ballot system. Soldiers were selected by this system in their age group 'to make up the size of the army fixed by the Legislature'.[4] The remainder of that age group was deemed to be an untrained reserve. The unhappy individuals selected, by chance, to this Gallic form of National Service were committed to serving in the Army for several years.

This tenure varied over time but, in 1832, Marshal Niel fixed it at seven years. This was time enough to wean the soldier from any civilian practices and would have so seriously damaged any civilian career ambitions that the probability was he would serve on as a volunteer regular soldier.

There was an adjunct to the ballot rules, and this allowed anyone selected to provide a 'substitute'. This system grew into a business and agencies were established to find volunteers, willing to be substitutes, perhaps discharged former soldiers. Insurance companies offered cover for those about to enter the ballot just as they did for fire, flood and theft.[5] Clearly, the system favoured the wealthy who, in effect, could buy their way out of the Army. Perhaps it was no more unpatriotic than the machinations of Americans, a century later, who sought to avoid Vietnam, such as Clinton, Bush Jnr, Trump et al.

The French Army, produced by the ballot system, did enjoy a degree of public approbation and it was seen by the middle classes to be a bulwark protecting society from proletarian revolution. On that basis, the Army had a quasi-police role and the culture of the French Army in 1868 put it at odds with 'any active and intelligent minority'.[6]

In 1870, half the standing French Army had between seven and twenty years' service. This had the effect of raising average ages across all ranks. Specifically, the average age of a lieutenant was 37, a captain 41 and a major 47. Some French junior officers were in their fifties and sixties. This officer corps was ten to thirty years older than their Prussian peers, physically unfit, intellectually blank and 'apathetic and inert'. These were not officers likely to take much interest in their men.[7]

In 1869, the standing French Army was marginally bigger than the Prussian, but the balance was tilted when the well-trained Prussian reserves were taken into account. A Prussian officer was reported to have said to a French officer, 'You may win in the morning, but we will win in the evening with our reserves.'[8]

Officers of *Garde Nationale, 190e Batallion*, 1870–71.

(*Paul Getty Museum, Los Angeles. Photo by André Adolphe-Eugène Disdéri, 1819–89*)

The French trained their officers at the three military colleges of Saint-Cyr, Metz and Saumur, for which the candidates were required to be both wealthy and well educated. Admission was by examination and the cost of tuition expensive.[9] However, the standard of teaching was abysmal, and graduates on leaving were well equipped with panache but less so with military vision and expertise. The deficiencies, bordering on professional illiteracy, of the French officer corps who were taken prisoner in 1870 amazed the Prussians.[10] The junior officers were, in the majority of cases, commissioned from the ranks and thus they had the experience and leadership skills that came with years of campaigning. Their junior rank was often belied by their advanced age. One of their number did rise to become a Marshal of France. This was the aforementioned François Achille Bazaine – of whom more later.

The officer cadre depended on seniority for promotion; suitability or merit were not factors ever considered. Niel tried to change the system, but he had to cope with an emperor who made quixotic, personal selections at senior level and invariably promoted the wrong man and put him in the wrong job. There was also the deeply ingrained conservatism of the French regimental culture, which deployed what it called Marshal Niel's 'expansionist tendencies'. Graduates from the Staff College were rejected by some regiments on the grounds that they were 'outsiders' and thus unversed in the regimental tradition.[11] This was a hidebound, inflexible organisation that would soon be put to the test.

Given the political climate it would have been prudent for the French to produce maps of the likely area in which it might fight. There were available maps of the border areas of Prussia but on the unlikely scale of 1:320,000. They were unusable, and so the solution was to make officers an allowance, so that they could buy more appropriate maps from bookshops.

This was symptomatic of the administration of the French Army of the mid-nineteenth century. It was negligible. It functioned on the basis of *le système D: en se débrouiller toujours*, which translates as 'we'll muddle through somehow'.[12] It was this cavalier attitude that had prevailed in 1859 when the French were engaged in operations in Lombardy. The first units to arrive had no blankets, tents, cooking equipment, fodder or ammunition. It was a national disgrace and Napoleon III signalled from Genoa, 'We have sent an army of 120,000 men into Italy before having stocked up any supplies there. This is the opposite of what we should have done.' How right he was, but incredibly, the French won the war and that victory was 'the justification for preserving a system which with all its faults had stood the test of time'.[13]

The Prussian victory over Austria in 1866 sent a further wake-up call to the Second Empire of Louis-Napoleon III, but it did not displace well-ingrained complacency. The French still did not identify Prussia as a threat, despite estimating Prussian strength at 1.2 million and their own at only 288,000. From this number had to be found assets to meet commitments in Mexico, Algeria and Rome. The Emperor determined that he needed a fully mobilised force of 1 million men, but how this manpower was to be raised was a contentious issue.

There were several options, one of which was to adopt universal, short-term service, much as the Prussians had. Some critics countered by calling for an extension of service by ballot from six years to nine. Others argued that the size of the Army was entirely a matter for the Legislature and nothing to do with Napoleon. Inevitably, money was a factor, as it always is.

The threat posed by Prussia was not considered or debated. Instead the size and organisation of the French Army was to be governed in a manner that was politically possible. The Army was to provide protection for a people who begrudged every penny spent on it, people who distrusted their national government and who were deeply divided politically across, broadly, class lines. Marshal Niel, a man of considerable intellect and with matchless military experience, brokered a solution to the manpower issue. He proposed the revival of the *Garde Nationale* (*GN*).

Back in 1851, when Napoleon III usurped power and took the throne, one of his first acts was to disband that organisation. The *Garde Nationale* had had a doubtful history that need not detain us here. Suffice it to say that Niel now saw it as comparable with the Prussian *Landwehr*. For most of its history the *GN* was perceived to be principally composed of middle-class men, defensive of their class interests. It was not part of the French Army, was only superficially trained, elected its officers, and was not under command.

Niel argued that the involvement of men of military age in the *Garde Nationale* would raise 824,000 and would be supplemented by 400,000 men of the *Garde Mobile*. This was composed of men of a military age who had previously obtained exemption from full-time military service and had four years in the reserve. Their annual training was limited to two weeks. The combination of all categories achieved the aim of 1 million under arms, albeit of mixed capability and commitment.

The debate raged. In January 1867 Marshal Randon, the Minister for War, complained, 'It will only give us recruits, what we need are soldiers.'[14] It was a platitudinous but negative statement that did not help. The Emperor was not impressed; he sacked Randon that same month.

With a slavering wolf at the door the politicians beat the army issue to death, but in January 1868, most of Niel's objectives were met: a period of five years with the colours and four with the reserve. Niel died in 1869, aged 66, and he would have been disappointed that, when war broke out in July 1870,

A *Garde Nationale* with Tabatière rifle – a breech-loading weapon converted from a muzzle-loader and issued to second-line troops.

the *Garde Mobile*, so critical to French defence, was 'unorganised, unequipped and untrained'.[15]

In 1866, as Prussia rampaged over Austria, it was the French Army who led the world in artillery technology, equipped with rifled cannon, albeit muzzle-loaders but of a design and manufacture supervised personally by Napoleon. Nevertheless, the age of the rifled and breech-loading weapons of all calibres had arrived and the performance of the Prussians at Sadowa hastened change.[16]

In France, M. Chassepôt had perfected a breech-loading rifle that was vastly superior to the Prussian Dreyse. It fired a lighter round, which allowed an infantryman to carry more ammunition, and was optimistically sighted for ranges up to 1,600 metres. Marshal Adolphe Niel, before his death, had embraced this first-rate weapon and by 1870, some 1,037,550 were in French armouries.

A further significant asset was the *mitrailleuse*. This was an early machine gun and an improvement on the Gatling gun. It became the first rapid-firing weapon deployed as standard equipment by any army in a major conflict. It had a range of 2,000 yards and fired 150 rounds per minute. However, it was never used to best effect and French generals deployed it in six-gun batteries and employed it as they would artillery. Only 210 were produced and, despite their potential, they were not the battle-winning device hoped for.

Napoleon III's world was adjusting to new technology; not least was that of the electric telegraph, which shrank the world and had become a potent military weapon. It speeded communication that hitherto had depended upon the speed of a horse or a ship. In concert with this advance in communi-

The revolutionary bolt-action breech of the Chassepôt rifle.

The *mitrailleuse* gun, on display in Les Invalides.

cations, the railways had speeded the distribution of forces and proved to be a logistic godsend. In France the rail network had expanded almost five-fold, from 2,289 miles (3,685km) to 11,137 miles (17,924km). Rail had been widely employed in the American Civil War. The Prussians and others learning from that experience could well see the advantages rail gave to mass troop movement.

The Prussian Helmuth von Moltke was probably the most capable of the mid-century European generals and, anxious to exploit Prussia's central position, realised that his country would be made immeasurably stronger if it constructed a network of new railway lines from its centre to the extremities of its borders. This was a move quite correctly viewed with alarm by some of its neighbours. Moltke pronounced that:

> Every new development of railways is a military advantage; for the national defence a few million on the completion of our railways is far more profitably employed than on our new fortressses.[17]

A measure of the difference that rail transport could have in Europe is exemplified by the French and Hapsburg empires' campaign on Italy, as far back as 1859. Then, 'railways moved troops into Italy within a fortnight, which would have taken sixty days to march the same distance'.[18] Unfortunately, and in that case, speed of deployment was not matched by logistic capacity.

The use of railways brimmed with advantages over the less attractive alternatives. Troops and reserve forces could be delivered to the scene of operations swiftly and would arrive rested and ready to fight. By so doing they satisfied Napoleon Bonaparte's fundamental principle that required 'a concentration of force at the decisive point'. The need to 'live off the land' while

Bismarck, Moltke and Roon – a powerful team. This 'photograph' is, in fact, a drawing with the heads superimposed. That is most evident with the figure of Bismarck on the left.

marching to the front was obviated and trains could carry all the logistic support required by their passengers en route. Resupply was simplified, the evacuation of wounded hastened, and survival rates improved. Leave could be granted in mid-campaign. A mixed blessing was the access that railways gave to the press.

On Niel's death in 1869, General Leboeuf was appointed and promptly promoted to be a Marshal of France. He allowed some of Niel's reforms to wither on the vine. Two of the most serious, bordering egregious, were his neglect of the *Garde Mobile* and his abandonment of the Central Commission on Military Movement, which had hitherto been making useful progress.[19] Like every military leader, of every generation, in every country he had to resist continuous assault on the funding of his military organisation.

Marshal Edmond Leboeuf (1809–88).

By July 1870, Leboeuf felt able to assure his political masters that the French Army was ready to face any adversary. His regular army numbered 492,585 and he anticipated being able to mobilise 300,000 of those within three weeks. The *Garde Mobile* was ostensibly 417,366 strong but, at best, only 120,000 of these, inadequately trained, individuals could be expected to rally to the colours immediately. Leboeuf was dangerously complacent. He was ready, but not to fight a foe like the Prussians. General Trochu, a thorn in the establishment's side, commented bleakly:

> As it had been for the Crimean War, for the Italian War, for the Mexican adventure, for all military enterprises of that era; that is to say, ready to fight successfully and sometimes with brilliance against armies constituted and trained like itself.[20]

Notes

1. Badsey, S., *The Franco-Prussian War 1870–1877* (Oxon, Osprey, 2003), p. 17.
2. Horne, p. 20.
3. Émile de Girardin, *La Presse* (Paris, 1870).

 4. Howard, p. 13.
 5. Trochu, L.-J., *L' Armée française en 1867* (Paris, 1887), p. 49.
 6. Howard, p. 15.
 7. Montaudon, J.-B., *Souvenirs Militaires*, 2 vols. (Paris, 1898–1900), Vol. 1, pp. 216–17, Wawro, p. 45.
 8. SHAT, Lb1 Renseignements Militaires.
 9. Chalmin, P., *L' Officier française 1815–1870* (Paris, 1958), p. 153.
10. Ibid., Annex No. 2.
11. Waldersee, Graf A. von, *Denkwürdigkeiten*, 3 vols. (Berlin, 1922), Vol. 1, pp. 69–70.
12. Howard, p. 17.
13. Ibid., p. 18.
14. Bapst, C.G., *Le Maréchal Canrobert* (Paris, 1898–1913), Vol. IV, p. 58.
15. Montaudon, J.-B., *Souvenirs Militaires*, 2 vols. (Paris, 1898–1900), Vol. II, pp. 34–5.
16. The conclusive battle of the Austro-Prussian War, 3 July 1866.
17. Earle, E.M., *Makers of Modern Strategy* (New Jersey, Princeton University, 1941), pp. 148–52.
18. Howard, M., p. 2.
19. Jacqmin, F., *Les Chemins De Fer Pendant La Guerre De 1870–1871* (Paris, 1872), pp. 18, 19, 45.
20. Trochu, L.-J., Oeuvres posthumes I: La Siege de Paris (Tours, 1896), p. 88.

Chapter Four

The Protagonists – The Prussians

The Prussians shared the French manpower issues but not to the same extent. The major military difference between the two nations was rather more cerebral. In Chancellor Otto von Bismarck and Generals Helmuth Karl von Moltke and Albrecht Graf von Roon the Prussians had three formidable individuals who were single-minded in their purpose to unite all the multiple German states into one nation.

In 1868, Prussia was a confederation of only the North German states. It would take the absorption of the Southern German states to form a German nation. The difficulty was that some of the Southern German states identified more strongly with Austria – which had just been ravaged by Prussia. The elimination of Austria as a military rival was, nevertheless, a step in the right direction towards the formation of a German state.

The tool with which Bismarck would build that state was the Prussian Army. He was an astute, ruthless and very determined politician and he made it his business to seek a *casus belli*, because he saw war with France as the unifying catalyst he needed. Moltke was the military thinker who deduced that the key to military success was efficient planning, administrative excellence and total discipline. It was Roon as Minister of War who would manage Prussia's military fortunes.

The education, training and commitment of soldiers in the Prussian Army was, in all respects, superior to that of the French. Junior officers were young men in tune with their soldiers of similar age. University students served for one year instead of the more normal three, and they

Otto von Bismarck, Duke of Lauenburg (1815–98).

were mobilised as and when required. The non-commissioned officers – the backbone of any army – were professional soldiers. They were drawn from, broadly, the middle class, and although pay was poor, they enjoyed an excellent pension on retirement. The bulk of any army is the 'private men' and the Prussian private was a well-educated, healthy individual, receptive to imaginative training.[1]

Moltke had been appointed Chief of Staff, as far back as 1857, and he had ample time to put his theories to the test. It was Moltke who broke new ground, when he identified a deficiency and devised a solution. He created the concept of a 'General Staff', a body of professional officers with disparate skills and experience who, when trained, would provide cohesive, timely and accurate advice to their commander. His work was observed by Baron Stoffel, the French military attaché in Berlin, who reported that Moltke focussed on the selection and training of staff officers. From them he demanded personal dedication and a willingness to meet his 'mercilessly high standards'. He recruited only the very best pupils from the *Kriegsakademie* and 'took only twelve of the top class of about forty'. Those forty were the cream of an intake of about 120.[2]

General Helmuth Karl von Moltke (1800–91).

Moltke's regime was rigorous, demanding and ruthless. He would return to regimental duty any officer who, at any time, failed to produce excellence. Despite his unbending and exacting rule, he generated in his students a degree of affection such that they were disciples rather than subordinates.[3] His graduates mixed time on the staff with regimental duty and by this means Moltke's philosophy permeated the entire Prussian Army. By 1870, most of the officers in senior command appointments had trained under Moltke. The French were fully aware of Moltke's creation of a General Staff but made no attempt to emulate his success.

Moltke had the responsibility to draw up war plans, a complex task given the many frontiers Prussia shared. He recognised that he had to arrange for the rapid deployment of vast numbers of men and a supporting logistic system – he concluded that rail was the answer. He faced up to the un-welcome fact that all had not gone well in the Austrian campaign just a few years before. It had been the logistics that had failed. Getting the men to the right place was one thing but ensuring that they had food, tentage, blankets and ammunition was another. In the predicted war with France, the magni-tude of the mobilisation and deployment was daunting. In 1870, the North German Confederation (Prussia) could field 15,324 officers and 714,950 men. The *Landwehr* would provide a further 6,510 officers and 201,640 men. Came the day, in 1870, and Roon was able to put into the field 1,183,389 officers and men.[4]

To facilitate mobilisation as expected, Moltke redirected part of the mili-tary budget from the building of fortresses to the railways. He took private railway companies under military control and thereafter their activities gave a high priority to military requirements. He appointed an Inspector General of Communications and a second senior officer solely to oversee rail movement. Any railway issues faced by the Prussians were as nothing compared to the shambolic situation faced by the French.

The introduction of the electric telegraph in the early 1860s was a game changer and Moltke embraced it wholeheartedly. He was among the first European generals who could see the manner in which the telegraph would hasten operations and assist in the coordination of formations. He made use of the system in the war with Denmark in 1864 and again in the war with Austria in 1866.

Prussian officers in plain clothes and posing as tourists had been conduct-ing reconnaissance in the French border provinces for some years. They evaluated the defensive capability of the French forts at Châlons, Metz, Sédan, Belfort and Strasbourg. They produced maps of the French provinces and they considered the logistic value of French towns. They established contact with like-minded people. Major Alfred von Waldersee, the military attaché in Paris, made it his business to strike up an acquaintance with the attractive mistress of Napoleon's principal aide-de-camp. The lady over time furnished all manner of useful information about the French Army.[5] The Prussians were not only prepared for war, they relished the opportunities a successful conflict would bring. Then, like a gift from the gods, a trivial issue arose that they were able to exploit.

It was all about the throne of Spain – and who should sit upon it.

The throne was vacant, and in early July 1870, Bismarck chose to advance the cause of a Hohenzollern candidate, one Prince Leopold of Sigmaringen (1835–1905), a member of the Swabian line of the Hohenzollern dynasty and the brother of Carol I of Romania. Chancellor von Bismarck persuaded Spain's *de facto* leader, General Juan Prim (1814–70), to support his candidate.

The London *Times* published on 8 July 1870 described it as 'a vulgar and impudent *coup d'état* in total contradiction of accepted diplomatic practice in handling such matters'. Leopold reluctantly accepted the throne but the French, fearing a Spanish/Prussian alliance, applied very intense diplomatic pressure.

As early as 11 July, the Prussian military attaché reported to Berlin that the French had begun discreet preparations for war. In his view the evidence was quite clear as orders for forage were being placed with American contractors, naval officers had been recalled from leave and military personnel were in the process of taking up positions with railway companies. Transport vessels were being prepared to collect troops from Algeria.[6]

King Wilhelm was quite rightly alarmed, and he gave instant but confusing orders for partial mobilisation, specifically, for the reinforcement of the fortresses at Mainz and Saarlouis. Moltke had designed a sophisticated mobilisation plan but, as it was explained to the King, 'military half measures on our part would evoke similar measures on the enemy side and we would be driven inevitably into war. If your Majesty believes that according to reliable reports of effective French measures war is inevitable, then only the mobilisation of the entire army at one stroke can be recommended.'[7]

This was not the time for Prussia to mobilise, but some checking of systems made sense and, on 12 July, it was confirmed that everything was in place. This came to French ears, and its intelligence network, now fully activated, confirmed that *Landwehr* personnel were being recalled. That same day, Leopold, just a pawn in this diplomatic manoeuvering, withdrew. The French having won this war of words then went a little too far. Through their ambassador they demanded that Leopold's candidature never be renewed.

The French ambassador, Count Vincent Bénédetti, had been vociferous in presenting his country's case to the King at Bad Ems. However, he had irritated King Wilhelm in the process, who summarily rejected the French demand. Wilhelm declined to meet Bénédetti again.

The King sent a telegram to Bismarck, in Berlin, on 13 July outlining the discussions with Bénédetti. Bismarck 'sharpened the tone of the despatch before handing it to the Berlin Press and expediting it to every capital in Europe'.[8] This became known as 'The Ems Telegram'. It has a little niche in world history because it was the instrument, manipulated by Bismarck, that led inexorably to war.

The situation concerned foreign governments witnessing this political pantomime and not least of these were the British. The French were disproportionately outraged at the publication of the telegram. It was a provocative

A DUEL TO THE DEATH.

France: 'Pray stand back Madam. You mean well but this is an old family quarrel, and we must fight it out.' (Punch, *23 July 1870. Cartoon by John Tenniel. Ann Ronan Library*)

gesture, but the language used was not such as to provide the desired *casus belli*. The Prussian response to the rising political temperature was to avow that 'so far as the Prussian Government is concerned the affair does not exist'.[9] This mendacious statement further inflamed French public opinion. However, on 14 July, when it was reported that Prussian reservists were being recalled and Prussian agents were buying horses in Belgium, French attitudes hardened still further.

On 15 July, and reacting to the news that, in Paris, war credits had been voted on, the King and Crown Prince read the Prussian mobilisation order to a cheering crowd in Berlin.

French Foreign Minister, the Duc de Gramont, did not have the skills to tone down the rising rhetoric, events moved quickly, and France declared war on Prussia on 19 July. *Punch* commented on the situation adroitly on 23 July: 'Thus by a tragic combination of ill-luck, stupidity and ignorance France blundered into a war with the greatest military power that Europe had yet seen, in a bad cause, with her army unready and without allies.'[10] France was entirely alone; Austria, Russia and Italy all declined to get involved. A Gallophobic Great Britain had more sympathy for its ally at Waterloo, a sympathy heightened when Bismarck provided *The Times* with the details of the French plan to subsume Belgium back in 1866.

Louis-Napoleon's decision to go to war with Prussia is among the most asinine military decisions in history. It ranks alongside Hitler's invasion of Russia in June 1941 and the Japanese decision to declare war on the USA in November that same year.

Notes

1. Montaudon, Vol. I, pp. 27–8, Wawro, p. 45.
2. Stoffel, E.G., *Rapports Militaires ècrits de Belin 1866–70* (Paris, 1871), p. 112.
3. Howard, p. 24.
4. Ibid., p. 22.
5. Waldersee, Vol. 1, p. 14.
6. Lehmann, G., *Die Mobilmachung Von 1870–71* (Berlin, 1905), p. 23.
7. Ibid., p. 25.
8. Horne, p. 37.
9. *Documents sur les Origines Diplomatiques de la Guerre de 1870–1871*, 29 vols., (Paris, 1910–32), Vol. XXVIII, p. 31. Hereafter referenced as *Guerre*.
10. Howard, p. 57.

Chapter Five

. . . and So, To War

Before war was formally declared the pundits were assessing the options. A consensus was that the French would take the first aggressive steps and advance into Germany, either to the north by way of the Palatinate or eastwards across the Rhine. The London *Standard* had promulgated the view that 'it seems impossible to our judgment that the Prussians will be ready to take the initiative'.[1]

War having been declared, the reaction of the French was mixed. In Paris there was excitement and enthusiasm bordering on hysteria. One publisher rushed out a *French-German Dictionary for the use of French in Berlin*.[2] His lack of business acumen was offset by his optimism. In the provinces reaction to war was more measured and, in Washington, the French ambassador, Lucien-Anatole Prévost-Paradol, had given consistent warnings of Prussian strength. He had been ignored: in black despair, on 20 July he shot himself. The French military attaché in Berlin, Baron Eugène Stoffel, sent similar warnings to Paris – he, too, was ignored, but lived with the rejection.

The original plan was to deploy three armies to Metz, Strasbourg and Châlons. At Metz, Marshal Bazaine, defeated in Mexico, was to be given a chance to redeem himself. At Strasbourg, the commander was to be Marshal de MacMahon, who had distinguished himself in Crimea almost thirty years before and was now the Governor General of Algeria. Marshal Canrobert, another Crimean warrior, was to command two corps at Châlons. France's generals were all second-rate; they had established their reputations in colonial conflicts, such as those in Algeria. These generals had not confronted a modern European army since the Crimean War (1853–56) and the brief and unpopular foray against Italy in 1859.

Marshal François Achille Bazaine (1811–88).

However, with war just around the corner, on 11 July, the Emperor asserted himself and directed that there be an immediate and complete reorganisation. The three armies were to merge into one single entity of eight corps and he would command it, personally. His displaced generals would command elements of this one army at corps level. The initial order of battle was:

Marshal Patrice de MacMahon	I Corps
Major General Charles Frossard	II Corps
Marshal François Bazaine	III Corps
Lieutenant General Paul de Ladmirault	IV Corps
Major General Pierre-Louis Failly	V Corps
Marshal François Certain de Canrobert	VI Corps
Major General Félix Douay	VII Corps
Major General Charles-Denis Bourbaki	Imperial Guards

These commanders ranged in rank (by the British equivalent), from major general to field marshal. They were a mixed group of varied quality. The leadership of a large army was a task for which Napoleon III was completely unqualified and unsuited. He was also a sick man, in constant pain, which sapped his mental and physical strength.

Marshal Patrice de MacMahon (1808–93), 6th Marquess of de MacMahon, 1st Duke of Magenta, later, President of France 1873–79.

Napoleon had a very capable, large fleet that employed state-of-the-art technology and was good enough to be viewed with suspicion by the Royal Navy of the United Kingdom. The French Navy had forty-nine ironclads. Of these, fourteen were frigates, capable of 14 knots and mounting twenty-four guns, and a further nine corvettes with 16mm and 19mm ordnance. The Prussians could not match this naval power, having only five ironclads and about thirty other minor vessels. For the French, the possibility of a military arrangement with Denmark, still smouldering over its 1864 defeat at Prussian hands, was an option to be examined. If successful it would be possible to launch operations against Kiel and Hamburg, perhaps even Hanover.[3] Napoleon gave directions to his naval staff to this effect before he left for the front.

In his new capacity, Napoleon sent Marshal Leboeuf, the Chief of Staff and, ostensibly, the professional head of the Army, a memorandum, on 23 July. In this he detailed his requirements, all of which needed immediate, very high-priced attention. These included a complete reorganisation of the logistic system, a reorganisation of the railway deployment plan, the creation of a requisition and remount service together with the provision of transport for all the civilian specialists and observers attached to the Army. There were many more demands of a similar hue. The list was long, very detailed and quite beyond the capacity of Leboeuf to satisfy. This was because most of the demands would require months, if not years, of study before they could be implemented – and then only if funds were available.

French mobilisation plans, such as they were, failed miserably and comprehensively. They resulted in scenes of indescribable chaos. For example, soldiers who lived in the north in Normandy, Brittany and Pas de Calais were sent to join regiments either in the far south or west. Men, everywhere, were travelling to the far corners of the country. Stations were jam-packed as men sought the right train. Supply wagons were abandoned in sidings, unable to reach their destination. Officers could not find the units they were to command; if they did find them, they were hopelessly ill-equipped, the soldiers' needs being in those abandoned supply wagons. Gunners were separated from their guns. Inadequate maps of Germany were distributed, but not of France. The all-enveloping scale of incompetence matched that which had been obtained in the Crimean War.

Bazaine was the senior marshal, but after his defeat in Mexico he had been traduced and treated poorly. Napoleon III had tried to placate him but had failed and for three years Bazaine had worn his resentment like a cloak. The Emperor now gave the Marshal temporary command of all units in Lorraine, but only until Napoleon arrived in station. Bazaine was responsible for nineteen divisions of infantry and cavalry, but he was constrained by explicit instructions that he should not take any initiative without direct orders from Paris – this added further insult to injury.

Napoleon fed Bazaine's resentment when he sent Marshal Leboeuf and General Lebrun to Metz and placed Leboeuf in overall command. Leboeuf was significantly junior to Bazaine and Napoleon's instructions could not have been any more insulting in an army in which seniority was everything. Bazaine was an indifferent general. He lacked a sense of urgency and any capacity for innovation. As history shows, this war ruined his already tattered reputation. Nevertheless, he was entitled to be accorded the dignity that his rank deserved.

On 28 July 1870, Napoleon III left Paris for Metz, where he assumed physical command of the newly titled Army of the Rhine. He had 202,448 men under his command and anticipated that his force would increase in size as the mobilisation took full effect.

His army waited on the German border, a posture in accordance with Napoleon's perception that the Austrian and Southern German states would soon join him in an assault on Prussia. That was no more than a pipe dream, because the Southern German states threw their weight behind Prussia, as they were obliged to do under treaty arrangements – a piece of intelligence that had bypassed the French.

A conference was arranged and Bazaine was in a dark and uncooperative frame of mind. He was irritated when the Emperor and his new commander, Leboeuf, pressed him for suggestions as to how the campaign might be conducted. He saw no reason to assist 'the major general' and the meeting failed to achieve its purpose other than to cement bad relations all round.

Prussian mobilisation was well advanced and had been effected relatively smoothly, certainly far more efficiently than that of the French. Moltke had under his control three armies and their initial composition in mid-July was:

> The 1st Army, under the command of General von Steinmetz, consisted of 60,000 men all told. It formed the right wing. The 2nd Army, commanded by Prince Frederick Charles, was the central force, 134,000 strong. The 3rd Army, under the command of the Crown Prince of Prussia, [with an] approximate strength of 130,000 men. The IX Corps, of the 2nd Army to form a reserve of 60,000 men in front of Mayence, for the reinforcement of the 2nd up to a strength of 194,000 men.
>
> On 19 July, the three armies numbered 384,000 men. There still remained the I, II and VI Prussian Corps, numbering 100,000 men; but they were not at first included, as railway transport for them was not likely to be available for about three weeks. The *Landwehr* troops were detailed to defend the coasts. It is apparent that numerically the German armies were considerably superior to the French. Inclusive of the garrisons and reserves, about 1 million men and over 200,000 horses were on the ration strength.[4]

Marshal de MacMahon was in command of the four divisions that together comprised I Corps, and he occupied positions near Wissembourg in Alsace (east and south of Metz). Canrobert of VI Corps, also with four divisions, was placed at Châlons to foil any Prussian thrust through Belgium; although the frontier was about 65 miles (105km) away, Canrobert would be able to move to a blocking position from Châlons. The overall French posture was to be defensive in nature and Marshal Niel's plans for an offensive towards Trier had died with him. Instead, General Frossard's II Corps waited on the German border, complying to his sovereign's master plan. Frossard personally favoured a rapid invasion of the Saarland but his ideas were rejected by Leboeuf, whose constant refrain was that 'the army needs more time'.

The world was holding its breath and waiting for someone to do something, somewhere. There was a view being expressed in the foreign press that

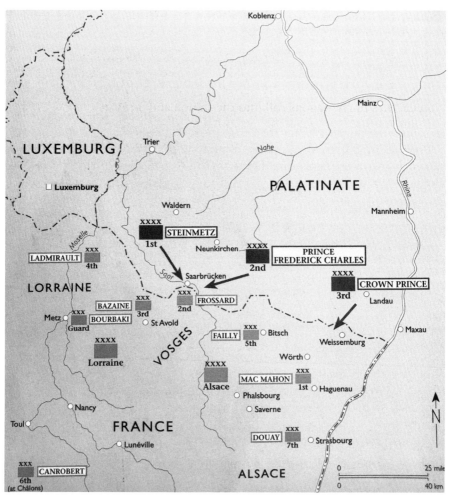

The disposition of forces on the French/German border, 1 August 1870. This map identifies the provinces of Lorraine and Alsace, which for many years were bones of contention between the two countries. (*Badsey*)

a swift French attack would not only stun and disorganise the Prussians, it might induce the Austrians, Italians and Danes to join the war on the French side. Marshal Niel had said before his death, 'The superior speed with which blows can be delivered, would offset any Prussian superiority in numbers.'[5] Niel's view presupposed an efficient build-up of French forces and that did not happen. The absence of strategic railways was now impacting on the French. The build-up of their forces was slow and badly organised. There were only four railway lines available to move the men, guns and logistic supplies to the border. On the other side the Prussians had six lines and a crisp organisation to manage them to best advantage. A British journalist observed the troop movement on the French side and wrote:

> you cannot conceive the difficulty of uniting even 100,000 men. If even 15–20,000 arrived each day it would take a week, but even that number is impossible because the cavalry needs horses and the artillery needs guns. Sometimes thirty wagons roll into the station and, after all the guns and equipment has been taken off, just fifty men step down.[6]

Napoleon was now under considerable domestic pressure to take offensive action, despite the deficiencies of his mobilisation. He had only 40,000 men at Strasbourg, not the anticipated 100,000. At Metz there were 100,000 men, not the anticipated 150,000, but those he had were ill-equipped. Canrobert's VI Corps was short of two full divisions and had neither artillery nor cavalry. Notwithstanding the domestic pressure, this was not an army capable of invading a powerful neighbour.

The Emperor was aware that Saarbrücken was only defended by elements of the Prussian 16th Division. He took note of Frossard's opinions and determined to attack and take the city. It was on 31 July that the Saar River was crossed, and on 2 August, battle was joined. The advance of Frossard's II Corps and Bazaine's III Corps of six divisions overwhelmed the Prussian defenders and the Chassepôt rifle proved its superiority over the Prussian Dreyse.

There was one small but significant engagement and that concerned a French platoon commanded by a Lieutenant Camille Lerouse. His platoon (about thirty men) was advancing in a skirmish line when it was confronted by a full Prussian company (about 100 men) that had emerged from some tree cover. The Prussians sought to envelope Lerouse's men. Outflanked and under heavy small arms fire the young officer ordered his men to seek cover, such as it was, in the furrows of a ploughed field.

He then gave his fire orders and the Chassepôts and superior marksmanship extracted a heavy toll on the Prussians who faltered. Lerouse roused his men to kneel and, from that position, they produced withering fire sufficient to cause the Prussians to break off and flee. A lone Prussian officer, ashamed by the flight of his men, stood, waved a flag and called on his soldiers to rally. He was 200 yards away when Lerouse fired two rounds at the officer, the second of which killed him. After the event Lerouse and his men were visited and congratulated by a flurry of senior officers who gifted cash to be split among the soldiers. Each man's share was about 60 francs, a significant sum in 1870 and several hundred in GBP at today's values.[7]

The capture of Saarbrücken was really no more than a skirmish and casualties were about eighty-five on each side. The city was not much of a prize and logistically it was a burden. There was only a single, readily defendable, railway line from the city into the heart of Germany. The rivers would not serve French needs as they ran roughly north to south along the border.

The taking of Saarbrücken was greeted in France with unabashed but disproportionate joy. It was thought to be the first of many victories but, in practice, it was to be one of the very few French successes in the war.

The loss of Saarbrücken was of minor importance to Moltke and he commented only briefly, making it clear that the French employed disproportionate force. He wrote:

> On 2 August three entire army corps were set in motion against three battalions, four squadrons, and one battery in Saarbrücken. The Emperor himself and the Prince Imperial shared in the enterprise. The III Corps advanced on Völklingen, the V Corps through Saargemünd, the II Corps on Saarbrücken.[8]

Within eighteen days, starting 16 July, Moltke had assembled 1,183,000 men and of these, 462,000 had been deployed along the French frontier. The Prussian mobilisation planning and execution was all that the French version was not. The senior Prussian commanders were the son and nephew of King Wilhelm: Crown Prince Frederick and Prince Frederick Charles. Together they had defeated the Austrians at Sadowa and so they had an enviable military track record. The Crown Prince assumed command of the 3rd Army in which troops from the Southern states would serve. These Southern soldiers presented a problem as the Crown Prince commented that they were 'ill-disposed towards us and quite untrained in our school'.[9] He had his doubts as to their efficiency against trained French troops.

Frederick Charles (hereafter called 'Charles' to avoid confusion) took command of the 2nd Army, which was vast, being composed of six corps as well as two independent cavalry divisions. Prince Charles was the most accomplished of the Prussian generals.

The 1st Army fell under the command of General von Steinmetz, who was already 74 years of age. He had acquitted himself very well in the war with

Crown Prince Frederick, later
Frederick III (1831–88),
Commander 3rd Army.

Prince Frederick Charles (or Karl)
(1828–85), Commander 2nd Army.

General Karl Freidrich von Steinmetz (1796–1877),
Commander 1st Army.

Austria just four years previously. Not unlike many old men, he believed that he had more than his share of wisdom. He was 'wilful, obstinate and impatient of control'. More importantly, he did not accept or practise the philosophy and planning of Moltke. One of his staff officers wrote: 'His judgement and activity had been affected and only his obstinacy remains.'[10] Eventually this intractable old man would reduce Moltke's plans to ruin.

King Wilhelm, a year younger than von Steinmetz, was a better-informed and more capable commander. He was the Commander-in-Chief and content to be advised by Moltke, although he expected all the bells and whistles that accompanied a commander-in-chief when he took to the field. Wilhelm's entourage included a host of military attachés, journalists and a veritable army of curious civilian observers who saw war as a form of entertainment. All of these people had to be transported, accommodated and fed.

Notes

 1. London *Standard*, 13 July 1870.
 2. Horne, p. 39.
 3. Howard, p. 74.
 4. *MMK*, p. 7.
 5. *Pall Mall Gazette*, 1 August 1870.
 6. *The Globe*, 27 July 1870.
 7. SHAT, Lb4, Histroff, 1 August 1870. Lieutenant Lerouse to Captain Depuy de Podio.
 8. *MMK*, p. 11.
 9. Frederick III, War Diary, pp. 7–10.
10. von Schellendorff, B., *Geheimes Kriegstagbuch 1870–71* (Bonn, 1954), p. 70.

Chapter Six

Wissembourg, Spicheren and Frœschwiller 4–6 August 1870

On page 1 it was suggested that *a siege situation is invariably the consequence of earlier battlefield reverses and, in every case, it is the cutting of the logistic chain that completes the investment* (author's emphasis). In the space of only six weeks (2 August to 19 September) the logistically illiterate French Army sowed the seeds for such a siege by dint of suffering a series of defeats that made the Siege of Paris an inevitable consequence. The pattern of future events was set in the first week of August, the events of which are outlined in this chapter. For the Francophile they make upsetting reading.

The modest success of taking Saarbrücken had had the effect of sapping the initiative of the French commanders and none was pursuing any further advance. In Metz a series of plans was formulated and abandoned. This had the effect of moving formations, exacerbating the logistic deficiencies, exhausting the soldiers, damaging morale – but all to no evident purpose.

Napoleon and Leboeuf had aspirations to send Ladmirault's IV Corps to Saarlouis and by so doing, dominate the entire Saar valley.[1] However, intelligence reports of '40,000 Prussians advancing from Trier' caused that plan to be abandoned. The source of the intelligence was the British journalists embedded with the Prussian force whose reports to London were sent uncensored.[2] The 'intelligence' was probably referring to the Prussian 1st Army.

Major General Ducrot, a key player in this story, was at this time commanding an unidentified division. His rise to the upper echelons of the French Army was meteoric and, within three months, he would be an army commander – full general. This is all the more inexplicable as he lost every engagement in which he participated. However, to be fair, that is a charge that could be levelled at almost all French generals of this period.

On 1 August, Ducrot either rejected, or was unable to accept, the information he was given about the strength of the force about to confront him. On that basis, he advised Major General Abel Douay, commanding 2nd Division, 'that the information I have received makes me suppose that the enemy has no desire to take the offensive'.[3] He could not have been more wrong because Crown Prince Frederick had two corps, the V and XI, under command and he was planning to cross the Lauter River and engage any French force he could bring to battle. Moltke observed, 'This stream affords an exceptionally strong defensive position, but on 4 August only one weak division and a cavalry brigade of the 1st French Corps covered this point, the main body of that corps being still on the march towards the Palatinate.'[4]

The night of 3/4 August had been wet. The Prussian soldiers, mostly Bavarian reservists, were cold, drenched and miserable as they crossed the frontier, in foggy, humid conditions, early on 4 August. They did not have far to march and advanced swiftly on Wissembourg, around which Douay had centered his weak division, only a few hundred yards from the Prussian border.

The town was logistically important to the French because the supply chain had broken down and troops were having to 'live off the land'. Wissembourg was a logistical asset, but a tactical death trap.[5] That August morning, about 80,000 men of the Prussian 2nd Army fell upon the French division of 8,600 men like the 'wolf on the fold', to quote Lord Byron. The French, unknowing, unexpecting and unprepared, were having breakfast. The imbalance in the two sides could only have one result. As soon as the Prussian artillery impacted on the pretty little town, the inhabitants demanded that their army open the gates and let the Prussians in. This was an unattractive and early example of the defeatism that was to be a feature of the French war effort.

Major Liaud, a battalion commander, reported on the interference of the civilian population who pleaded with his men to cease their 'useless defence' and who refused to provide directions through the labyrinthine streets of the town. When the major sent men onto rooftops to snipe the enemy the mayor berated him for 'causing material damage'. The fighting ceased when a large group of implacable citizens opened the Haguenau gate and invited the Bavarians inside.[6] Isolated groups of French soldiers of the 74th Regiment fought on in a hopeless cause, and although they inflicted severe casualties, they were all eventually eliminated.

Major General Charles Abel Douay was killed in the encounter. At Wissembourg, 1,000 Frenchmen died, 1,000 were wounded and the same number were made prisoner. Fifteen guns and four *mitrailleuses* were captured. Prussian losses were 91 officers and 1,460 men killed and wounded.

The Prussian soldiers were fascinated to see dead and wounded *Turcos* (colonial African). These North African soldiers of the 1st Algerian Terailleur Regiment had performed very well and their marksmanship had taken a toll of the Bavarian infantry as it closed upon the walled town. The victors were much impressed by the quality of captured Chassepôts that had been used to such effect by the Algerians.

Crown Prince Frederick, the victor at Wissembourg, views the corpse of Major General Charles Abel Douay. (*Anton von Werner, 1888*)

The fact that these weapons were sighted for ranges up to 1,600 metres was less a testament to French marksmanship, perhaps more the advertisement of an ambition. Even in the twenty-first century, engaging and hitting a man-sized target, with non-optical sights, at that range is speculative. That said, Nicolaus Duetsch, a Bavarian lieutenant, reported that, while inspecting his platoon on the banks of the Lauter River, one of his infantry men threw up his arms and cried out, '*Ich bin geschossen*' (I am hit). The bullet can only have come from the walls of Wissembourg, more than 1,300 yards away on a foggy morning.

The distinctive tac-tac-tac of the *mitrailleuse* had been heard that morning and the ghastly effects of its fire were readily evident when some of the dead were viewed. The gun did not traverse in the manner of later generation machine guns and its concentrated fire was focussed on one single target at a time. The impact of thirty rounds on a man's frame literally tore him into shreds. One Bavarian officer commented, 'few are wounded by the *mitrailleuse*. If it hits you, you're dead.'[7]

The Chassepôt, although a factor in the battle, was not employed to best advantage. It gave the French the ability to keep enemy infantry at long range – say 600 yards or more – and the capacity to extend their front. Instead its soldiers were grouped, were vulnerable to artillery, and fought at shorter ranges that reduced the potential advantages of the weapon.

It could be argued that this was an entirely avoidable disaster for the French and that it was the result of complacency and inadequate logistic support that caused the concentration at Wissembourg. In addition, deficient intelligence combined with imprudent defence of a river line proved to be calamitous. This defeat was to be symptomatic of others that followed.

Two days after Wissembourg, Marshal de MacMahon positioned himself between Wœerth and Frœschwiller (53 miles (85km) from Saarbrücken) and called forward V Corps, commanded by General Pierre de Failly, to support him. Failly was slow to react and, once again, the sense of urgency so important in operational matters was missing. Later, Failly, when obliged to defend himself, pointed out that his men had had a long day's march on 5 August and that they needed rest before they were fit to march and fight again. Be that as it may, Failly's tardiness meant that de MacMahon, instead of having 77,600 men, had only 48,000. He faced an estimated 89,000. It did not augur well, despite the strength of the French position on the Frœschwiller ridge. The map on page 43 shows the nature of the country.

de MacMahon was unconvinced of any forthcoming attack on his position and sufficiently so to enquire, mildly, of Failly, 'On what day and by what route will you be joining me?'[8] de MacMahon's confidence and complacency matched that of the dead Douay. It extended to his not requiring his men to dig in, accepting that there was no need to post sentries, allowing his men to frequent the taverns in nearby villages and to water their horses in the Sauerbach River.

The cavalry of the Prussian 3rd Army (now enhanced by II Bavarian Corps) had not exploited the victory at Wissembourg and did not know of de MacMahon's presence at Frœschwiller. When de MacMahon was eventually able to identify his potential opponent, he mistakenly thought that he had the advantage of numbers and was confident that his four divisions could not only hold their ground but also pose a threat to any Prussian move towards Strasbourg.[9] He was gravely misled on the relative strength of the two forces, but he did have the advantage of holding the high ground.

> The broad meadows of the River Sauer all lie within effective range of the commanding slopes on the right bank; and the long-ranging Chassepôt fire could not but tell heavily. On the French side of the river the terrain was dotted with vineyards and hop-gardens, which afforded great advantages for defensive purposes.[10]

The fighting that had now begun at Wörth was broken off after about half an hour, but the artillery of both sides had been engaged. The sound of cannon

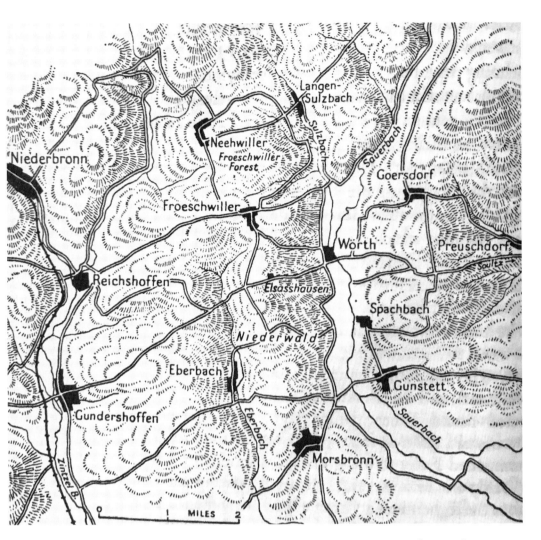

MILES

fire had been the signal for Hartmann's II Bavarian Corps, to advance from Langensulzbach, a village approximately 12 miles (19km) south of Wissembourg. This II Corps was soon engaged in a brisk fight with the French left flank. The French on their side had advanced on their right where they made contact with XI Prussian Corps.

In the early stages, the battle around Wörth ebbed and flowed, with neither side able to make significant headway. Attacks were launched, repulsed, and launched again. A critical event had been when the guns of the Prussian V Corps were able to cross to the west bank of the Sauer River, taking advantage of the bridgehead won by XI Corps. At about the same time, near Morsbronn, the French committed two Cuirassier and one Lancer regiments. This was, emphatically, not cavalry country; it was wooded, broken ground.

With great elan, about 1,000 men and horses focussed on a formation of the 32nd Infantry Regiment that was manoeuvring in the open, and charged. The Prussian infantry excelled; it stood fast and fired upon the fast-approaching horsemen, emptying many saddles. Only a handful of the cavalrymen reached the 32nd and broke through the line. These survivors then encountered the Prussian 13th Hussars, who completed the execution.

The crossing of the Sauer was not now being contested and the Prussian XI Corps fought its way up into the wooded slopes of the Niederwald, and by early afternoon was secure on the northern edge of the forest, where it linked up with V Corps. The hamlet of Elsasshausen was stormed and burnt. Just beyond the village there was fierce hand-to-hand fighting in and around a small copse, just south of Frœschwiller.

de MacMahon, seeking room to manoeuvre, initiated a thrust to the south and the Prussian units around Elsasshausen were swiftly pushed back into the Niederwald. A counter-attack restored the Prussian position. French cavalry was deployed again and with the same dismal result. They suffered appalling losses, achieved nothing and were no longer a force to be reckoned with.

de MacMahon had by now discovered, to his cost, that his adversary was at least as strong as he was, and he was outmanoeuvred in this major battle. The will to win was greater in the Prussian Army than in the French. The Prussian losses were 489 officers and 10,000 men. The French losses included 200 officers and 9,000 killed, wounded or taken prisoner. In addition, 33 guns and 2,000 horses were lost.[11]

Despite the heavy losses the Prussians held the ground and claimed victory, whilst de MacMahon acknowledged defeat and led his survivors towards Châlons. The Prussians were so exhausted and depleted that they were unable to pursue the retreating French.

The shattering defeat at Wissembourg on 4 August had initiated a juggling of French formations, the result of which was that the French fell back from Saarbrücken. Two days later, Lieutenant General Charles Frossard, commanding II Corps, took up a strong defensive position at Spicheren on the French right wing. The topography lent itself to defence and although, ostensibly, the French line seemed to be stable, the reality was that the frontier was covered only thinly, and the divisions were 'too widely scattered to give mutual support'.[12] There were only two corps held in reserve and Moltke could have attacked anywhere along the line and achieved a break-through but, perversely, he chose to assault the strongest of the French positions, that at Spicheren.

Leboeuf recognised that the extension of his forces in a linear formation along the frontier made command and control difficult. Accordingly, he split it into two commands – the right and left wings. The right wing was to be commanded by de MacMahon, who had I, V and VII Corps. The left wing of II, III and IV Corps answered to Marshal Bazaine. On paper, this seemed to be a neat solution, but control of an army-sized formation required the injection of skilled staff officers to coordinate and administer about 100,000 men and their materiel. This new arrangement denied the 'wing commanders' any control over the administration of their command. Napoleon's headquarters was located at Metz and he retained personal command over VI Corps and the Guards. The effect of the reorganisation was to create confusion as to who was to do what, when and where. Army headquarters at Metz issued orders that contradicted those issued elsewhere and that compounded the confusion.

On the Prussian side Steinmetz was proving to be a difficult bedfellow for Moltke. He resented Moltke's orders restraining individual operations and which insisted on a coordinated army-wide plan. Undeterred by common sense, Steinmetz sent one of his corps directly towards Saarbrücken – in a straight line that cut across the axis of the 2nd Army and separated the infantry of the 2nd Army from its cavalry. Neither formation was in contact with the French – it was probably just as well. Von Moltke was very displeased and when Steinmetz offered an explanation for his ill-disciplined behaviour, Moltke made a note on the despatch: 'would have exposed the 1st Army to defeat'.[13] It was remarkable restraint in the circumstances.

The Prussian assault on Spicheren had nothing to commend it. This was a battle in which the French held all the tactical cards. The heights of Spicheren projected into the valley of the Saar, forming a spectacular bluff that dwarfed the foothills between them and the river and commanded the country for 20 miles (32km) around. Their eastern slopes were covered by the forests of the Stiftswald and Gilferts, and any assailant penetrating these woods emerged at the crest of a ridge only to find a steep and narrow valley barring access to the French position and the village of Spicheren.[14] To the west, the country sloped down to the Forbach-Stiring valley, through which threaded the road and rail link from Metz to Saarbrücken. The French position at Spicheren dominated egress from and to this valley from a spur called the Rotherberg. This feature had vertical cliffs on three sides. Rotherberg was a key feature as it gave line of sight over the valley below. General Charles Frossard and his II Corps were well ensconced in an enviable defensive position.

Initially, Prussian probes, which started at 1000 hrs, were easily repulsed and soon the hillsides were decorated with Prussian dead. By 1330 hrs, the battle was developing along lines less favourable to the French and Frossard telegraphed to Bazaine that he needed support. Action was initiated, but there was no sense of urgency and the support never arrived. Frossard was alone, facing much more than just von Kameke's division. Frossard still had numerical superiority, but there were 42,900 Prussians intent on climbing his hill and, critically, they had massive, well-directed artillery support. A feature

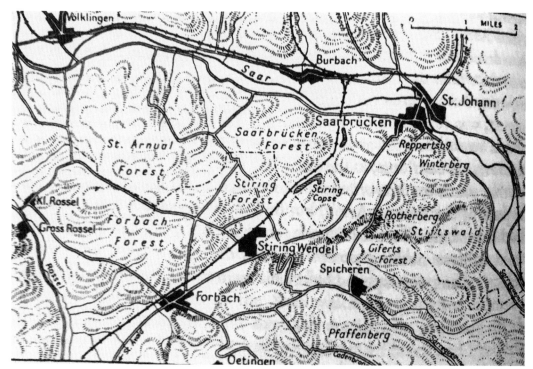

The juxtaposition of Saarbruken and Spicheren (4 miles (6km) south-west). (*Howard*)

of this battle was the efficiency of that Prussian artillery which dealt whole-sale death from a range outside that of the Chassepôt or the *mitrailleuse*. The artillery of the Prussians more than offset any numerical disadvantage. At 1730 hrs, Frossard signalled again and told Bazaine, 'My right, on the heights, has had to fall back. I am gravely compromised. Send me troops quickly and by every means.'[15]

The 14th Division of the Prussian VII Corps was under the command of General Georg von Kameke, and he, with only lukewarm support from his corps commander, stumbled into an attack on the only point in the French line that had a defensive depth of more than one corps. Indeed, Frossard had four divisions of Bazaine's III Corps available for support and within striking distance of Spicheren if needed. There were 54,000 confident Frenchmen waiting for von Kameke.

As it was, and against all expectations, the Rotherberg was scaled and taken. Prussian attacks, although costly, carried the day. When eventually, sometime after 1900 hrs, French reinforcements arrived, they faced survivors of the Spicheren battle streaming away from the heights.[16] Horne judged, disap-provingly, that 'if the French had been worthy of their salt the day would have been turned into a Prussian disaster'.[17]

The 'butcher's bill' at Spicheren cost the Prussians 4,500 and the French 2,000, but a further 2,000 were taken prisoner. Losses were less than half that at Wœerth, but the effects were much greater. The morale of the French

Army was lowered and got all the lower as there followed a series of 'retreats' that could not be dignified as withdrawals.

Three battles in the space of two days required both sides to consider what lessons had been learnt. The Prussians recognised that massed infantry attacks, with men shoulder to shoulder, may have bred an initial confidence. However, rapidly opening gaps in the ranks had the reverse effect. Massed infantry was easy meat for Frenchmen armed with the most excellent Chassepôt. Those same Frenchmen realised that their obsolescent artillery was no match for the Prussian Krupp guns, which had the capability to eliminate strongpoints and assets such as closely grouped *mitrailleuses*. Professor Sir Michael Howard took the view:

> The achievements of the German gunners on 6 August heralded a new age of applied technology in war; the disasters to the French cavalry emphasised that an epoch in warfare was now ended … On this battlefield, as henceforth on all others in Western Europe, the only choice before horsed cavalry lay between idleness and suicide. But the lessons which now seem so evident in retrospect, the armies of Europe would take fifty years to learn. Only the very clear sighted could have seen the triple significance of 6 August 1870: the collapse of cavalry; the transformation of infantry; and the triumph of the gun.[18]

Notes

1. *Guerre*, Vol. V, pp. 70–3.
2. Ibid., p. 296.
3. *Guerre*, Vol. IV, p. 6.
4. *MMK*, p. 12.
5. Howard, p. 100.
6. SHAT, Lb5, Mersebourg, 19 December 1870. Chef de Bataillon Liaud du 2e Bataillon du 74 de Ligne, Wawro, p. 102.
7. Wawro, p. 99.
8. *Guerre*, Vol. VII, p. 4.
9. Ibid., Vol. VIII, p. 54.
10. *MMK*, p. 18.
11. Ibid.
12. *Guerre*, Vol. VII, p. 88.
13. *MMK*, p. 199.
14. Howard, p. 90.
15. *Guerre*, Vol. VIII, pp. 17–18, 96.
16. Maistre, P.A., *Spicheren* (Paris, 1908), p. 352.
17. Horne, p. 42.
18. Howard, pp. 118–19.

Chapter Seven

Prussia Invades, Metz Invested

Bismarck and Moltke were aware that a large land mass, such as France, would be impossible to occupy and garrison. Accordingly, they determined that their objective was Paris, the seat of government. This confined Prussian military operations to a relatively small portion of France, but it allowed for the efficient concentration of force and logistic support, as the map shows.

The three defeats in the first six days of August were a very serious setback for the French but, at this stage, the aspirations that Napoleon, Leboeuf and Bazaine entertained of invading Prussia were still being polished. The likelihood of a massive incursion by the enemy was rejected. In Metz, the reality of the situation had not yet struck home.

Meanwhile, in early August 1870, the exuberant mood in Paris, generated by the capture of Saarbrücken, had swiftly evaporated, to be replaced by anger – focused on the Army and the Royal House. Prime Minister Émile Ollivier, was under great pressure to 'do something'. The Empress Eugénie, who had been for many years the power behind Napoleon, applied a steady hand to the tiller and by so doing reduced the heat in the debate. Nevertheless, Ollivier realised that after less than eight months in office, he was running out of time and that his likely successor was Major General Louis-Jules Trochu, whom he approached. On 7 August, Trochu, characteristically, declined political office.

Trochu was an unusual officer who had been denied a field command on the outbreak of war. This was because he had published a book entitled *L'Armée Française en 1867*, which had outraged the French establishment with its frank, bordering on brutal, assessment of the French Army. Trochu exposed a system that allowed men of 50 and 60 years of age to re-enlist, chronic ill-discipline, unrestricted drinking and abysmal training standards. It was an excoriating document that stripped away years of complacency.

The book told it as it was, warts and all. It ran to ten editions in only a few months, and was a smash hit with the French public and with at least some members of the Army. The consequence was that it triggered Trochu's removal from the War Office and his further employment was on half pay.

On 7 August, Napoleon and Leboeuf took the train from Metz the 29 miles (47km) east to St Avold, where Bazaine had concentrated his corps. The situation was very fluid and before the two men had even left St Avold station,

The area of France eventually occupied by Prussia.

they heard that the Prussians had taken Forbach, and St Avold was now being threatened. This was a hammer blow for the Emperor, and in a state of moral and physical collapse, he ordered the entire Army to move to Châlons. By dint of the decision he took at the railway station, he had acknowledged defeat.[1] Soon after, this order was rescinded and instead the Army was directed to concentrate around Metz. This was going to be difficult for de MacMahon and impossible for General Douay (the brother of the man killed at Wissembourg), who was obliged to stand fast at Belfort. Canrobert was to return to Paris and there construct a new army.

Frossard of II Corps, having heard of the defeat at Frœschwiller, and without reference to anyone else, decided to fall back to Metz anyway. His soldiers were wet, cold, tired and very hungry. They had abandoned their cooking equipment and tents, and they had lost contact with their line of supply. No rations were available, local purchase was not immediately possible, and even when it was, on 8 August, they had no means of cooking. The parlous state of II Corps was indicative of the whole Army, in which inadequate administrative systems, always third-rate, had now completely collapsed.

In Paris, Ollivier had instigated the activation of 450,000 reservists and his plan was to form, from this inadequately trained mass, two new corps. The XII Corps was to be commanded by Trochu and located at Châlons. The XIII Corps was to remain in Paris, under the command of Major General Joseph Vinoy, who had been recalled from retirement.

These two officers, unemployed when war broke out, were to have a great impact on the events that followed. Their appointments coincided with the extraordinary proclamation that there was a 'state of siege' in Paris – the first time that such a possibility had even been breathed aloud, and now it was being publicly proclaimed. Soon after, on 9 August, Ollivier resigned and his post was taken by General Charles Guillaume Cousin-Montauban, 1er Comte de Palikao (hereafter referred to as Palikao). His tenure was very short, only twenty-four days, but during that period he laid claim to have enhanced de MacMahon's army in Châlons to 140,000 men, created three new army corps and thirty-three new regiments. He also took credit for enlisting

Major General Joseph Vinoy
(1803–80).

Major General Louis-Jules Trochu
(1815–96).

100,000 *Gardes Mobile*. The quality of these new formations and the training of the 100,000 men were highly problematic.

Palikao was nothing if not committed and energetic, and it was he who suggested that the Army of Châlons should march at once to support Bazaine near Metz. For that to succeed, it would require splendid staff work to arrange the logistics, the order of battle and the order of march, all to be executed at great speed as there was not a moment to lose. In reality, it was a task way beyond the capability of de MacMahon and his army, in which morale was very low; the supply system had broken down to the degree that some men had no boots. Many men had had only cursory 'training'. This army was not anxious to tangle with the Prussian 3rd Army and its 4th 'Army of the Meuse', both of which were getting closer to striking distance.

It made more military sense for de MacMahon to fall back to defend Paris, but that measure was politically unacceptable as it savoured of defeat and could spark yet more civil unrest in the capital.

A commendable sense of urgency swept Paris as all fit, single men from the ages of 25 to 35 were deemed subject to enlistment. The anger in the streets gave way 'to a spirit of self-sacrifice and resolution'.[2] However, Prussian 'spies' were being hunted and several innocent individuals were badly treated.

On 9 August, Bazaine and Leboeuf had assembled four corps on the French left wing on the banks of the Nied River, about 10 miles (16km) east of Metz. The move to this position had been accompanied by confusion, bordering on panic. There had been constant alarms that required soldiers to 'stand to', and feeding was, at best, a haphazard operation. There was no effective rear guard and the cavalry contribution was nil. This cavalry moved very slowly, was disinclined to leave infantry protection, culled no information on the enemy, or his location … and it continued to rain.

On 10 August, Trochu put pen to paper and wrote:

> the essential conditions for all sieges, imperatively necessary for this one, is that the struggle should be supported by a relieving army … to act by repeated attacks against the Prussian Army which would, as a consequence, be incapable of a complete investment and to protect the railways and major roads from the south by which the city would be provisioned.[3]

The letter was not a flash of brilliant original thought, but its importance is that Trochu at least recognised that the war was going badly and that siege conditions could possibly be in force soon. He saw Bazaine's army in Metz as the saviour of the situation, but he warned that, while at present there were still three roads open between Metz and Paris, in four days' time that would be reduced to two, and within eight days only one would remain. Moltke was, of course, entirely au fait with that situation and was determined to exploit it.

Moltke was manipulating his three armies as an entity and his aim was to confront the French at Metz. Moltke's greatest difficulty was not the French; it was *Generalfeldmarschall* Karl von Steinmetz, always a recalcitrant, rebellious subordinate, commanding 1st Army. His relationship with Moltke was poor and even worse with Prince Charles. There were only two roads upon which the nine corps of Prussians could advance towards Metz. Road discipline was of paramount importance, but von Steinmetz claimed priority, and complained bitterly that the Prince was using *his* roads.[4] The Prussian cavalry was, like the French, failing in its role and it was its laxness that had allowed Frossard to disengage his II Corps so adroitly.

On 12 August, the Emperor abdicated his command and passed it to Marshal Bazaine – not the safest pair of hands. Bazaine opted to move into the fortress of Metz. On 14 August, while making that short move, he was engaged, at Borny-Colombey, by elements of the Prussian 1st Army. It was a battle that neither side wanted, but once committed, had little option but fight it out. Borny was only about 3 miles (5km) from the sanctity of the fortress. Borny was not a mere skirmish; it was a serious battle, with high losses on both

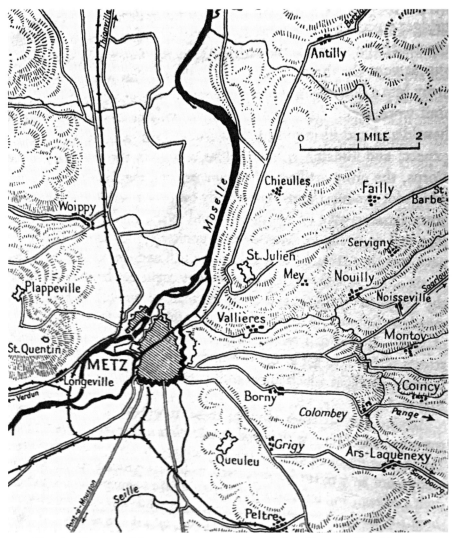

The significance of Metz as a communications hub is illustrated by this map. Borny is shown just to the east of the city.

sides. The Prussians lost almost 5,000 killed and wounded, the French some-what fewer, about 3,500. Both sides claimed victory. Moltke described it thus:

> When, at four in the afternoon, the break-up of the enemy was per-ceived, General von der Goltz (commanding 26 Infantry Brigade) with the advanced guard of the VII Corps struck him in the act and wrenched from him Colombey and the Château d'Aubigny on his right flank. But,

at the first cannon sound, the French columns immediately turned about, fully equipped for fighting, and eager, after their many previous disasters, to break the spell by a desperate effort. Castagny's Division threw itself in greatly superior force upon the weak German detachment in the isolated position of Colombey, which held its own only by the utmost exertion.[5]

When Bazaine withdrew into Metz he did not envisage ever being besieged. His intention was to rest, re-equip his men and then return to the fray. Metz was no more than a staging post. It was easy to get in but, as Bazaine would soon discover, getting out was an entirely different matter.

One outline order from Bazaine was for his force to 'fall back' to Verdun. That said, he retired to bed and left no instructions for his staff. While he slept the medieval streets of Metz were crammed with men, guns, 4,000 wagons and over 10,000 horses. It was an administrative mess. To reach Verdun all would have to be evacuated from the city and across the Moselle River. It was not until 1000 hrs on 15 August that any specific orders were issued to put that into effect. A new factor in the movement of the force was that many of the temporary bridges across the river had been washed away, the river being swollen by continuous heavy rain.

A division of II Corps that had been mauled at Spicheren was to remain in Metz to garrison the fortress. The balance of II Corps and VI Corps forming the left flank were to head off to Verdun by way of the Mars-la-Tour road. IV and III Corps, the right flank, were to move via Doncourt and Verneville. The Guards were to provide a rear guard and the cavalry were to protect the flanks.

The first problem was managing the departure of 160,000 men and their equipment from the city in their formation order. There was only one route out, a steep road that debouched onto the plateau of Gravelotte. The exodus was a protracted affair and progress was very slow. At one point it had taken the better part of two days for the French to move less than 10 miles (16km). The rain had stopped and it was now uncomfortably hot.

Late on the afternoon of 15 August, a cavalry patrol from the 1st Hanoverian Dragoons, by chance, ran across the vanguard of the French Force near Vionville. The information was passed swiftly to Prince Charles, who seized the opportunity and ordered his III Corps, commanded by General Constantin von Alvensleben, to block the French advance along the Verdun road. The Prussian force was grossly outnumbered – 30,000 against 160,000 – of which, only 80,000 could be brought to bear. Battle was not joined until the morning of 16 August, when the Prussian III Corps defeated the weakened French II Corps near Vionville, captured the village and, by so doing, sealed off any

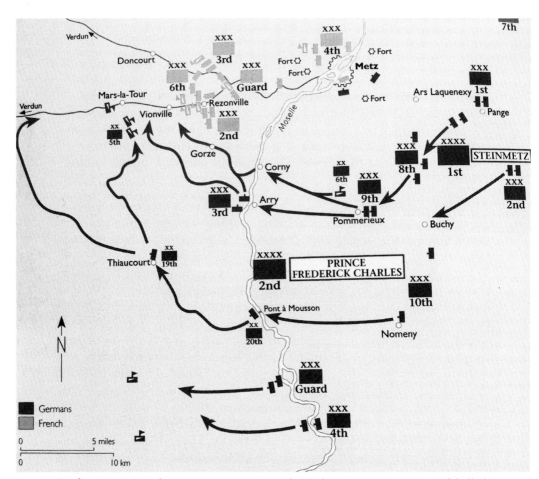

Deployments around Metz, 14–15 August. (The 10th Prussian Corps is mis-labelled, it should be 11th Corps.) (*Badsey*)

escape route to the west. It was a magnificent feat of arms by von Alvensleben when, for over four hours that afternoon, his corps confronted four French corps and denied them movement to the west. He was reinforced by the XI Corps, and by late afternoon the Prussian block was firmly based.

Losses had been equally shared; the Prince lost 4,421 dead, 10,411 wounded and 971 missing, a total of 15,803. The French lost 1,367 dead 10,120 wounded, and a staggering 5,472 missing. These were either dead or prisoners of war.

The French had numerical superiority but were handicapped by Bazaine, their overly cautious commander. In a difficult situation he rode from unit to unit encouraging the men but not taking any of the decisions expected of a leader.

The French claimed victory at Mars-la-Tour and so did the Prussians. The latter had a stronger case as they had completely thwarted the French aim to move to Verdun. In Paris, the news from Metz on 16 August provoked extreme republicans and generated civil disorder. There was 'a serious insurrection in the area of La Villette'.[6] Public buildings were attacked – not least fire stations, in which several firemen were killed. This was an early taste of things to come. An instigator of this purposeless violence was a man called Émile Eudes, who was sentenced to death for the part he had played. However, events overtook the judicial process and Éudes escaped the guillotine. The events of 16 August signalled, to some, that the Second Empire was at risk.

That same day, Napoleon arrived in Châlons in a third class railway carriage. What he saw caused him to have a rethink. This army was little more than an undisciplined mob. Exhausted, dirty and drunken soldiers reeled around the streets, the brothels were doing good business and everywhere there was no sense of purpose. The officers who gave an order were likely to be ignored, and so they did not bother. At the heart of indiscipline lay eighteen battalions of *Gardes Mobile* who were chanting republican slogans such as '*Vive L' Empereur!*' '*Un-deux-trois!*' '*Merde!*'[7] They were clearly not an asset, but a liability, and were shepherded back to Paris. de MacMahon tried to cobble together a viable force from what he had left in Châlons, assisted by Trochu.

The stalemate at Mars-la-Tour, resulting from the battle, led directly to a further bloody encounter at Gravelotte-St Privat on 18 August, about 6 miles (10km) west of Metz. The French 'Army of the Rhine' took up what Bazaine perceived to be a strong defensive line on high ground with ample cover. He was now facing the full strength of two Prussian armies, 188,332 officers and men, and 732 heavy guns. The early Prussian attacks by von Steinmetz's 1st Army endorsed Bazaine's perception – it was a strong position, very strong. The casualties inflicted on the infantry of 1st Army by Chassepôt-armed Frenchmen with *mitrailleuse* in support were enormous. Notwithstanding the losses, the Prussian 2nd Army provided support. It pressed home its attacks and at 2000 hrs St Privat was taken. The Prussian losses were 20,160, of whom 5,237 were killed. The French lost 12,275 killed and wounded. Bazaine bore the responsibility, not for losing the battles of Gravelotte and St Privat but for not winning them when 'he had victory within his grasp'.[8]

The next morning, Bazaine led his battered but very large army back to Metz, from where it would not emerge until the fortress surrendered on 27 October.

Bazaine and his staff calculated that they had sufficient food for the civilian population for a little over 100 days. However, feeding the 197,326 members of the optimistically titled 'Rhine Army' was a different matter and the likelihood was that they could only survive for forty-one days.[9]

Moltke had ringed Metz with his 1st Army and elements of 2nd Army. Siege is a manpower-intensive matter and Metz was no exception. Bazaine

The cemetery of Saint-Privat, near Metz, 18 August 1870. The cemetery was a bloody battlefield; when it was captured it heralded the French defeat. Painted by Alphonse-Marie-Adolphe de Neuville in 1881. The picture had a considerable impact on the French public after the war, and it earned the artist the title of 'Officer of the Legion of Honour'. (*Ann Ronan Picture Library*)

took up residence in the smart suburb of Ban-Saint-Martin, where, inexplicably, he withdrew from contact with his subordinates. His army sat, drank, played cards and waited. A breakout was expected but, day by day, the Prussian grip on Metz became tighter and stronger.

The IV and VI Corps had both been mauled at Gravelotte, but the remainder of the Army was in relatively good order, although confused as to the reasons for this patently defensive posture. On 23 August, Bazaine sent a signal to de MacMahon saying he intended to break out, and as the next chapter will reveal, this signal was a 'game changer'. In Paris there was a very positive response to Bazaine's breakout plan and morale in the capital, always volatile, rose accordingly.

The re-equipping inside Metz was quickly achieved but there was one insuperable deficiency, and that was in officers. On 23 August, a drunken sergeant of the 63rd Regiment shot his sergeant major dead for upbraiding him.[10] This was a most extreme case of ill-discipline, but an early manifestation of the problems caused by a shortage of officers. Bad behaviour was rampant. One officer commented, 'Our troops need severe discipline; far too many are *pillards* [looters] or *trainards* [stragglers], they sneak out of camp and have begun to defy their NCOs, complaining that they lack orders, food, wine or ammunition.' Siege conditions had only just started to apply in Metz, but early signs of anarchy did not augur well. Meanwhile, the Army waited for its leader 'to play some master stroke'.[11]

The reality was that Bazaine was hopelessly out of his depth. Master strokes were not to be found in his intellectual armoury. The fact is that the Marshal was of limited ability, something that became increasing evident as the siege of Metz ran on.

If Bazaine intended to break out, he could not afford to delay. There appeared to be two avenues open to him. He could strike out to the north and meet up with de MacMahon at Montmédy or cut south and wreak havoc across the Prussians' supply line. On 26 August, he opted for the north-eastern route up the right-hand bank of the Moselle. However, the planning for this operation was as mediocre as ever. As an example of appalling staff work, no provision was made for the breakout force to carry bridging equipment. Two of Bazaine's senior officers called on him on the evening of 25 August to urge the cancellation of the operation for two good reasons. First, there was insufficient ammunition for a series of protracted engagements. Second, the whereabouts of de MacMahon were unknown, as was his ability to meet the breakout force.

Bazaine vacillated, but did not cancel the operation, which commenced at 0400 hrs on 26 August. Then, with tens of thousands of men engaged in the opening moves, Bazaine called a conference of his senior commanders and invited them to hear the arguments put to him the previous evening by General Coffinières de Nordeck and Colonel Soleille, the artillery commander. This was an incredible episode. Minutes were taken at the meeting and from those it is evident that complete confusion reigned. These corps commanders were unused to being consulted by Bazaine, and none had a grasp of the wider strategic picture.[12] The consensus was that the Army in Metz was performing a useful function in tying up almost two armies of Prussians and that the fortress would be a useful bargaining chip when peace talks were opened – it might even ensure the retention of Lorraine.[13] While these talks were being conducted the soldiers were trying, with only limited success, to clear the jammed streets of Metz in torrential rain.

After everyone had had a chance to express an opinion, Bazaine cancelled the operation. The French host was ordered to turn around and retrace its footsteps. The confusion and frustration were all enveloping. It took twenty-six hours for the wet, miserable, discontented, hungry soldiers to return to what was termed their 'quarters'.

On 30 August, a message dated 22 August from de MacMahon reached Bazaine. It was in response to Bazaine's message of 19 August. It had been overtaken by events because it said, 'I will be in on the Aisne the day after tomorrow where I shall act as circumstances allow to come to your help.'[14] The message was sufficient to persuade Bazaine that the earlier aborted operation should now be resurrected, and it should start the following day with a force of five army corps – say 100,000 men. Having rehearsed the exercise only four days before, the exit from Metz should have been like silk.

It was not.

Disorder was prevalent although, initially, the French enjoyed some small success. The Prussian outposts at Colombey were taken but then, inexplicably, the Prussians saw their foe halt and cook lunch! There was a marked lack of any sense of urgency and it enabled Prince Charles to redeploy his army to meet the threat. The French objectives were the villages of Servigny and Noisseville. These unimportant villages had no specific strategic characteristics and were no more than reference points on the map. However, the battle that followed has come to be known as the Battle of Noisseville. It was here that, once again, the guns of the Prussian artillery, 114 of them, swung the balance. Bazaine contributed no leadership to the contest and, at 1100 hrs on 1 September, when French troops were obliged to withdraw from Noisseville, he ordered all his formations to withdraw back into Metz. The breakout had failed; there would be no meeting with de MacMahon. French casualties were 3,379 soldiers and 145 officers. The loss of those officers was particularly critical. The Prussians losses were of the same order, amounting to 2,850 soldiers and 126 officers.

Unbeknown to Bazaine, de MacMahon and his men were fighting for their lives in and around Sédan, and the chances of relief had been reduced to zero. Bazaine's fate and that of his men was on his shoulders.

Notes

 1. Ibid., p. 124
 2. Ibid., p. 122.
 3. Trochu, L.-J., 10 August 1870, in a letter to the French War Council. Quoted by Horne, p. 48.
 4. *MMK*, pp. 207, 212, 214.
 5. German General Staff, *The Franco-German War 1870–71* (1881), Part 1, Vol. 1, p. 29.
 6. Horne, p. 47.
 7. Ibid.
 8. Howard, p. 182.
 9. *MMK*, p. 160.
10. SHAT Lb12, 23 August 1870, II Corps, 3rd Division.
11. Howard, p. 259.
12. Minutes kept by General Boyer, reproduced in Bazaine, *Episodes*, pp. 164–7. Howard, p. 261.
13. D.T., I, p. 56.
14. Bazaine, F.A., *Procès Bazaine* (*Capitulation of Metz*, Versailles, Paris, 1873), p. 177.

Chapter Eight

Beaumont and Sédan
29 August–27 October

Moltke now reorganised his forces. Steinmetz, for long a thoroughgoing pain in the posterior of Prussian progress, was removed from command of 1st Army and appointed Governor of Posen (now Posnan). Moltke created a new 4th Army composed of XII Saxon Corps, IV Corps, the Prussian Guard and remnants of 2nd Army. This new formation he entitled 'The Army of the Meuse'. It was 86,000 strong and under the command of Crown Prince Albert of Saxony.

On 21 August the orders were given for a further advance, and two days later, both 3rd and 4th Prussian armies moved westward, on the assumption that Bazaine was secured in Metz by Prince Charles and his amalgam of 1st and 2nd armies.[1] There were two fortresses that were obstacles in their path, those at Toul and Verdun. Both could easily have been circumnavigated but Moltke chose to bombard them into surrender. He expended a small mountain of gun ammunition in the process but failed in his aim. He was unaware of de MacMahon's position, but a cavalry patrol found Châlons to be deserted and evidence that equipment and supplies had been destroyed.

Meanwhile, de MacMahon was ordered to set out with his 'Army of Châlons' to Rheims, where, he was assured, all manner of supplies would be available to make up his deficiency. Unfortunately, when he reached Rheims railway station, he found that all the supplies were piled up

Crown Prince Albert of Saxony (1828–1902), Commander of 'The Army of the Meuse'.

haphazardly. There was no management and distribution system to make best use of these critical assets.

At a meeting in Rheims with Eugène Rouher, President of the Senate, a most influential politician, de MacMahon made it clear that 'it is impossible to rescue Bazaine, he has no munitions, no supplies, he will be forced to capitulate and we will arrive too late'.[2] Rouher was obliged to accept the soldier's appreciation of the military situation. He realised that it was only de Mac-Mahon's army that stood between Bismarck and Paris. Rouher published a proclamation giving de MacMahon command of all military assets in and around Paris.

On 23 August, unexpectedly, Bazaine sent a message that he was going to break out and join forces with de MacMahon. This apparently simple statement of intent was the spanner in the works of legend. Inevitably, de Mac-Mahon was then redirected by his political masters to the fortress town of Montmédy on the Belgian frontier. This was a likely rendezvous with Bazaine. Speed was going to be key to success. Speed is not a characteristic of large armies and it was even more difficult to achieve if the advance was contested.

Nevertheless, good soldier that he was, de MacMahon set off for Mont-médy with four days' rations. He took with him the Emperor, a man no longer in command of anything and a political ruler in name only, 'like an unwanted parcel in the baggage train of his army, a phantom racked with pain, forbidden to return to his capital and with no other option but to chase after his nemesis'.[3]

The failure to fully replenish supplies in Rheims left de MacMahon's men little option but live off the land by foraging. Those are the polite terms – actually, remorselessly pillaging the surrounding countryside is more accurate.[4] The movement of this army, along a previously unexpected axis, presented the inadequate logistic system with a challenge far beyond its capability. Logistic deficiency was the motivation for the Army of Châlons when it 'diverted from its route and marched 18 miles [29km] further north, at right angle, to Rethel' on the Aisne River to draw from railway stocks.[5] It was not until 26 August that the Army was able to resume its advance to the east. It was little wonder that the Prussian cavalry had been unable to find the French. de MacMahon signalled to Bazaine, saying, 'I do not think I can move much further east without having news of your plans, for if the Crown Prince's army marches on Rethel I shall have to fall back.'[6] Late on 26 August, the Prussian cavalry found the Army of Châlons – to be more accurate, the French VII Corps, commanded by General Douay. Douay, thinking he was in contact with the main body of a Prussian army, halted and the entire army, behind him, was obliged to halt too.

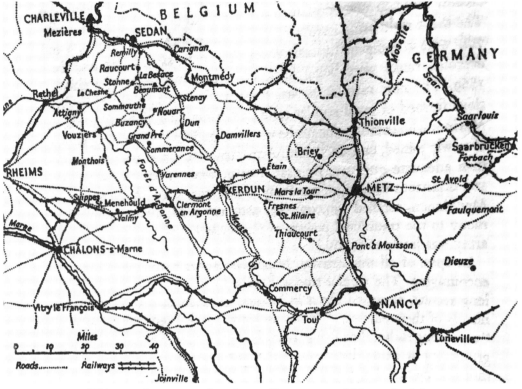

This map shows part of north-east France, over which much of the Franco-Prussian war was waged. (*Howard*)

By the evening of 27 August, the Prussians were in a commanding position. They had occupied Châlons and Rheims, having crossed the Meuse River at Dun and Stenay. de MacMahon abandoned the operation to reach Montmédy and resolved to move north and withdraw to Mézières, 10 miles (16km) west of Sédan – it was his only avenue of escape. (See map above, top left.)

de MacMahon advised Palikao, the short-serving Prime Minister, of his intentions and brought down a political firestorm on his head. First he received a formal response at 0100 hrs on 28 August. It read:

> If you abandon Bazaine, revolution will break out in Paris and you will, yourself, be attacked by the entire enemy force ... You have at least thirty-six hours' march over the Crown Prince, perhaps forty-eight; you have nothing in front of you but a feeble part of the forces that is blocking Metz ... Everyone here has felt the necessity of releasing Bazaine and the anxiety with which we follow your movements is intense.[7]

This is a prime example of a politician, albeit a general, seeking to take military decisions without the facts and without any appreciation of the realities on the ground. Palikao, a military man, should have known better. However, he knew nothing of the existence of the 4th Army of the Meuse, and was unaware that its cavalry was already skirmishing with the Army of Châlons. He thought that de MacMahon had only to deal with the Prussian 3rd Army, which was, indeed, still some way off. Palikao followed up this message with a plain and simple order:

> In the name of the Council of Ministers and the Privy Council, I require you to aid Bazaine, taking advantage of the thirty-six hours' march you will have over the Crown Prince of Prussia.[8]

This was an order, a foolish one, and it sealed the fate of the Army of Châlons. But de MacMahon knew that his duty as a soldier was to follow that order. The Emperor protested weakly, but the situation was such that neither he nor, for that matter, de MacMahon were in command of their fate. 28 August was yet another wet day and de MacMahon's troops trudged towards river crossings at Remilly and Mouzon. For the two corps to the north, this presented no particular problem and Lebrun's XII Corps crossed at Mouzon without difficulty. I Corps made similar progress and reached Raucourt about 6 miles (10km) further west.

For de MacMahon's other two corps it was a much more difficult exercise because they were in contact with the enemy. VII Corps was under constant attack by Prussian cavalry and made very slow progress to its objective. Failly's V Corps was isolated because it did not receive the orders. The courier bearing the instructions was later found to have been taken by the Prussians. The result was that Failly continued eastwards towards Stenay until he ran straight into the Saxon XII Corps – fully deployed and prepared for instant action.[9]

Moltke had observed the changes of axis of each French formation and, predictably, moved his military chessmen around the board. He had taken control of the bridge at Stenay and thus barred any approach to Montmédy. He was sufficiently well placed to send back to Metz the two corps previously called forward from Prince Charles. The 3rd Army was fast reaching the centre of activity. It was Moltke's intention to trap de MacMahon between the anvil of the 4th Army of the Meuse and the hammer of the Crown Prince's 3rd Army.

Failly stumbled head-on into the left wing of the Saxon Corps and there was a brisk exchange of fire, at a cost of several hundred lives, after which V Corps withdrew 7 miles (11km) towards Beaumont, a small village 15 miles (24km) south-east of Sédan. The journey took six hours, and the men were exhausted and wet when, eventually, they rested. However, incredibly, they posted no sentries, dug no trenches, unsaddled all horses and did not deploy their guns. One does not have to be a Staff College graduate to spot the fundamental mistakes.

Early on 30 August, three Prussian corps – V, XII and IV Corps – an army no less, advanced through thickly wooded country unchallenged. By first light the vanguard was able to observe the French V Corps' encampment. There were no sentries, the guns were parked neatly, and their horse teams were tethered nearby. Smoke from breakfast fires drifted skywards. Some Prussians felt it was unsporting or unfair to attack such a peaceful scene.[10] However, some activity in the French encampment was sufficient for the watchers to put scruples aside, and the artillery of the Prussian IV Corps burst into voice. The falling shells created instant confusion, but Failly's soldiers reacted commendably and, in places, drove the Prussians back into the woods. However, in the camp and the adjacent village, all was in turmoil. Equipment was being loaded onto wagons, horses were being harnessed, wagons and guns jammed the streets. There was panic, and that is contagious.

Civilians and soldiers fled the scene and headed for Mouzon and very soon thereafter the entire corps joined in the flight. Withdrawal has always been one of the more difficult military operations; it calls for cool heads, excellent coordination, precise timing and faultless communications. All of these were in short supply that summer morning. From the chaos, slowly a modicum of order was established, and a limited but coherent defence was organised. Failly moved about a mile further north towards Mouzon, where his defence

The modern bridge at Mouzon.

demanded a formal set-piece attack from the Prussian IV Corps and Guard Corps. The gunfire had alerted Failly's comrades in other formations, but they were unable to assist. Douay was 6 miles (10km) away and completely engrossed in getting his VII Corps across the Meuse. Lebrun's XII Corps, having already crossed the Meuse at Mouzon, was in a position to help and the commander brought his guns to bear on the Prussians.[11]

de MacMahon vetoed the move of a division from XII Corps back across the river to assist Failly and declared that V Corps must fend for itself. Failly's men fought courageously, but it only delayed the inevitable. Failly was outnumbered, outflanked, and as discipline broke down his men streamed towards the bridge at Mouzon. Here there was a scene of despair and carnage. The narrow bridge across the Meuse was jammed, and men and horses plunged into the river. It was only Lebrun's gunners that prevented a massacre. This became known as the Battle of Beaumont. The French lost forty-two guns and about 7,500 men, the majority from V Corps. Prussian losses were about half of that.

de MacMahon ordered his army to move 10 miles (16km) north-west into the fortress of Sédan. It was his intention to gather his force, reorganise and re-equip where possible. Having con-solidated he could then determine his next move. He realised the demoral-ising effect that constant retreat was having on his troops and possibly considered Sédan a suitable place to make a stand.[12] Any decision to stand at Sédan did not win complete approval because, by doing so, he was putting all of his eggs into one vulnerable basket.

General Ducrot, now commanding I Corps (vice de MacMahon), having been positioned on the high ground behind the town considered the situation and commented, '*Nous sommes dans un pot de chambre, et nous y serons emmerdés.*' This might be translated as, 'We're in a chamber pot and they are going to shit on us.'

He was coarse, concise, and quite correct.

Major General Auguste-Alexandre Ducrot (1871–82).
(*Franz Robert Richard Brendamour*)

While de MacMahon was wrestling with events outside Sédan, back in Metz, Bazaine had launched the first of his attempts to break out, in a foray now known as the Battle of Noisseville.

Bazaine telegraphed a message to Napoleon III, who was with de Mac-Mahon on 1 September saying that he had been repulsed at Noisseville and was again in Metz, with little reserve of field artillery ammunition, meat or biscuit. He added that conditions within the fortress were very insanitary, which threatened the lives of his many wounded.

Failly, of V Corps, in the Army of Châlons, had not been having a good war and the Government had decided to replace him with General Felix de Wimpffen, the Governor of Oran and an old soldier who had been itching to get into the fight since war was declared only six weeks before. Napoleon confirmed his appointment and, on 28 August, de Wimpffen lunched with Palikao and was given a rundown on the situation – at least as Palikao saw it and from the comfort of a Parisian dining room. The next day de Wimpffen received a message from the Ministry of War. It said: 'In the event of any mishap befalling Marshal de MacMahon you will take command of the troops

The site of, perhaps, the most critical battle of the Franco-Prussian War. Note the village of Bazeilles. After the battle, a POW camp was established in the area of Iges, top left in the loop of the Meuse.

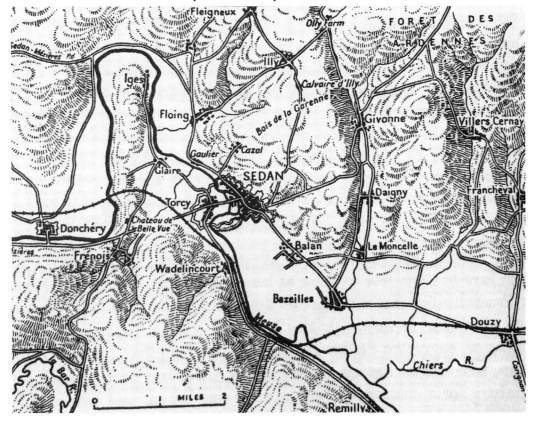

now under his orders.' He reached Sédan by train on 30 August, just before the investment was complete.

By 1 September the Prussians had completely surrounded Sédan. There was no way out, food was in short supply and Ducrot's prediction had proved too unhappily accurate. Sédan was a fortress in name only. Its fortifications were built in the seventeenth century and were no match for modern artillery. It was small and could not possibly accommodate a large garrison. de MacMahon distributed his formations in a tight circle to the north-east of the town, making best use of the high ground. The Meuse River gave a measure of protection to the south-west. The future of Paris was dependant on the two French armies. However, one was caged in Metz, the other surrounded at Sédan. The very future of the French state was at risk.

On 1 September, riding south-east towards the small village of Bazeilles about 2 miles (3km) from the fortress, Marshal de MacMahon was wounded by a shell fragment. He handed over command to Ducrot, the most experienced and capable of his corps commanders, but not the most senior. Unfortunately, Ducrot was not privy to any of the strategic or even tactical plans for the Army. Nevertheless, he decided that it was still possible to get out of the trap and he issued orders to move to the west.[13]

At this point Ducrot had resistance from some of his immediate staff officers but, more importantly, from General Barthélémy Lebrun of XII Corps, who was sufficiently senior that his view had to be considered. After a spirited debate Ducrot exerted his position as army commander and ordered Lebrun to withdraw his men from Bazeilles and move westwards. It was at this point that a furious de Wimpffen appeared, bearing the message and authority he had been given from the Ministry of War. He pronounced that he was in command and promptly countermanded Ducrot's orders.

Ducrot had no illusions as to the gravity of the situation but he was unable to convince his new commander, who insisted that 'we need a victory'. 'You will be very lucky, *mon general*,' Ducrot replied, 'if this evening you even have a retreat.'[14]

The last forty-eight hours in Sédan were marked by matchless courage, grotesque incompetence and, in the case of de Wimpffen, boundless optimism and splendid leadership. But having claimed command, he now was to have ownership of defeat.

The victory of the Prussian armies at Sédan was inevitable, so much so that Moltke's staff found a suitable vantage point from which King Wilhelm could view the battle. It was on a hillside, south of the Meuse, and the King was not alone. In his entourage he had amongst others a collection of German princelings, foreign military attachés, newspaper correspondents, not least

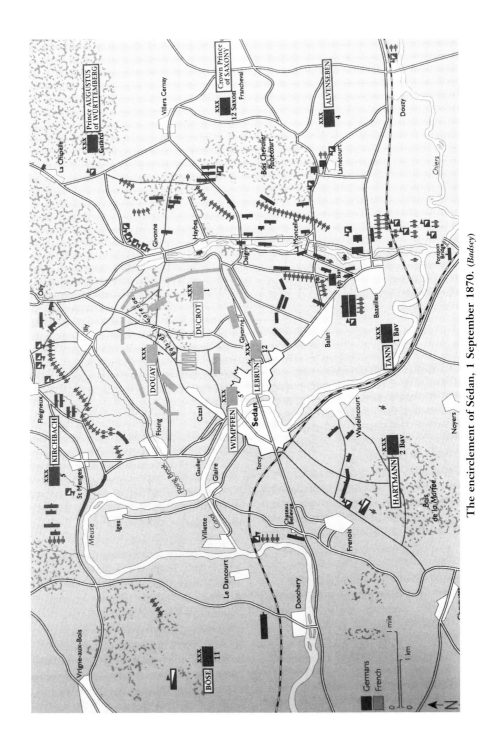

The encirclement of Sédan, 1 September 1870. (*Badsey*)

Mr W.H. Russell of the London *Times*, General Sheridan from the USA and the Russian General Kutusow. Colonel Walker represented the UK. Bismarck and Roon were accompanied by a coterie of aides. There was a festive atmosphere as the spectators watched Prussian artillery do its lethal work and bring an end to the Second Empire.

The soldiers of the Army of Châlons were now in that chamber pot mentioned by Ducrot; it was nothing organic that poured down upon their heads. It was a well-directed, persistent, artillery bombardment. Prussian artillery drenched each French position in turn and wreaked death and total destruction around the town and on the high ground above it. It was a stunning demonstration of destructive power and 'never before had gunfire been used in war with such precision'.[15] Napoleon rode around the battlefield under this fire and it was presumed, by many, that he sought a soldier's death. However, he was denied even that. He had only humiliation ahead of him.

The French cavalry rode into oblivion in a display of extraordinary corporate courage that achieved nothing, except the grudging admiration of the Prussian soldiers who had shot them from their saddles. At 1630 hrs on 1 September the barrage by ten batteries lifted, and the Saxons and troops of the 3rd Army advanced into the Bois de la Garenne, on the high ground to the north of the town. They found the totally demoralised, bemused and defenceless remnants of three divisions, former adversaries, but now quite incapable of any resistance. Moltke, watching from that hillside, commented:

> long columns of French could be seen pouring down on Sédan from the surrounding heights. Disordered bodies of troops huddled closer and closer in and up to the fortress, and shells from the German batteries on both sides of the Meuse were constantly exploding in the midst of the chaos. Pillars of fire were soon rising from the city, and the Bavarian riflemen, who had pushed forward through Torcy, were preparing to climb the palisades at the gate when, at about half-past four, the white flags were visible on the towers.[16]

Those soldiers who had fled from the Bois de la Garenne down the hill to the fortress found that the doors were locked against them and, as they huddled together, so the Prussian artillery rained down.

At the top of the hill, Lieutenant Josef Krumper was horrified by what he found in the Bois de la Garenne. The French had built breastworks from their backpacks. These had been scattered by the artillery barrage and partially concealed the many dismembered corpses of the French soldiers. French artillery pieces were upended together with *mitrailleuses*, their crews lying dead around them.[17] The wounded were 'mutilated, dying men, mostly artillery casualties, without arms, feet, legs, many with open skulls with their brains oozing out. The screams were horrible.'[18] A Bavarian captain gazed, then vomited, at the sight of a French gunner who had been dismembered by razor sharp shrapnel and blast, 'he had only a head chest and one arm'. Nearby was a pile of flesh, it was the remains of a general and his staff. Totally anonymous in death. A Saxon officer was ordered to identify the dead but all he could find was a on a scrap of underwear bearing the label 'General T'.[19]

The 3rd Army closed in from the north and west, the Saxons from the south, and by about 1700 hrs the guns on both sides fell silent. The capitulation of the French was the subject of negotiation in which the defeated had no cards to play, and the victors were determined to extract full measure from their stunning victory. There was an exchange of formalities in which the aspirations of Napoleon III were floated. He asked that his army should march out of Sédan, under arms, with baggage and full military honours, having given an undertaking not to take up arms against Prussia or her allies for the duration of the war. Bismarck, now very much in control of events, dismissed this optimistic proposal out of hand.

When Napoleon's emissary General Reille rode back from his meeting with Bismarck he brought with him the Prussian terms, which were draconian: the surrender of the entire French force as prisoners of war. Failing that, Moltke's now 250,000-strong army with 500 guns would annihilate all the Frenchmen still standing.

Wimpffen was loath to take on the responsibility for negotiations and asked Ducrot to accept the job. Ducrot replied, 'You assumed the command when you thought that there was some honour and profit in exercising it ... Now you cannot refuse.'[20] Wimpffen then did his best, but he had no cards to play. His appeal for generosity fell on deaf ears. Instead, he was given a lecture by Bismarck, who judged:

> France was not a stable country with whom war could be conducted on a limited eighteenth-century basis. French political restlessness had menaced the stability of Europe for eighty years, her military ambition had troubled Germany for two hundred.[21]

Bismarck warmed to his theme and added that *if* France had a sovereign established on a throne in a stable fashion, he *might* be able to trust in the gratitude of the Emperor and his son and set a price on that gratitude, *but* French governments were kaleidoscopic and untrustworthy. There was more along the same lines and, in a nutshell, the French would pay the full price for their defeat. In Bismarck and Moltke, the Prussians had two implacable, ruthless agents. There was not an iota of sympathy for the French – who, after

266. 1870. BAZEILLES — Ruines de la Grande Rue au lendemain de la Bataille

A view of the village of Bazeilles, pictured after the battle in which it was destroyed –
turned to commercial advantage by a photographer.

all, had declared this war. After the event one commentator summarised as
follows:

> the command was assumed by General de Wimpffen, who pressed with
> all his available forces towards the south-east. Indeed, of the three or four
> chiefs who directed that day the movements of the French, the first had
> apparently no plan; the second adopted, and sought to execute, a plan
> which the third caused him to abandon; and the third was still making
> unavailing attempts to carry out *his* plan, in exact opposition to that of his
> predecessor, when the fourth, in the person of the Emperor, came for-
> ward, and seeing that there now remained but one plan – caused the
> white flag to be hoisted.[22]

A bit unkind, superficial perhaps, but crushingly accurate.

Despite the totality of defeat, Napoleon III still entertained hopes of
retaining his crown, but to do so he would need the remnants of his army to
quell revolutionary elements. He rode out to Donchery to appeal monarch to
monarch with King Wilhelm. Bismarck intercepted the Emperor. He was
subject to an hour's harangue and was disabused of any idea of marching out
of Sédan other than as a prisoner. Eventually Napoleon was granted access to
Wilhelm, who made no effort to conceal his pleasure at Napoleon's plight.
He regarded Sédan as payback for Tilsit – a reference to the French-imposed

treaty of 1807 that had annexed half of Prussia's territory and population.[23] They do say that 'revenge is a dish best served cold', and this was a fine example. Napoleon wept and was dismissed.

Wimpffen had no doubt that he would bear the blame for this catastrophic defeat, and in a vain attempt to diffuse the responsibility, he insisted that all of his generals sign up, formally, to Moltke's terms. Lebrun, Ducrot, Douay, Dejean and Forgeot were all signatories to a Prussian-drafted armistice document. The formalities were concluded at Chateau de Bellevue, between Sédan and Donchery.

The fighting, and now the talking, was over, but at Sédan there were prisoners to herd into confinement, dead to bury, and wounded to treat. The losses on both sides were as follows:

	Prussia	France
Dead	1,310	3,220
Wounded	6,443	14,811
Missing		2,107
Captured	nil	104,000
Total	9,860	120,000

In addition, the French lost 558 guns, 6,000 horses and 1,000 wagons.[24] In terms of battle casualties, this was nothing like as costly as others in the brief

La Moncelle was a small village outside Sédan that saw some of the fighting. Today, it remains a small village, with a population of approximately 132.

4. - Bataille de Sedan. - Un épisode du combat de La Moncelle, 1ᵉʳ Septembre 1870

campaign. However, the French lost much more than men and materiel at Sédan. The enormity of the Prussian victory and its consequences started to be realised by both sides. The balance of power in Europe had completely changed; the road to Paris was wide open and total victory lay ahead.

Notes

1. Ibid., p. 239.
2. *Enquête parlementaire sur les Actes du Gouvernement de la Défense National: Depositions des Témoins* (Versailles, 1873), pp. 238–9. Hereafter referenced as *DT*.
3. Horne, p. 49.
4. *Guerre, Armée de Châlons*, Vol. 1, Annexes 166–77.
5. Howard, p. 195.
6. *Guerre, Armée de Châlons*, Vol. 1, Annexe 251.
7. Ibid., 278–9
8. Ibid.
9. Howard, p. 198.
10. Defourny, P.G., *La bataille de Beaumont*, (Brussels, 1872), p. 108.
11. Howard, p. 202.
12. D.T., pp. 37–40.
13. Ibid., Annexes 78–91.
14. Lebrun, B., *Souvenirs Militaires 1866–70* (Paris, 1895), pp. 111–12.
15. Howard, p. 217.
16. *MMK*, p. 98.
17. Wawro, p. 223.
18. BKA HS 856, Landwehr – Lt Josef Krumper.
19. SKA ZGS, 158 Lieut. Hinuber 'Tagebuch'.
20. Ducrot, A.A., *La Journée de Sédan* (Paris, 1871), pp. 51–3.
21. Wimpffen, E.F., *Sédan*, (Paris, 1871), p. 239.
22. Edwards, H.S., *The Germans in France* (Stanford, London. Re-printed 2019), p. 126.
23. Waldersee, Vol. 1, pp. 93–4.
24. Clodfelter, p. 185.

Chapter Nine

Sédan: The Aftermath

Bismarck and Moltke were not idle and within half an hour of signing the surrender documents at Sédan on 2 September, the General had issued his orders for the move on Paris, 130 miles (209km) away. Bismarck did not prevent the initiative, but he did have reservations. He commented sagely and privately to his son, 'My wish would be to let these people stew in their own juice and install ourselves comfortably in the conquered provinces before advancing further. If we advance too soon that would prevent them falling out among themselves.'[1] Bismarck's justifiably negative attitude towards France was going to be a feature of the following six months and way beyond. His negativity was shared by the German press, who exhibited a very strong anti-French view. Participants in the war were of the opinion:

> They must be made to feel what it means to challenge a peaceable neigh-bour to a struggle for life or death. The whole French nation must be made sick of fighting, no matter whether a Napoleon reigns or an Orléans or a Bourbon or anything else.[2]

General Count von Roon, the Prussian War Minister, was in no doubt, and he wrote:

> We can, for the sake of our people and our security, conclude no peace that does not dismember France, and the French Government . . . There-from necessarily follows the continuation of the war till the exhaustion of our forces.[3]

Field Marshal Leonhard Graf von Blumenthal, the chief of staff to the Crown Prince in 3rd Army, made a major contribution to the success of that army and was a very seasoned old soldier. He was forthright in his views and said:

> They should treat the French as a conquered army and demoralise them to the utmost of our ability. We ought to crush them so that they will not be able to breathe for one hundred years.[4]

In all the German states there was unrestrained rejoicing at the victory. At Bonn University, 1,000 students flocked to the colours. The German press reminded its readers of the fourteen French invasions of German soil from 1785 to 1813; there was fervent hope for further victories.

During the evening of 3 September, in the *Corps Législatif,* Palikao was obliged to confirm the worst rumours that, indeed, Sédan had fallen. This prompted Jules Favre to table a motion calling for the abdication of the Emperor – now a prisoner. The motion did not pass, but in the streets of Paris, disbelief and anger were the two emotions most expressed. There were very few shouts of *'Vive l'Empereur'* to be heard.

In Paris, there was general acceptance that, with the Emperor a prisoner, the monarchy no longer functioned and there was no evident support for the Prince Imperial, the heir apparent. *Ipso facto*, a republican situation existed. It followed that there was a need for a new head of state. The national government was in disarray but determined that power should pass to a 'Council of Regency and National Defence' (CRND). This later was more usually referred to as the 'Government of National Defence' (GND) and, in this text, the latter nomenclature is used.

This did not satisfy the militant hard left, for which the overriding priority was the formal overthrow of empire. Hastily, and to appease that hard left, a republic was proclaimed in Paris. This was a decision taken by a small group without anything resembling a vote. They were a miniscule minority of its population of 2 million. The population of the country was 37 million, but the views of the other 35 million were not considered, not even for a moment. It was agreed by the Chamber of Deputies that the GND should be formed from the deputies elected by the Department of the Seine. This was 'a decision which had the advantage of not only asserting the primordial Parisian right of governing France but of placing power in the hands of the moderate Left'.[5] The GND was composed of the following:

Léon Gambetta	Minister of the Interior and Minister of War
Jules Favre	Vice President, Minister of Foreign Affairs
Ernest Picard	Minister of Finance
Clément Duvernois	Minister of Commerce
Admiral Léon Fourichon	Minister of the Navy
Jules Ferry	Prefect of the Seine
Jules Simon	Minister of Education
Adolphe Crémieux	Minister of Justice
Étienne Arago	Mayor of Paris
Gustave Dorian	Minister of Works and Armaments Production
Henri Rochefort	Minister without Portfolio

Rochefort was accepted into the Government after the attempted coup of 31 October as a show of good faith to extremist republicans, but resigned his position in November 1870. The formation of the GND had the unexpected effect of dividing the city into three constituent parts. There were the

Ferry, Picard, Simon, ?, Arago, Thiers, Favre, ?, Gambetta. (*E. Appert*)

Bonapartists, who favoured the retention of the crown, and the republicans, who took a strong counterview and who formed the Council.

These republicans, who were now in control of civil life in Paris, were further divided into 'moderate' and 'radical' elements. The moderate wing sought a prompt armistice with Prussia and a return to normalcy as soon as possible. The radicals saw the situation as a contest between 'proletarian virtue and thieving monarchy'.[6] They opted for a *guerre à outrance* (total war). The 'strategy', such as it was, was to assault the enemy in such a manner as to inflict sufficient casualties that it could be ejected from France, despite the cost. This was unadulterated, unachievable, military nonsense. However, it found favour with those who wished to abolish 'moderation' and establish the 'rights of all' in order to collectivise property and to found a totalitarian state, solely devoted to the interests of the proletariat.[7]

From the earliest days of the siege dissent between the different republican factions, who held sway in the city, was a constant threat to good order. The promulgation of extremist views was exemplified by three men, each of whom edited a news sheet. These men, who had considerable influence on public opinion, were: Louis Auguste Blanqui, a 65-year-old long-term revolutionary who had been in and out of prison since 1849 and who edited *La Patrie en Danger*; Louis Delescluze controlled *Le Revéil* and took a similar hard left political line; and Félix Pyat was the editor and publisher of the most scurrilous news sheet, significantly entitled *Le Combat*. Pyat had spent twenty-nine of his sixty years in prison. He was an anarchist who propounded violence for political ends, and he was not open to compromise. He presented a significant threat to whoever sought to govern France – unless it was him and his associates. Despite the vehement political leanings of Pyat and his friends they were, nevertheless, vocal and fervent patriots.

Despite the obvious threat to the Government of France by the militant Reds it is curious that at no time was any degree of censorship introduced, or even considered. The press covered all shades of political opinion and so the pious hope of the GND was that the public would be exposed to a balance of views and would respond accordingly. Many years later, and learning from the French experience, in Leningrad one of the first steps taken was the confiscation of wireless sets and the cutting of telephone lines. Information, such as it was, was a very carefully controlled resource.

This was by no means the first flowering of 'communism'. Historically, it was a political philosophy that had surfaced from time to time but never took root. Karl Marx propagated communist theory and his brand became known as Marxism. Marx and Engels wrote:

> The communists disdained to conceal their views and aims. They openly declare that their ends can be attained only by the forcible overthrow of all existing social conditions. Let the ruling classes tremble at a communist revolution. The proletarians have nothing to lose but their chains. They have the world to win.[8]

To a Parisian peasant who had little or nothing material, lived in squalor, was cold and hungry and was now threatened by a Prussian assault, the attractions of *La Commune* are self-evident. As this text will show, the 'forcible overthrow' of which Marx wrote would come to pass ere long.

The next day, crowds formed, and the chant was '*Déchéance!*', which, literally, means 'lapse', but in this context, 'abdicate'. The writing was on the wall for the Second Empire. The military position was dire because everyone knew that Paris was the next Prussian objective. A product of public anger was spy fever in which suspected Prussian agents were hunted down. There was no call for evidence; pure speculation was enough for the mob to restrain citizens going about their lawful business. A woman was arrested on the basis that she was Madame Bismarck. An American and his daughter were detained while sketching in the Bois. A pigeon flying from the garden of the Anglo-American school was deemed sufficient reason for the school to be closed and searched. Marshal Jean-Baptiste Vaillant, who headed the 'Fortifications Committee', was seized by a mob who interpreted his viewing of the city defences as 'spying'. It was a serious incident and Vaillant came very close to being summarily executed. One speculative investigation led to the death of a sewage worker who was stalked by 'three hundred members of the *GN* and, when he emerged from his unsavoury place of work, was blown to pieces'.[9] The

Louis Blanqu (1805–81).

Félix Pyat (1810–89).

Louis Delescluze (1809–71).

atmosphere in Paris was volatile and there were countless other absurd over-reactions with attendant mob behaviour.

On 4 September 1870, the situation was that de MacMahon's disarmed French Army was marching into captivity, bearing its wounded. It was destined, in the short term, for an internment camp at Iges, located in a loop of the Meuse that bounded three sides (see the map on page 65). There was a canal on the fourth side. The few prisoners who attempted to escape by swimming the Meuse were shot. Many of the French arrived drunk, having been supplied with wine by the local population during their march. On arrival, the exhausted soldiers found that they had very few tents and little cooking equipment, and firewood was in very short supply. The men and their officers had to sleep on the mud in torrential rain. Little wonder this ghastly establishment was called *le camp de la misère*. Starvation became a factor in the health of the 104,000 soldiers as the Prussians were overwhelmed by the extra mouths they had to feed. A few weeks later, when Metz fell, the population of the camp swelled to over a quarter of a million men, of whom 17,200 died there of wounds or disease.[10]

As the Emperor was taken into captivity his soldiers turned their backs on him, a cruel affront to a sovereign who only 'meant well'. Napoleon was making his way to the palace of Wilhelmshöhe, near Cassel, Germany. He travelled in a carriage at the head of a line of wagons filled with all the accoutrements that go with monarchy and was attended by a coterie of aides and servants. Napoleon had asked of Bismarck if he could leave France by a different route to that of his soldiers. He wanted to travel by way of Belgium, which would avoid an embarrassing passage through the French country-side.[11] It was a modest request and swiftly granted.

It was recognised that the void left by Emperor Napoleon had to be filled by a president. The only, generally acceptable, candidate was General Louis-Jules Trochu. He was the recently appointed Governor of Paris and was not overly enthused at being offered the presidency. He sought assurance that the new government would defend what he saw as the three essentials of a civilized society, namely religion, property and family. The commitment to the defence of the country was assumed and, on that basis, he accepted the post on 4 September 1870. His tenure was to be only five months.

Trochu's abiding aim was to avoid civil dissent and unnecessary military action leading to bloodshed. He hoped to achieve these aims and secure national honour along the way. He was content for Moltke to attack the redoubts of Paris and although confident that any attack could be resisted, he had no illusions as to the deficiencies of his men that would be ruth-lessly exposed if they confronted the enemy in the field.

The abolition of the police, who had pursued all republicans during the 2nd Empire, had been an early aim of moderate republicans. However, Trochu quickly discovered that, in the real world, someone had to maintain civil order. This was because there were any number of hard Reds, like the three named above, who were calling for insurrection and were actively instigating 'terror' against the new regime. These Reds eschewed democracy, capitalism and monarchy, and announced that their aim was to establish *La Commune*, a regime in which all wealth and property would be shared.

Louis Adolphe Thiers was not a member of GND because, canny politician that he was, he was able 'to look over the hill'. He realised that, eventually, GND would have to be party to a humiliating capitulation. He did not want to be associated with failure because he had a keen eye on his personal, political future.[12] Nevertheless, he was content to play a part and when Jules Favre asked for his support, he readily gave it. On 9 September, he set off on a tour of European capitals to enlist support for France.

His first diplomatic encounter was in London, where he met Granville Leveson-Gower, the 2nd Earl Granville (whose Christian name was confusingly the same as his title). Granville listened, but apart from accepting a commercial relationship and agreeing to the supply of arms, offered nothing more. Thiers then moved on to St Petersburg and Vienna and had no more success there.

France was on its own.

On 11 September, the North German Confederation Government, in effect, Prussia, pronounced that 'it could enter into relations with the former Emperor whose government is the only one recognised'. It added that it was prepared to deal with Marshal Bazaine, who by now had been besieged in Metz for almost a month and had been put in command by the Emperor. Then there was a 'but': the German Government could not justify dealing with a group that 'up till now represents only a part of the Left Wing of the former Legislative Assembly'.[13] Years later, Moltke wrote:

> A number of men combined in Paris, who, without consulting the nation, constituted themselves the Government of the country, and took the direction of its affairs into their own hands. In opposition to this party, Marshal Bazaine, with his army at his back, could well come forward as a rival or a foe; nay, and – this was his crime in the eyes of the Paris Government – he might restore the authority of the Emperor to whom he had sworn allegiance.
>
> Whether he might not thus have spared his country longer misery and greater sacrifices may be left undecided. But that he was subsequently charged with treason obviously arose, no doubt, from the national vanity

of the French, which demanded a 'Traitor' as a scapegoat for the national humiliation.[14]

In early September 1870, the worsening situation, seen from a French perspective, had the effect of energising preparations for a possible siege of Paris. About a quarter of a million French soldiers were either prisoners of war or were to be prisoners sometime in the near future. It was only six weeks since Napoleon III had embarked, with the highest of hopes, on a war in which everything, to date, had gone seriously wrong.

Facing the grim realities, the authorities had designated empty spaces in Montmartre as graveyards, where graves were dug in anticipation. In the city centre, gun parks were established and the treasures of the Louvre were crated up and moved by train to Brest. *Les grandes horizontales* continued their business, but their less well-connected sisters in trade were taken off the streets and forcibly employed in workshops. Property was requisitioned, the Opera House became a military depot, and the Gare du Nord became the home to a flour mill. Theatres were converted into hospitals.

The fact had to be faced that, if Paris were to fall into German hands, further resistance would be, at best, sporadic guerrilla war conducted in the face of waning public support. Although the need to defend Paris was unchallenged, it was not the place from which the defence of France could or should be conducted. The Government of National Defence was unable to manage the affairs of the nation from a city under siege. However, and notwithstanding the practicalities, only a small number of the GND members had supported a move to the provinces before encirclement.[15]

After the fall of Sédan the *Mobiles* of the Seine returned to Paris, where their appalling indiscipline made them little more than an unmanageable mob. Nevertheless, they lacked nothing in self-confidence and earnestly believed that, man for man, they were vastly superior to their Prussian counterparts. It was on this basis that they eschewed any practice of the military arts. They were untrained and luxuriated in that status. The value of these men, militarily, was minimal but politically they presented themselves as a potent 'Red' force.

Membership of the *Garde Sédentaire* was originally restricted to those on the electoral roll and it was similar in structure to the *Garde Nationale*. At its formation the *GN* was intended to be a bourgeois, counter-revolutionary militia. However, as a consequence of its enormous expansion it had morphed into something else. With its leadership in the hands of elected officers it was a potent threat to any government of which it did not approve

There were other volunteer armed formations, all of which conducted their military activity quite divorced from the formal chain of command. Among these were the *Légion des Volontaires de France*, which found its member-ship from among Polish émigrés. *Les Amis de France* recruited from among the Belgian, Italian and British communities. For those of an academic or literary bent then the *francs-tireurs de la presse* could and would satisfy their academic and martial aspirations. In late September 1870, Paris was filled with hundreds of thousands of men who were largely uncontrolled and of mixed political aims, and all were provisioned with firearms. The GND had a tiger by the tail.

In any siege the highest priorities are the provision of food and water. All else is secondary. This being the case, those about to be besieged have a direct interest in ensuring that there are no unproductive mouths to feed and that food stocks are measured, stored and kept secure. This is not an area that can be 'played off the cuff'. It is a sound policy to expel non-productive passengers.

At Leningrad, the Russians started making arrangements two months before von Paulus invested the city. Twenty per cent of the population was sent away and, in anticipation of what lay ahead, food rationing was imposed on those remaining. The Russians may have learned from the French because, in Paris, arrangements for a siege were rather more cursory.

In Paris, far from reducing the population of the city, it was actually allowed to increase. The *Corps Diplomatique* left en masse and among their number was the British ambassador, Richard Bickerton Lyons, 1st Earl Lyons GCB GCMG PC. He abandoned the several thousand British residents to their fate and left without a backward glance.

However, as fast as people boarded trains to a destination outside the war zone, so others flowed in. It was bizarre that in the midst of a savage war, people of all nationalities flocked to a city that was in imminent danger and, even more bizarre, that the authorities permitted their admittance and their residence. Estate agents capitalised on the extraordinary influx of visitors and, for example, advertised as follows: 'Notice for the benefit of English gentle-men wishing to attend the Siege of Paris. Comfortable apartments, com-pletely shell-proof, rooms in the basement for impressionable persons.'[16]

Among the influx of foreign visitors was Henry Labouchère. He had an interesting life. He was described as, 'lover, wit, cynic, stage manager and diplomat'.[17] He was an MP and, as a republican, had earned the unbridled enmity of Queen Victoria. He lost his seat in Westminster and soon there-after inherited £250,000. This was a vast fortune, which in 2020 equates to £345 million. With his new-found wealth Labouchère bought a 25 per cent share in the *Daily News* and he appointed himself the Paris correspondent. He was good at his job; his despatches trebled the circulation of the paper. He was a shrewd observer of Parisian affairs.

These were very strange times indeed and the behaviour of some, residents and visitors alike, was surreal. The notable diplomatic exception was the American ambassador, Mr E.B. Washburne, who emerged from the war with an enhanced reputation. He conducted himself in the most dignified and exemplary manner. During his eight years in post, he established a reputation not only for his diplomatic integrity but also, during the war, for the manner in which he provided humanitarian support for neutrals and Germans, as well as his own countrymen.

Paris was fortunate in having as Minister of Commerce the capable Clément Duvernois, who set to work centralising all food stocks – a daunting task in which not everyone gave him their unqualified support.

Elihu Washburne (1816–87), the American ambassador 1869–77.

The Bois de Boulogne, by now with many fewer trees, became positively bucolic. The Paris correspondent of the *Manchester Guardian* reported: 'As far as the eye can reach, over every open space down the long avenue all the way to Longchamp itself, nothing but sheep, sheep, sheep! The South Downs themselves could not exhibit such a sea of wool.'

In the Bois it was estimated that there was a sheep population of about 250,000, and of oxen, 40,000. The grassed city squares became grazing areas. There was, however, a marked deficiency in milch cows, which was to have a serious effect on children in the future.[18] In order to deprive the Prussians, farmers brought all their produce into the city and carts of cabbages, pumpkins, potatoes and leeks trundled in through the fortifications to be added to Duvernois's larder. In order to deny the Prussians anything and everything, hunts were organised to seek out and slay any game, feathered or furred, they could find.

The GND had no idea how many people there were in Paris and, on that basis, was unable to calculate with any accuracy how long it could withstand a siege. Early estimates were that there was probably enough flour and grain to subsist for about eighty days. Winter was fast approaching and the availability of fuel was not thought to be an issue as stocks were plentiful. The perception

Leon Gambetta (1838–82).
(Painted by Leon Bonnat in 1875)

of the GND was that, at worst, Paris might be invested for a month. Then, the new armies, being raised in the provinces, would drive the Prussians from the gates.

That was yet more military pie in the sky.

Meanwhile, a second French army was still bottled up in Metz by the Prussian 1st Army, supplemented by elements of the 2nd Army. The French, incarcerated in Metz, had no evident means of either escape or relief. The Prussian 3rd and 4th (Army of the Meuse) armies, after their crushing success at Sédan, were now marching on Paris to bring this one-sided war to its inevitable conclusion. There were very few neutral observers who could see any other result to this ill-considered exercise in French hubris.

On the approach to Paris the Prussian 6th Cavalry Division reached Leon and the town capitulated without a fight. A few French soldiers were taken prisoner together with twenty-five guns and stores of arms and ammunition.

> 2,000 *Gardes-Mobile* were dismissed to their homes on parole to take no further part in the war. While friends and foes were assembled in large numbers in the courtyard of the citadel, the powder-magazine blew up, having probably been intentionally fired, and did great damage both there and in the town. The Prussians had fifteen officers and ninety-nine men killed and wounded; among the wounded were the Division-Commander and his general-staff officer. The French lost 300 men; the commandant of the fortress was mortally wounded.[19]

On 15 September, those who opposed Trochu, and who had been drenching him with suggestions as to his conduct of public affairs, formed the 'Central Committee of the Twenty Arrondissements'. This body went as far as publishing a manifesto that proposed, among others:

> municipal elections and the control of the police, the election and responsibilities of all magistrates to be placed in the hands of those

municipals, absolute rights of the Press to hold meetings and form affiliations, the expropriation of all essential food stuffs ...[20]

Despite the fact that the full weight of two Prussian armies, now approaching, would soon be levelled at the city, initially defence was accorded a low priority as men of all bents manoeuvred for political power. There was a host of aspirants for public office, many of whom seemed to have been motivated more by personal advancement rather than by love of *La Belle France*.

A number of key appointments had been made. Those individuals, named previously, became the hub of the new Third Republic. There was the need for a president to fill the vacuum left by Napoleon III, and Trochu had been an unwilling appointee.

Gambetta emerged as the strong man in this new government and it was evident that, despite his arrogance, he had marked leadership qualities. In Lyons and Marseilles, power had already been seized by republicans of one hue or another and there was a possibility of the nation fragmenting. Urgent steps had to be taken by the new government to regain public trust and bind the social and political structure together. Gambetta was the right man in the right job. It occurred to the new government that its mandate would be enhanced, and would give it a stronger moral basis, if there were to be a national general election.

The members of the GND could only tolerate a democratic election if the populace voted the 'right' way – a type of democracy much favoured by the European Union 150 years later. Nevertheless, it was decided to hold an election on 2 October because it was recognised that only a *democratically elected government could sign a peace treaty* (author's emphasis). The problem was that history showed that the majority of French citizens had previously rejected the philosophy of republicanism and favoured a monarchist state, and had done so since 1848.

Moltke called a meeting at Château-Thierry-sur-Marne, on 15 September, where he outlined his plan for the investment of Paris. The Army of the Marne, commanded by the Crown Prince of Saxony, was detailed to secure the northern perimeter of Paris. The 3rd Army, under command of Crown Prince Frederick, was to swing round and position itself south of the city. On 17 September, the encircling manoeuvre was put into effect and the Saxons were surprised at the lack of opposition. The following day, Crown Prince Frederick crossed the Seine south of Paris and then cut the railway line to Orléans.

Moltke was pursuing a dangerous course. He had 223,000 infantry and 24,000 cavalry, and these men were to be spread very thinly around a 50-mile (80km) perimeter. The General was hoping the French would not realise just how vulnerable his armies were, as they presented their flanks to the French while taking up position. An immediate sortie by Trochu on the flanks of the widely dispersed Prussians would be deeply damaging.

Moltke was betting on the early fall of Metz and the release of Prince Charles's army from that siege in order to take his place at this one. Moltke's intelligence staff had calculated that Paris had only sufficient food for ten weeks at the outside – on that basis it would all be over sometime before Christmas.

The GND gave some thought to the French position on a peace treaty. Unfortunately, its deliberations were divorced from reality and its conclusion was wildly optimistic. It was determined that it would not surrender 'an inch of soil or a stone of her fortresses'.[21] The Germans might have a view on that.

The Empress Eugénie – who had been a tower of strength during the Second Empire and who had tried to insert steel into Napoleon's backbone – now realised that she would have to leave France for ever. She was aided in her escape by the ambassadors of Italy and Austria. She fled to England, escorted by Sir John Burgoyne, and died there, in Farnborough, Hampshire, in 1920.

Jules Favre (1809–80). His negotiating position with the Prussians was, 'not an inch of soil or a stone of her fortresses' would be surrendered.

Any hopes that the French had of a swift and painless exit from this war were soon to be dashed when, eventually, Jules Favre was grudgingly granted an audience with Bismarck. The meeting was on 18 September and the investment of Paris was imminent.

Favre was more than a little put out when, instead of being greeted as the representative of a major power, he was treated with scant respect. He was viewed as only a member of a despised nation that had a historical record of aggression and had initiated this latest war.

The meeting did not start well and for Favre it got worse, much worse. Bismarck laid his cards on the table and made it clear that he intended to establish a frontier that would provide protection from future French attacks. On that basis, Strasbourg, the province of Alsace and a large slice of

Lorraine would be taken to include Belfort, Toul, Metz and Château-Salins. These unequivocal demands stunned Favre. Bismarck was not yet finished; he concluded by saying that, as and when Paris fell, and before food was delivered, France would have to surrender one of the protective forts that ringed the city. There would also be major financial reparations.

At this final demand Favre collapsed, and he made no attempt to ameliorate the terms imposed by Bismarck. He made no counter-offer, probably because he did not have one. He reported saying: 'I made a mistake in coming here. It is to be an endless struggle between two peoples who ought to stretch out their hands to each other. I had hoped for another solution.'[22]

Perhaps the crushed Favre had missed a trick? If Bismarck's aim was a secure frontier, Favre might have sought a mutually acceptable, diplomatic arrangement without the employment of implied force. It was a long shot, but Favre did not air it. Unfortunately, he did not represent France and did not have the authority of any other than that provided by his colleagues on the GND. In short, Favre had no democratic mandate, no 'clout' – and Bismarck was well aware of that.

A factor in Bismarck's implacable posture was the resentment of 200 years of French aggression that had left countless old scores unsettled. Alsace and Lorraine had been German territory until 1582, and he wanted them back.

The Prussian armies faced only sporadic and uncoordinated attacks as they advanced on Paris, any barricades erected on their axis were easily swept aside. The soldiers were obliged to forage for food and the indigenous population were in no position to object. By 15 September, the Prussian Royal Head-quarters had reached Château Thierry, about 56 miles (90km) from Paris.

In the provinces there was remarkable enthusiasm to confront the Prussians and local defence committees were formed and liaised with others geo-graphically close. In Nice, Marseilles and Lyon, feelings ran so high that anarchist activists brought all three cities close to revolution. Gambetta worked hard to keep the lid on political extremism while at the same time seeking to coordinate military opposition to the advancing Prussians. Across the country the demands for arms to be made available were incessant. There was an abundance of small arms in the military arsenals, but an obstacle to piecemeal military activity was the local, resident military commanders. These worthies waited for legal commands from the Minister of War. The Prefect of Haute Marne voiced the view that his military colleague was 'the greatest obstacle to any initiative in defence that I have met'. He was not alone and, in places such as Lyon, frustration boiled over into civil disorder. Here, a General Mazure refused to accept that the old order had been turned on its head. He was so hidebound in his refusal to act without an order that the Prefect arrested him and kept him confined for two weeks.

General Joseph Vinoy's XIII Corps had been marching to Sédan but the swift fall of the fortress gave Vinoy good reason to reverse his troops and return to Paris. It was a long, desperate journey. By 9 September, Vinoy was able to parade 43,068 men and 13,567 horses together with his artillery and supply train.[23] From this point Vinoy provided the backbone of the defence force. However, his troops did not inspire confidence. They were bedraggled, jaded and dispirited. Physically exhausted, they had no quarters and so their beds were on the damp earth in an encampment on the site of the Great Exposition, held only three years previously. The forces available to Trochu for the defence of Paris were a mixture ranging from the professionally competent to the untrained, ill-disciplined and criminal.

About 60,000 were competent soldiers, and included in that number was Vinoy's XIII Corps, a collection of escapees from Sédan, and 13,000 French naval personnel including marines and gunners, all bearing their personal weapons. There were other uniformed individuals who could play a part; they were the firemen, policemen and customs officers. Around 100,000 *Gardes Mobile* from the provinces had rallied to Paris but their training had only been sparse at best. Among the 100,000 were twenty-eight battalions of Breton *Mobiles* who did not speak French. They were, accordingly, held in contempt by the Paris *Garde Nationale*, who considered themselves to be several cuts above the *Mobiles*, although the *GN* was far from being an elite force by any measurable standard. The *GN* had been 24,000 strong when war was declared, and it was rapidly expanded to 90,000 in the early weeks of the war.

The GND made the registration of all men between the ages of 21 and 40 mandatory. With immediate effect, those serving in the *GN* were to be paid 1.5 francs per day. It seems unlikely that such a modest sum was a motivator but, to universal surprise, 350,000 able-bodied men came forward. That posed the question, why were these men not enlisted on mobilisation?

These vast numbers were impossible to administer and train. Trochu commentated, 'We have many men but few soldiers.'[24] So, Trochu had about 500,000 men with which to defend his city, but their quality and political adherence was unmeasured. There was no filter to weed out rogues, vagabonds and thugs. They were all under arms.

General Sheridan, from the USA, who was observing events from the Prussian side noted that, as the Prussian Army moved towards Paris, 'there were two almost continuous lines of broken bottles along the roadside all the way down from Sédan'. The Prussians were relaxed and well refreshed.

About 4½ miles (7km) south-west of the centre of Paris is an area of high ground called the Châtillon plateau. Today, much of it has been built over but, in 1870, it provided a splendid view of the city. It was the single most dominating feature and was held by General Ducrot's XIV and XIII Corps.

Ducrot, by dint of his appointment to command an army, assumed seniority over General Vinoy. This created some high-end irritation because, until Ducrot s appointment, Vinoy had enjoyed ten years' seniority over his new commander. Thereafter, Vinoy advertised his dissatisfaction at every opportunity. Ducrot was on thin ice as he had allegedly broken his parole, having escaped from Sédan. Bismarck had made it clear that if recaptured, Ducrot would be shot.

Ducrot was in a position to identify the vulnerability of the Prussians as they moved insouciantly across his front, their flanks fully exposed. Ducrot urged Trochu to allow him to mount a major assault but was given leave only to 'probe the Crown Prince's flank but with the greatest circumspection'. That is an apology for an order, and it begs the question, what was the aim of a mere probe? Long after the event, Trochu excused himself by claiming that Ducrot wanted to implement 'an act of high military imprudence that, if permitted, the Siege of Paris might have ended there'.[25] Indeed, with a decisive strike, in force, well timed and with artillery support, the French could have inflicted a wound on Moltke's force that would have altered the course of the war.

Trochu as the head of a Republican Government was obliged to treat his colleagues of the moderate left with particular deference. He was well aware of the rising social unrest in the city and, as Governor/President, his overriding aim was to avoid civil war. Any military decisions he took were strongly influenced by the issue of civil disorder. His watchword was 'caution', and it was caution that coloured his instruction to Ducrot.

Just after first light on 19 September, Ducrot prepared to launch his Zouaves in the agreed modest 'probe'. These were not the seasoned soldiers who had won plaudits in the past and established a regimental reputation for steadiness and courage – these were, for the most part, young, unbloodied recruits. The issue of their ammunition had been a muddled affair, and that had been unsettling. The young soldiers waited nervously for the order to attack but the Prussians, who were alert to the situation, pre-empted Ducrot and opened brisk and effective artillery fire. It was unnerving for the Zouaves; it was their first time under fire. They panicked and fled. Fear is contagious and an adjacent battalion of *Gardes Mobile* was affected, and in their panic, opened fire, mistaking the Zouaves for Prussians. The Zouaves who were not running to the rear returned fire.

It was a shambles.

Ducrot galloped up to the scene and by force of his personality managed to restore a vestige of order, but the initiative and the day were lost. Elements of Ducrot's force moved into the Châtillon redoubt but its water source had been destroyed previously and so their long-term position was untenable.

At 1600 hrs, Ducrot abandoned the heights together with nine guns. He had suffered 723 casualties, the Prussians 444. By the simplistic measurement of casualties this was not a major battle, but it was a critical one.[26] A wonderful opportunity to inflict heavy damage on the enemy had been hopelessly fumbled and a humiliating withdrawal was the result. Moltke wrote, long after the event:

> The enemy, by half-past eight … advanced to renew the attack on Petit Bicêtre and the Bois de Garenne. They were received with a destructive musketry fire, and not even General Ducrot's personal influence could persuade the troops, who were young recruits, to go forward. The Zouaves posted about the farm of Trivaux were finally thrown into such confusion by some shells falling among them that they hurried back to Paris in headlong flight. General Ducrot had to abandon his attempt. His divisions retired in evident disorder on Clamart and Fontenay [both now suburbs of Paris] under cover of the artillery and of the cavalry, which had resolutely endured the hostile fire; pursued at their heels by the German troops.[27]

The retreating troops were soon thronging the streets of Montparnasse and Edmond de Goncourt, and a French novelist who was present during the Siege of Paris commented that the soldiers claimed to be 'the only survivors of a body of two thousand men'. At much the same time and place, a *Mobile*

Prussian officers survey Paris from the Châtillon heights on 19 September 1870, south-west of Paris, near Sceaux and Fort Montrouge (see map on page 90).

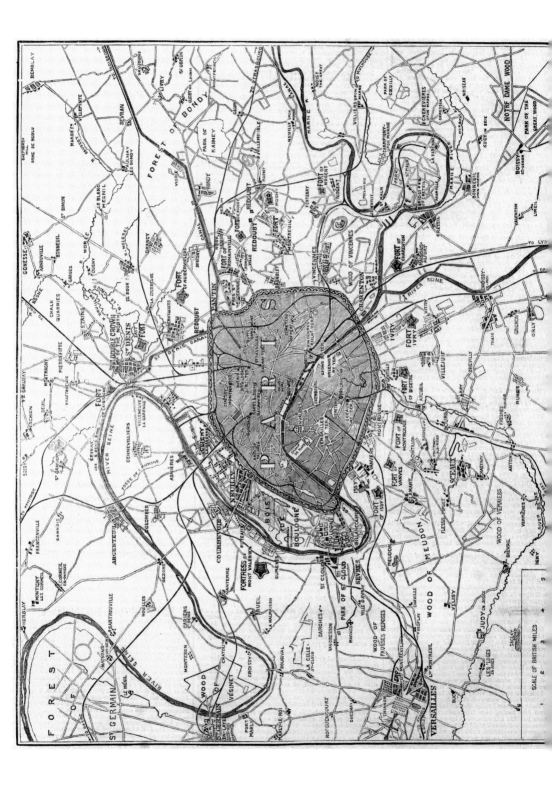

related that the Prussians 'numbered 100,000 in the Bois de Meudon'. Goncourt dealt in fiction, and he judged that the accounts he was hearing were the product of 'the madness of fear and the hallucinations of panic'.[28]

Moltke, on the other hand, had two experienced, well-led, well-equipped, well-supplied armies. He was unable to match Trochu's 500,000 in number, but he outstripped him in the quality and the commitment of his individual 240,000 soldiers. When Metz fell, as it surely would, he would be able to redeploy his 1st Army of 154,000 men, and if Strasbourg fell too, then von Werder's 40,000 could be added to the pot. Moltke was a military scholar, and he might at this time have considered the words of Sun Tzu, who wrote: 'The worst policy of all is to besiege walled cities.'[29]

Notes

1. Bismarck, in a letter to Herbert Bismarck, 7 September 1870, Howard, p. 229.
2. Verdy du Vernois, J., von., *With the Royal Headquarters in 1870–71* (London, 1897), pp. 61, 108.
3. Roon, A.T.E. von, *Denkwürdigkeiten* (Breslsu,1897), Vol. III, p. 214.
4. Blumenthal, C.C.A., von Graf., *Journals of FM Count von Blumenthal for 1866 and 1870–71* (London, 1903), p. 119.
5. Howard, p. 225.
6. Wawro, p. 233.
7. Ibid.
8. Marx, K., Engels, F., *The Communist Manifesto*, Chapter IV (London, The Communist League, 1848).
9. Horne, p. 68.
10. Fermer, D., *Sédan, 1870: The Eclipse of France* (Barnsley, Pen & Sword, 2008).
11. Busch, M., *Graf Bismarck und seine Leute Wöhrend des Krieges mit Frankreich* (Leipzig, 1878), p. 159.
12. Fermer, D., *France at Bay 1870–71* (Barnsley, Pen & Sword, 2011), p. 17.
13. Howard, p. 251.
14. *MMK*, p. 104.
15. *DT*, Vol. I, p. 548.
16. Horne, p. 67.
17. Ibid.
18. Ibid., p. 64–5.
19. *MMK*, p. 120.
20. Horne, p. 92.
21. Reinach, J., *Dépêches, Circulaires, Décrets, Proclamations et discourses de Léon Gambetta* (Paris, 1886), Vol. 1, pp. 9–12.
22. Favre, J., *Gouvernement de la Défense National* (Paris, 1871–75), Vol. 1, pp. 156–87.
23. Jacqmin, F., *Les Chemins de Fer pendant La Guerre de 1870–1871* (Paris, 1872), Vol. 1, p. 145.
24. Horne, p. 62.
25. Horne, p. 77.
26. *GGS*, Vol. 3, Appendix LXI.
27. *MMK*, p. 124.
28. Goncourt, E. & J., de, *Journal 1851–95* (Paris, 1896), Horne, p. 78.
29. Sun Tzu, *The Art of War*, c.500 BC.

Chapter Ten

September: Investment of Paris and the Fall of Strasbourg

For the Prussians viewing the defences Paris from the heights of Châtillon it was a daunting sight. The fortifications of Paris had been constructed in the 1840s but since then the world had moved on, evidenced by Herr Krupp's breech-loading artillery. The effective range of Prussian artillery in 1870 was double that of any army in 1840.

Trochu had at his disposal 3,000 of the old smooth-bore, muzzle-loading guns, of which about half were deployed on the massive fortifications that surrounded the city. These defences were 30 feet high and divided into ninety-five bastions. In front of the stone walls there was a broad moat at a minimum 30 feet wide and over 10 feet deep. This was, in reality, a deep, wide ditch that accentuated the height of the stone walls (as in the photo below). To service the awesome Paris fortifications a railway ran behind the walls to provide supplies and to hasten reinforcements to any position under threat. Built into the walls were seventeen gates, twenty-three minor road crossings, eight railway crossing points, five crossing points for rivers or canals, and eight 'posterns', which are small pedestrian gates. All of these penetrations of the great wall, potential weaknesses, were given priority for defence.

The fortifications around Paris had a circumference of about 38 miles (61km).[1] This circle was 4 miles (6.5km) deep, and every building in this zone was prepared for defence, but unmanned, with loopholed walls and clear lines of fire. Between 1 and 3 miles in front of the walls there was a chain of sixteen stoutly constructed forts, each equipped with between fifty and seventy heavy guns with ample, ready-use ammunition. All the forts were placed in commanding positions and were mutually supporting. The fort at Mont-Valérien was the most formidable. It was atop a hill on the northern loop of the Seine.

By any yardstick, Paris presented Moltke with a very significant obstacle. The city defences imposed on him the need to man about 50 miles (80km) of trenches and defended locations if he chose to besiege Paris. The manpower bill to do this was enormous and the logistic support would put his system under strain.

Moltke was fully aware of the strength of the fortifications he faced – his officers had examined them in fine detail only three years before. He had no illusions as to the task that lay ahead. The Prussian general was faced with an interesting military dilemma and he had two options. First, he could select a point in the French defences and, assuming that the defending troops would be thinly spread, employ his artillery to strike with enormous force and create a breach in the city wall. He would then advance, street by street, well knowing that in urban battles, the odds are on the defender. If and when he had overcome armed resistance, he would have to garrison the city and exert iron control over the population. It was a very unattractive option that would require massive manpower – and one that he swiftly rejected.

His second option was to invest the city, cut its logistic lifelines and starve the inhabitants into surrender. This process would take months, during which he had to sustain his armies deep in hostile territory. It would be uncomfortable, especially as winter was fast approaching, but casualties would be minimal, and success was assured.

By mid-September 1870, Parisians, although they still entertained high hopes for the relief of Metz, were nevertheless expecting to be assaulted by Prussians, their bayonets dripping with French blood. The Parisians were ready for it – or so they thought.

In the week of the encirclement of Paris the news from the strategically important fortress of Toul was not good. The fortress sat astride one of the

Fortifications near Porte de Versailles. Here the 'moat' is about 30 yards wide and much deeper than 10 feet, but it is also bone dry.

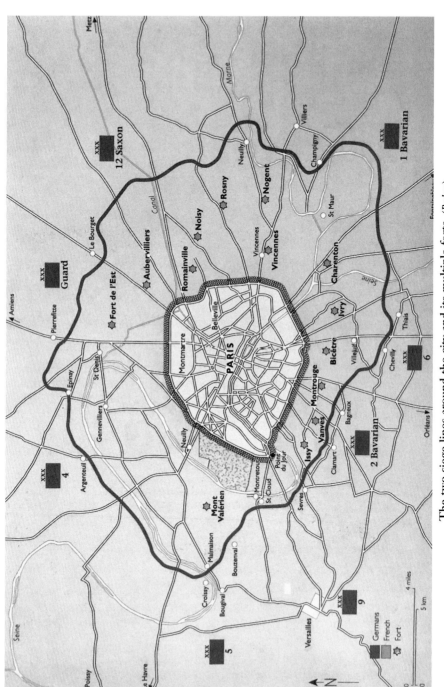

The two siege lines around the city and its multiple forts. (*Badsey*)

only two railway lines between Germany and Paris, and were it to fall into German hands, the logistic support of Moltke's armies would be greatly enhanced.

The fact that Moltke halted his armies and merely invested Paris and cut off its contacts with the wider world frustrated some and gave others the chance to express widely divergent opinions. It bored the remainder into apathy. Sieges are boring for all concerned. It was thus in Metz. Rarely do investments end in unrestrained bloodshed and, in many cases, recent history shows that a siege is usually lifted after negotiation – Metz and Strasbourg being relevant examples.

This book is being written while the 2020/21 Covid-19 'lockdown' is being applied throughout much of the world. Today most of the population is equipped with the full range of digital media that is overwhelming it with information. Telephones, television and computers are present in almost every home. In addition, the print media is still running at full tilt. Despite a reduction in political, social and sporting news, it still manages to fill its pages every day. Many correspondents, with 20/20 hindsight, explain what HM Government has done wrong in the recent past, and what it must do in the immediate future.

In contrast, Paris was awash with hard-left invective, rumour and speculation. The dearth of accurate, timely information fed the all-pervading frustration and boredom in Paris.

In 2020, there are some parallels with Paris of 150 years ago, not least the boredom. Henry Labouchère had watched the preparations for siege conditions and wrote, before the investment, in the *Daily News* under the byline 'The Besieged Resident'. In one piece he commented, 'I presume if the siege lasts long enough, dogs, rats and cats will be terrified.' He had no idea just how prescient his remark was. Although a mere visitor, Labouchère was much given to making ill-considered political speeches. His friend and fellow staunch republican Sir Charles Dilke feared they might be arrested as Prussian spies.[2] The pair were at odds with the British establishment but were at ease among like-minded people in Paris, that September 1870.

Inside the fortifications Trochu knew that time was not on his side and before the arrival of the Prussians he had applied himself to the enhancement of his defences. Twelve thousand labourers were put to work laying electrically fired mines, improving the earthworks, clearing fields of fire and placing barrages across the Seine. In the Bois de Boulogne, magnificent old trees were felled for fuel and building material. There was a sense of purpose and urgency for some, but for others, 'a visit to the fortifications had replaced a drive in the Bois as the smart Parisienne's Sunday-afternoon entertainment'.[3]

The GND had been catapulted into power before they, individually, had the opportunity to consider their fundamental aims and they had no chance to formulate any common policy over the myriad issues that faced them. They had no strategy and their status was entirely dependent on the whims of the Parisian mob.

The GND had appreciated that there was a possibility that Paris might be invested, but judged, on no evidence, that it would be only a temporary situation. That was not a view shared by the diplomatic corps and the representatives of all the European powers, who had promptly voted with their feet. Only the American minister, the Papal Nuncio and the ambassadors of several minor powers held fast.[4]

Moltke and Bismarck had, so far, achieved all their aims. However, in siege situations, the norm was for the besiegers to outnumber the besieged by something such as 3:1. Back in Paris, in late September 1870, Trochu had the capacity to move vast numbers of men to any point on his perimeter and from there launch a surprise, and overwhelming, assault on the thinly held Prussian line.

The Prussian armies made themselves as comfortable as conditions would allow. Around the perimeter of Paris, front-line trenches were dug and strongpoints constructed. However, the principal line of defence was a continuous belt of linked strongpoints almost as formidable as that which confronted them. Any physical gaps were covered by fire. Buildings were joined by communication trenches; elasticity and flexibility of manpower was the aim. Villages, long since abandoned, were fortified and north of the city the fields were flooded by the breaching of canals. The forward trenches were thinly held; they were the tripwire that, when alerted, would bring into action the bulk of their comrades who were making best use of the shelter afforded by any building with a roof. The cavalry divisions ranged far and wide behind the front line, deterring the *francs-tireurs* and seizing whatever food and materiel that could be requisitioned. Moltke had no intention of assaulting the city and none of bombarding it but, ever the pragmatist, he sent for siege artillery in case he might change his mind.[5]

The French did not allow the building of fortifications by the Prussians to proceed unhindered and they brought down regular harassing fire that did more for French morale than damage to their targets. Curiously, there was a measure of social contact between the soldiers of both sides. Germans took no action against French civilians scavenging for the remnants of their potato crop. The two sides patronised the same bakers and taverns, albeit at different times, informally agreed. Prussian soldiers exchanged their rations, slanted information and newspapers for brandy.[6] These newspapers were seized upon and their content re-edited and distributed throughout Paris. In one case, a three-week-old paper, *Journal de Rouen*, was greeted with an enthusiasm that would have been accorded to the reappearance of the Ten Commandments.

In Paris there was scant information about anything, and that was the major contribution to the dangerous boredom. After the event, 'Many who underwent the siege considered in retrospect that this was a worse privation even than the subsequent food shortage.'[7] It follows that, in that situation, the city was susceptible to rumour and counter-rumour and the absence of authentic news was a malignant psychological element in the Parisian atmosphere.

The Prussians' position was testing because, prior to 19 September and the investment, Trochu had ordered a 'scorched-earth policy'. Over a perimeter of 50 miles (80km), any building, livestock, food, canal, railway, bridge and forest had been destroyed.[8] Even the Bois de Boulogne had not been spared.

The GND had done little to regulate the issue and consumption of foodstuffs, although grain was taken into public ownership and the slaughter of cattle was subject to control. It was necessary to institute meat rationing in early October. Although bread quality declined, its consumption was not rationed until the last few weeks of the siege. Food prices rose to levels far beyond the means of the multitude of poor who faced starvation.[9]

The oxen and sheep were a finite resource and the good citizens of Paris and its army slaughtered and ate the beasts in a surprisingly short time. The meat ration had to be supplemented by horsemeat, which, as survivors of Metz could aver, was not to everyone's taste. But even unpalatable horsemeat rose in price and reduced in availability.

There were other players adding to that logistic pressure, and these were the *francs-tireurs*, which translates as 'maverick'. *Francs-tireurs* were the product of gun clubs in the east of France that were formed in 1867 at the time of the Luxembourg crisis. The members practised with rifles and the assumption was that, in time of war, they would act as militia. Their military status was complicated by the fact that they wore no uniform and could not be readily identified as being 'military'. Their organisation was wholly civilian in nature as they elected their own leaders. Forty years after the war, they were described as 'at once a valuable asset to the armed strength of France and a possible menace to internal order under military discipline'.[10] *Francs-tireurs* were usually deployed in small bands and were early exponents of what is now called 'revolutionary war'. The *francs-tireurs* 'paralysed large detachments of the enemy, contested every step of his advance, and prevented him from gaining information, and their soldierly qualities improved with experience'.[11]

These unregimented, volunteer irregular soldiers conducted their operations against the Prussian supply chain with some considerable success. The *francs-tireurs* were treated as terrorists and their capture led, invariably, to a swift and summary execution.

> The Germans reacted to *francs-tireurs* ambushes with harsh reprisals against the nearest village or town, where they killed civilians. Whole regiments or divisions often took part in 'pacifying actions' in areas with significant *franc-tireur* activity; this created a lasting enmity and hatred between the occupying German soldiers and French civilians.[12]

Two of the milder examples of retribution were when a Saxon officer was killed on a road near Beauvais and the town was forced to crippling financial reparations, and when fire was opened on a Prussian patrol near Héricourt, the village was burned to the ground.

There was local support for the *francs-tireurs*, not least in Alsace and Lorraine, where armed volunteers had been organised from 1868. As early as 15 August, they were in action against Prussian cavalry crossing the Moselle. As the situation developed around Sédan, the 3rd Army came under fire from *francs-tireurs*. The Crown Prince commented, 'Single shots are fired generally in a cunning, cowardly fashion, on patrols, so that nothing is left for us to do but to adopt retaliatory measures by burning down the house from which the shots came.'[13] One hundred years later, Captain Chuck Reindenlaugh, an American officer, wrote home from Vietnam and commenting on Vietcong activity, said:

> Imagine a football game in which one of the teams is conventionally uniformed and observes the rules of play. The opposing team, however, wears no uniform and in fact has been deliberately clothed to resemble spectators. This team plays by no rules, refuses to recognise the boundary markers or the Ref's whistle and, when hard pressed by their own goal, the team's quarter back will hide the ball under his shirt and run into the spectator boxes and defy you to find him.[14]

This suggests that, in guerrilla warfare, nothing much changes. There are still no 'rules', nor has the hostility that formally organised soldiers have for their irregular opponent. However, in 1870, the uniform issue was important and the *francs-tireurs* realised that their survival might depend on being part of a uniformed force, no matter how loosely organised. There were 300 units, with about 57,000 members. The Government voted funds for their pay and, by so doing, changed their status. Within months, different units wore different uniforms, some of which were theatrical in the extreme. The ranks were swollen by foreign volunteers as men from England, Spain, Poland, America and Italy flocked to join the battle. One of these was the Italian revolutionary, Giuseppe Garibaldi. He was something of a mixed blessing.

He was past his soldiering best, overweight and unwell. His revolutionary zeal was far in excess of that of the members of the Government of National Defence and it made him an uncomfortable bedfellow.

The Prussians had, by now, 'established a reputation for prompt and sometimes indiscriminate retaliation'.[15] Under this ruthless regime some local authorities were obliged to collaborate, and their population became passively acquiescent. This was less so in the Vosges and border area, where Prussian troops had to be assigned with the specific task of eradicating *francs-tireurs*.

Some thought that the wider employment of *francs-tireurs* might obviate the need for new armies and that the interdiction of the Prussian logistic tail could bring about its defeat. On 21 September, Admiral Léon Fourichon, the Minister for the Navy and the Colonies, advised all local commanders as to the employment of their *francs-tireurs* and *Mobiles*. He suggested that their role was to harass the enemy ... to obstruct him in his requisitions ... above all to carry out *coups de main* and to capture convoys, cut roads and railways, and destroy bridges. He added that these troops must wage real partisan war.[16]

There is no doubt that the *Mobiles* and *francs-tireurs* were a potent force, but they were neither the Vietminh nor Vietcong, whose brand of successful guerrilla warfare was on a completely different level. Nor did they have the leadership of a logistic genius like Giap. The irregular forces were a factor, but they were never going to be capable of defeating a disciplined, well-led Prussian force.

On 23 September, Toul was obliged to surrender: '109 officers were released on parole, 2,240 rank and file were taken prisoners.'[17] The railway line from Germany opened – a significant logistic plus for the besiegers. Strasbourg would fall only a week later. News of these two victories were broadcast widely and celebrated by the Prussians. They made every effort to be sure that the news was communicated to Paris.

The isolation of the city was completed when the Prussians dredged up a submarine cable from the bed of the Seine on 27 September and, by doing so, cut off communications between the GND in Paris, its shadow organisation in Tours and all its provincial capitals. The Government was now unable to govern France.

On the French/German border the fortress city of Strasbourg had been attacked on 14 August and besieged by an army of 40,000 men, raised in the Grand Duchy of Baden, and commanded by General August von Werder. These troops were from just the other side of the Rhine and so were close neighbours. The garrison, of what was considered to be one of the strongest forts in France, was 23,000 strong, but of these, 7,000 were *GN* militiamen.[18]

The strength of Strasbourg was a myth. It was a medieval city and in no way fortified to a degree that it could resist a nineteenth-century army equipped

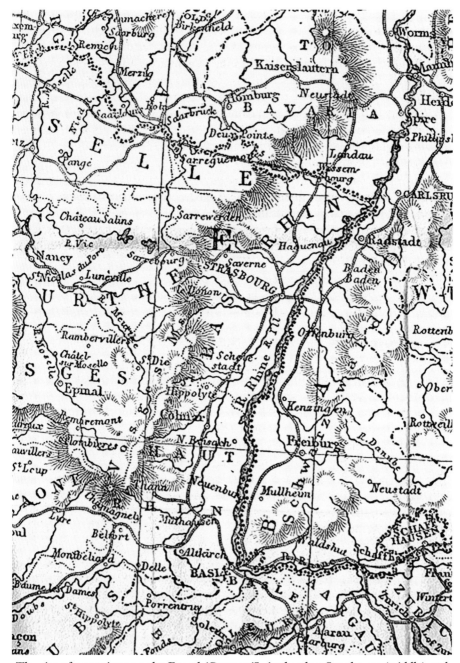

The site of operations on the French/German/Swiss border. Strasbourg (middle) and Belfort (bottom left) were both besieged by the Prussians.

with state-of-the-art artillery. There were no underground shelters either for people or ammunition. The latter was stacked in the open and vulnerable to the plunging fire of Prussian guns. The defenders had only 250 obsolete, smooth-bore guns of fifteen different types and calibres. There was, however, a dearth of gunners with the ability to operate the guns. Fortunately, there was food for sixty days and bread for six months.[19]

Once battle was joined it was, again, the Prussian artillery that held sway. During the six-week siege, 202,099 high explosive shells rained down on the ancient and beautiful city. The French, under the command of General Jean-Jacques Uhrich, were stunned to hear of the surrender of Sédan and the capture of the Emperor. The encirclement of the Army of the Rhine in Metz depressed morale even further. Ambitiously, the garrison made several sorties, but these achieved nothing.

In the meantime, their fortifications were being systematically reduced to rubble. The citizens of the city, who had lost 448 houses in the bombardment, urged Uhrich to surrender. They also suggested paying von Werder 100,000 francs for each day *he did not shell the city*.[20] On this and other occasions, the bombardment of a civil population was counter-productive in that it hardened opposition. This was a factor when the bombardment of Paris was proposed.[21]

In Strasbourg, the surrender option seemed to be sensible, and especially so when, on 19 September, the first of the city's fortifications fell into Prussian hands. On 27 September, Uhrich opened negotiations with von Werder and his garrison surrendered the following day.

The Prussians lost only 177 killed and 715 wounded – a small price to pay for such a politically important prize. French losses were 861 killed and an unknown number of wounded, probably about 3,000. A total of 3,023 Strasbourgers died during the siege, from a variety of causes. This was about 2,056 more than would have been expected in peacetime.[22] Clearly, disease and deprivation were as lethal as gunfire. Also, 17,562 prisoners were taken and marched into grim prison camps like that at Iges. The materiel losses were significant and included fifty locomotives, 1,277 field guns and 140,000 rifles. The consequences of this victory were that railway lines to the French interior became available and von Werder's 40,000 men were now available, either to tighten the noose around the Parisian neck or confront the new armies Gambetta hoped to raise in the provinces.

The loss of Strasbourg was a further blow to the GND, which had established a 'shadow government' at Tours. This was led by Isaac Crémieux and he was supported by senior officials carrying on the work of their respective ministries.[23] It was an unsatisfactory arrangement because the Paris Government continually obstructed or overruled that in Tours. A decision, taken on

24 September, to cancel the election planned for 2 October exacerbated already strained relations.

On 29 September, ten days after the investment of Paris, the *francs-tireurs* were placed under formal military command. This had become necessary to quell the murderous indiscipline that they had been displaying to 'the terror and the ruin of the countryside which they should have protected'.[24] At times their appalling behaviour exceeded even that of the Prussians.

The historian Isabel Hull saw 1870–71 as a precedent that changed the German Army's behaviour towards civilians and irregulars. She wrote, 'It was the origin of a ruthless military culture centred on "military necessity", which

The *Neptune*, the first balloon used to carry mail during the Siege of Paris, being prepared for launching, 23 September 1870.

The ruins of Strasbourg, 30 September 1870.
(Deutsch-Franzosischer Kreig, Belagerung von Strasbourg)

led to the subsequent atrocities in German colonies and during the First World War.'[25]

There is a counterview. Alexander Watson opined:

German actions were neither unusual nor was their conduct out of place, compared to other contemporary armies' norms of violence; if anything, they were milder, and therefore attempts to present the atrocities as a prelude or pointer to Nazi genocide and annihilation warfare in eastern Europe three decades later lack credibility.[26]

The Parisian newspapers were not inhibited by any lack of information and they stoked the rumour mill assiduously. On 29 September, for example, it was reported that the Prussians were in retreat towards the coast. Quite why this powerful dominating force that had swept all before it should retreat and in such an unlikely direction was not explained.

Earnest Picard, a member of the Council, was a proponent for the censorship of the press and said so frequently and publicly, but he was opposed by his colleague Jules Favre. The rumour mill ground on, adding daily to public disquiet. However, by late November and after ten weeks of siege, even the uncompromising Favre conceded that the newspapers were making Trochu's attempts at the even-handed government of Paris impossible.[27]

Ambassador Washburne wrote in his diary in late September, after only two weeks of siege, 'I wish there could be a balloon to come in, for this absence of intelligence from the outside world is becoming unbearable.'[28] He, like so many others, was quite unable to carry out his function because Paris was not now the centre of government and had not been so since 27 September. Washburne's diplomatic relationship was with the government of Napoleon III, not with the unelected Government of National Defence, whose writ was now limited to the confines of one city and whose authority was about to be the subject of attack.

Trochu, with his 500,000 men under arms, was under pressure to 'do something'. The something was anticipated as being military in nature but for what purpose was unclear. A social phenomenon of the Siege of Paris and home to the 'do something' campaign was the role played by the 'Red Clubs'. These establishments had been proscribed during the recent days of empire but, in late September, a number reopened as watering holes and were espoused by the under-employed *GN*. These clubs were a substitute for the theatres, low-cost restaurants and cafés. They provided entertainment and a degree of mental stimulation. They were hotbeds of anti-government rhetoric and ill-considered political and military philosophy. One observer commented:

> It is touching to see how these flocks of men are duped by the printed and spoken word, how marvellously deficient is their critical faculty. The sacrosanct word 'democracy' is able to fabricate a catechism even richer in miraculous fairy stories than the old ones, and these people are quite ready to gulp it down devoutly.[29]

That is the view of an educated, liberal-leaning individual. Reading between the lines one can detect a hint of contempt that he, a member of the bourgeoisie, had for the lower-class Parisian. This attitude was widespread, but the sentiment was warmly reciprocated. The hard-left publications of Pyat, Delescluze and Blanqui all attributed to the membership of the clubs an influence beyond their worth. This was to the extent that Pyat advised President Trochu that he should 'consult the clubs' before he embarked on any operation. The officers of the *GN* were elected by the members and so the clubs were the site of electioneering by prospective officers.

One of those successfully elected was Gustave Flourens. He was a committed revolutionary who had sought to raise a rebellion against the Empire on 7 February. It failed and Flourens had to flee to England, which he thought 'could be great, if only she had no Lords and no Bible'. When Napoleon III was captured at Sédan, Flourens hurried home. He managed to get himself elected to command a battalion of 500 men, a role for which he was totally ill-equipped. He was an extrovert and flamboyant poser, given to colourful uniforms of his own design and with a surfeit of self-confidence. Sarah Bernhardt, the actress, was one of many who fell under his spell.

Gustave Flourens (1838–71).

She described him as 'full of dreams and utopian follies. He was tall and nice-looking. He wanted everyone to be happy and everyone to have money.'[30]

Trochu was beset on all sides but he did not lack resolve, and removed from office Jacques Mottu, the aggressively atheist mayor of the 11th arrondissement, whose behaviour had become just too extreme to ignore. He had ordered the removal of crucifixes from schools and hospitals in his arrondissement – this in France, one of the most devotedly Catholic countries on earth. Mottu had also forbidden church attendance and he closed religious establishments, evicting nuns and priests.[31]

Trochu despatched Mottu to the political back benches and, in order to appease those calling for 'something to be done', he acquiesced at General Vinoy's plan to mount an 'offensive reconnaissance' on 30 September. This was to be up the left bank of the Seine to storm the villages of L'Hay, Thaïs and Chevilly (now Chevilly-Larue). Chevilly is less than 6 miles (10km) from the centre of Paris. 'Offensive-Reconnaissance' is a contradiction in terms and nonsense. Military men, the world over, go through a mental checklist before they embark on an operation. In the UK it's called an 'appreciation of the situation' and the first question is *always* 'what is the aim?' It might be something like, take that hill or capture that bridge, or clear the enemy from ... Once the aim has been selected the operation is equipped and manned to satisfy that aim. There is no deviation from the aim and no caveats. Vinoy did not go through that simple thought process and committed his 20,000-man force against the entrenched, well-found Prussian VI Corps. Quite what Vinoy hoped to achieve has never been explained.

There was no 'reconnaissance' element in this sortie but plenty of ill-directed offence. The villages were not of any great strategic value and, if taken, would have to be held and supported logistically. In the event, the operation, dignified as the Battle of Chevilly, was a miserable failure. The French were obliged to withdraw, having suffered 2,100 casualties and achieved nothing.[32] Prussian losses were 441.

The Chevilly debacle is a firm indication that Trochu's plans for the defence of Paris were not woven into a single cohesive French military strategy. French military affairs were completely devolved. Bazaine continued to hold Metz but was passive. Gambetta was making arrangements to leave Paris for Tours, and from there organise new armies. Trochu had a multitude of men under his command but no apparent intention of using them productively.

The President and General wrote in his memoirs: 'I had no idea of strategy and none of tactics. I had no object in view except to get the Germans involved in another Saragossa.'[33] This was an extraordinary admittance to be made by a general with a lifetime in the Army.

General Trochu was no longer a functioning president and, by his own admission, he was not a functioning general either. He was, in effect, only the nominal Governor of Paris. It prompts one to ask, how did Trochu rise through the ranks of the French Army and become a general? Men, brave men, died at his behest, and that of other inadequate officers such as Bazaine and Ducrot. The system that produced military mediocrities of this ilk had failed France.

Notes

1. Howard, p. 319.
2. Horne, p. 67.
3. Ibid., p. 64.
4. *Guerre, Investissement de Paris*, Vol. 1, pp. 22–3.
5. *MMK*, pp. 324–6, 334.
6. von Schnellendorff, P. Bronsart, *Geheimes Kriegstagebusch 1870–1871* (Bonn, 1954), pp. 183, 189.
7. Horne, p. 87.
8. National Archive (US) Ser. Set 1789, Bismarck to Washburne, 29 October 1870.
9. D.T.I., pp. 419, 421.
10. *Francs-tireurs* (*Encyclopaedia Britannica*, 1911 edition), pp. 15–16.
11. *Encyclopaedia Britannica*, 1911.
12. Ibid.
13. Pelet-Narbonne, G. von, *Cavalry on Service* (London, 1906), p. 322.
14. West, R., *War and Peace in Vietnam* (London, Sinclair Stevenson, 1995), p. 31.
15. Howard, p. 251.
16. Ibid., p. 249.
17. *MMK*, p. 131.
18. Chrastil, R., *The Siege of Strasbourg* (USA, Harvard University Press, 2014), p. 110.
19. Howard, p. 273.
20. Chrastil, p. 214.
21. Howard, p. 275
22. Flach, J., *Strasbourg après le bombardment 2 Octobre 1870–30 Septembre 1872* (Strasbourg, 1873), pp. 1–2, 95.
23. Ibid., p. 237.

24. DO 1, p. 413.
25. Hull, I., *Absolute Destruction: Military Culture and the Practices of War in Imperial Germany* (Ithaca, NY: Cornell University Press, 2005), pp. 117–30.
26. Watson, A., 'Unheard of Brutality. Russian Atrocities against Civilians in East Prussia, 1914–1915' (*Journal of Modern History*, 86, No. 4, 2014), pp. 780–825.
27. Favre, J., *Gouvernement de la Défense Nationale* (Paris, 1871–75), Vol. III, p. 297.
28. Ibid., p. 88.
29. Goncourt, Journal.
30. Bernhardt, S., *My Double Life* (Wilhelm Heinemann, now Penguin, 1907), p. 220.
31. Wawro, p. 234.
32. Vinoy, J., *Siège de Paris* (Paris, 1872), pp. 183–98.
33. Trochu, L.-J., *Oeuvres posthumes*, Vol. II (Tours, 1896), p. 273. (A curious and irrelevant reference to the battle fought in 1710. There were no Germans or Prussians involved; only Austrian troops.)

Chapter Eleven

October: Civil Disorder and the Fall of Metz

October was a tumultuous month in the Franco-Prussian War, both militarily and politically. There was activity of one sort or another in Paris, Le Bourget, Orléans, Tours, Metz and various European capitals. In order to put all of these disparate activities into their proper perspective this text deals with each in its chronological order. This does involve some mental acrobatics on behalf of the reader as the scene changes, but it is hoped that juggling these events in this manner will provide a coherent overview. However, the siege and capitulation of Metz, which culminated during October, is treated as a single entity, at the end of this chapter.

* * *

Trochu was still being persistently pressed by Flourens, who demanded to know why the enemy had not been attacked daily since the siege began. He considered the Chevilly sortie to have been insufficient and insisted that the vast military potential of the *GN* was not being properly exploited.

Eventually, on 5 October, having raised a head of steam, Flourens, leading a body of 10,000 *GN*, attempted a coup. The mob marched to the Hôtel de Ville (Town Hall). Flourens wore one of his absurd uniforms and the mob was accompanied by bands, which, at intervals, played the *Marseillais*. Flourens confronted Trochu and claimed that he represented the entire *GN*, and it was on that basis that he presented a number of demands. These included an immediate sortie by the *Garde*, the re-equipping of the *GN* with Chassepôts, new uniforms, municipal elections and the recruitment of Garibaldi, the Italian revolutionary, to aid the cause.

Trochu, to his credit, handled the volatile, possibly dangerous, situation with aplomb. He explained that 'purposeless sorties by large masses of un-disciplined men ... were hazardous'.[1] Gustave Dorian, the Minister of Works and Armaments Production, was present, and he told Flourens, 'I could more easily give you cannons than Chassepôts.' Trochu's quiet courtesy to the inflated Flourens surprised witnesses to the encounter and reported that the General/President closed the conversation by telling Flourens, 'Your place is on the ramparts and not in the Hôtel de Ville.'[2] The *Garde* withdrew noisily, booing Trochu and the unpopular General François Tamisier, who had been appointed, on 6 September, to be the overall commander of the *GN*.

The Government of France, having shifted to Tours, found communication with Paris impossible. The delegation in Tours assumed the governance of the country and it was this situation that persuaded Léon Gambetta, on 7 October, to take the unprecedented step of flying out of the city in a balloon. He was the Minister of the Interior and was best able to deal with the ramifications of an election if one were to be held. He was, in addition, anxious to continue his crusade to raise new armies in the provinces.

For Bismarck, finding someone to negotiate an armistice with became all the more difficult. Trochu's responsibilities were effectively limited to Paris. Gambetta, in Tours, was still only a member of the GND and not able to represent France. The Emperor was a prisoner and Bazaine was incarcerated in Metz. Maintaining the siege seemed to be the only course open – perhaps something might turn up?

Gambetta was an energetic, charismatic man, an outstanding public figure and better employed outside Paris rather than cooped up inside. His flight was not the first example of the military use of the third dimension. They had been used for observation for over a hundred years. As far back as 1799, the French Balloon Corps had been disbanded by Napoleon I.[3] Nevertheless, the aerial element would be a present in every siege from this date forward. Eugène Godard, a French aeronaut, made the arrangements for Gambetta's flight.

This flight was a hazardous undertaking as the balloon was made of varnished cotton and filled with highly flammable coal gas. It made a very large target and was susceptible to small arms fire. The balloon was subject to the vagaries of the wind and there was no possibility of a return journey. In the event, Gambetta took with him as much official mail as the balloon would carry. After Gambetta's, there were sixty-four further flights and only five of these fell into enemy hands. A total of 164 passengers, 381 homing pigeons, and about 11 tons of messages, including 2.5 million letters, were taken from Paris by balloon during the siege. The homing pigeons were not a success: 320 were launched but only fifty-nine ever made it back to their home in Paris.

The day after Gambetta's flight there was a further major demonstration mounted by the *GN*. Flourens kept a low profile and his place was taken by a miscellany of hard-left republicans led by Eugène Varlin and Théophile Sapia. The atmosphere was different, ball ammunition had been issued and there was a scent of suppressed violence in the air. This was less a demonstration, much more the early manifestation of revolt. Trochu had had prior knowledge of the event and had taken the precaution to call forward 'loyal' troops from the middle-class arrondissements. There was a confrontation between two large groups of armed men – all of whom were, ostensibly, members of the same *Garde Nationale*.

It would only take a single spark to cause a massive social and military conflagration. Théophile Sapia, one of the most extreme participants, was thought to be likely to strike that spark and his own side, recognising the danger he presented, seized him – then they handed him over to Trochu. This was an unexpected turn of events and a fortuitous period of drenching rain was enough to quell the last glimmer of revolution, at least it was on 8 October. Sapia faced a court martial but, to Trochu's irritation, he was acquitted.

Émile de Kératry, the Chief of Police, who had been in office only since 4 September, wanted to pursue Flourens and Blanqui. However, to arrest these two high-profile 'Reds' would be a risky business and Trochu forbade it. de Kératry was outraged, resigned and caught the next balloon out of Paris. Blanqui held forth in his newspaper, proclaiming mildly and accurately that:

> the good Germans will await phlegmatically the end of our cattle and our flour. After which the Government of National Defence will declare in unison that Paris has defended itself heroically, and that it is now time to think of the *pot-au-feu* … October 8th will mark in history the day that the first article of the capitulation of Paris was written by bourgeois bayonets; the others will follow of their own accord.[4]

Labouchere, who had observed events of 5 and 8 October, wrote ominously, 'What will be the upshot of this radical divergence of opinion between the two principal classes which are cooped up together within the walls of Paris, it is impossible to say.' His apparent pessimism was remarkably prescient.

Gambetta made an immediate impact as he toured 'free' France. By force of personality Gambetta was able to persuade the various shades of republicanism to unite in a common cause – that of victory. Gambetta assumed control over the Ministry of War in addition to his already onerous duties as Minister of the Interior (Home Secretary in British terms). In this latter appointment he was responsible for the mobilisation and equipping of the *Garde Nationale*. As War Minister he was responsible for their deployment.[5]

His eloquence and fervour won him support even from those who had previously opposed him. Soon after his safe return to terra firma and ensconced in Tours, Gambetta issued a proclamation, in which he said:

> We must set all our resources to work – and they are immense. We must shake the countryside from its torpor, guard against stupid panic, increase partisan warfare and, against the enemy so skilled in ambush and surprise, ourselves employ ruses, harass his flanks, surprise his rear – in short, inaugurate a national war … Tied down and contained by the

capital, the Prussians, far from home, anxious, harassed, hunted down by our reawakened people will be gradually decimated by our arms, by hunger, by natural causes.[6]

This was stirring stuff and perhaps that consummate historian, Sir Winston Churchill, took note seventy years later, when he delivered a similar message to a beleaguered nation. Gambetta was not inhibited by any need to conform to the previous norm and, in the face of considerable opposition from seasoned and wise officers in the Ministry of War, he declared:

I have determined to quit the usual paths. I wish to give young active chiefs capable by their intelligence and their energy of renewing the prodigies of 1792. Therefore, I have no hesitation in breaking with the old administrative conditions.[7]

Throwing out the old and introducing the new, without a trial, is a calculated risk. The Ministry of War was soon in some disarray and Gambetta made mistakes – he was, after all, exercising massive control over a discipline in which he had no expertise. Enthusiasm was not, in itself, enough, but it helped, and he pursued, energetically, the raising of new armies and with some success.

Gambetta wasted no time and by 10 October his 'Armée de la Loire' was engaged with the Bavarian I Corps of General von der Tann. Initially they met outside Artenay. It was little more than a skirmish, but nevertheless, von der Tann took four guns and about 850 prisoners. The baptism of fire for the Army of the Loire had been nothing to celebrate. However, Artenay was a prelude to the much more significant battle for Orléans on 11 October.

The French commander of the newly formed XV Corps, the elderly General Joseph Édouard de La Motte-Rouge, decided to withdraw behind the Loire, and there he positioned 15,000 men on the right bank of the river. It was a position that afforded a good defence. The French commander knew that he was obliged 'to cling onto Orléans. To lose it would end his military career and force Gambetta's government delegation (in Tours) to flee further south.'[8] The French consolidated their position behind the steep embankment of the Orléans/Le Mans railway line, behind stone walls and in the abundant stone houses available to them. They should have been able to contain von der Tann, but 28,000 men and 160 guns, coupled with sound leadership, Prussian determination and drive, carried the day. Taking the city gave von der Tann access to all the accumulated stores and, more importantly, a treasury of railway rolling stock with which to enhance his logistic train. Moltke commented:

The French rear-guard had lost in retreats alone 1,800 prisoners; but it had covered the retreat of the main body of the Army of the South for a whole day against superior forces, with praiseworthy determination. In the open field, where skilful handling of masses is possible, it would soon have been defeated; but in street-fighting unflinching personal courage is all that is needed in the defender, and the latest recruits of the newly created French levies did not lack that attribute.

de La Motte-Rouge paid for his defeat. Gambetta demanded that he be tried by court martial but was dissuaded from this extreme measure by wise voices in the Ministry of War. Instead, he agreed to replace him with General Claude d'Aurelle de Paladines. This officer was exactly the medicine a defeated army needed. He visited every regiment, spoke to the men, reminded them of the military traditions that they were charged to uphold and did not conceal the realities of their situation. In a nutshell, d'Aurelle de Paladines was a leader, and a good one. His energy and ebullient personality raised morale and by so doing transformed 'a leaderless, demoralised rabble into a disciplined and reasonably confident army'.[9] He moved his XV Corps into Salbris in the department of Loir-et-Cher, approximately 33 miles (53km) from Orléans and, on the face of it, a safe haven in which to regroup.

d'Aurelle, an old school soldier, did not admire Gambetta or his style, but he actively loathed his right-hand man de Freycinet and his aggressive, simplistic doctrinaire approach to matters military. d'Aurelle exercised correct professional caution and his every move was considered. He declined to accept the daily instructions from his civilian, unelected superior.

A decree published on 12 October ordered every canton to find a battalion, every arrondissement a legion and every department a brigade. These units were to be raised and equipped by the civil authorities. It was at this stage that they were then placed under the Ministry of War for initial training and discipline.

The aim was to relieve Paris.

There is no doubt that if, and it was an 'IF' in capital letters, Gambetta's

General Claude d'Aurelle de Paladines (1804–77).

'Armies of the South' could be equipped, trained, well led and skilfully deployed, they could create havoc in the Prussian logistic chain – not least if they could cut the rail link that ran from Nancy through Toul, Châlons and Meaux.[10]

At this early stage Bismarck was determined to bombard Paris into submission because he realised that the longer the city was invested the more the international standing of Prussia was degraded. The power and speed of the Prussian Army had raised qualms across Europe. In Florence, the Italian Foreign Minister confided in the British ambassador the view that 'Germany must be stopped! A united Germany with sixty million people and with France annihilated? What will become of the balance of power?'[11]

Internationally, views of the situation were mixed. Tsar Alexander II was providing tacit moral support to Bismarck in return for a promise to assist in restoring access to the Black and Mediterranean seas (denied by post-Crimean War treaties). Only two nations, the USA and Spain, had recognised the Government of National Defence as being the legitimate Government of France.

French naval supremacy gave access to the arsenals of Britain and the USA, whose arms manufacturers exploited the opportunity to offload stocks of obsolescent rifles. There was an embarrassment of riches as the products of eighteen different manufacturers were unloaded: Enfields, Springfields, Spencers, Sniders Winchesters, Remingtons et al.[12] There was a range of calibres and the provision of ammunition and tying it into a rifle that could discharge was a different logistic issue. This miscellany of indifferent firearms was given to the *GN* – who bleated for Chassepôts.

In the matter of artillery provision France was well served, domestically, by its foundries and arsenals at Bourges, Toulouse, Rennes, Nantes, Lyons and Besançon. They had the capacity to meet the demand, although they were not able to produce to the quality of Herr Krupp. During the war, 1,500 guns had been called for and 1,270 had been delivered – the balance came from the UK and the USA. However, it was not a shortage of guns, but a dearth of gunners that was a constant problem.

French needs were not limited to small arms and artillery; there was an urgent requirement for uniforms, saddlery, boots, blankets and tentage. These were available domestically, but the commercial imperative held sway. Those deputed to purchase commodities on behalf of their department to fit out their component of the *GN* or *Mobiles* found themselves competing in a sellers' market. The consequence was that the readiness of the French auxiliary army was patchy.

It was the training of *GN* and the *Gardes Mobile* that was the Achilles's heel of Gambetta's new armies. This host of men was sent to 'hastily constructed camps in ill-chosen sites that were seldom ready to house the floods of men sent to them, accommodated them at best in miserable discomfort'.[13] The training, such as it was, was cursory. An English journalist visited a camp near Boulogne and, soon after, filed a report for his paper that read:

> The scene was simply ludicrous. The officers, with one or two excep-tions, kept aloof, talking with their friends … Many of the men were engaged in position drill. Then they formed in battalion, and performed sundry evolutions in so clumsy a manner that the officers gave it up in despair, split the battalion into squads of six and ten men and ordered skirmishing again … 'It is difficult to teach what one is ignorant of oneself,' remarked one officer to another.
>
> Of discipline there was none. The men never saluted their officers, and spoke to them with easy and in some cases impudent familiarity … Everything about them was dirty.[14]

It was with these assets that Gambetta entertained expectations of defeating the Prussian Army and relieving Paris and Metz from siege. Gambetta could not work single-handed, and he quickly recognised and enlisted the talented Charles de Freycinet as his close associate. Freycinet was an engineer with a quick mind and a flair for administration. He became Gambetta's 'pleni-potentiary in matters operational as well as administrative'.[15]

Gambetta's style did not endear himself to the Army, now being mobilised, and especially not to the most senior soldiers. General Louis d'Aurelle de Paladines, writing two years later of the events of late 1870, said of Gambetta that 'he was to offend it daily, by his harshness, his demeanour, his com-plete ignorance of hierarchical principles which he had determined to tread under foot'.[16]

d'Aurelle was clearly deeply aggrieved. He was expressing his own opinion in a book (that sold very well) and made no claim to reflect the views of others. However, it is probable that his opinion was shared by fellow senior officers. At this difficult time, Gambetta needed all the friends he could find. It is blindingly obvious that, when trying to form and deploy armies, winning the hearts and minds of the generals who will lead those armies is a high priority. Gambetta failed in this respect and his unpopularity worked against him. He overplayed his hand.

The new armies being formed to relieve Paris did not lack the raw material. There was manpower in abundance. Ignoring the army penned up in Metz and the almost 500,000 men under siege in Paris, there was still a further million men of military age able to serve. Manpower was not the issue; in fact, such a number raised several problems. First was the training of this multi-tude, the where and with what? Second, its dressing, equipping and billeting.

Third, and possibly the most important, how was this mass to be led, where were the officers? On 16 September, just after the decree was issued the local military commander in Blois reported that he had 940 men under command and was expecting another 1,500. To lead and train this 2,440 he had six officers, and nineteen NCOs.[17]

In Paris, Ambassador Washburne was able to strike comparisons with the US Civil War and Washington DC after the Battle of Bull Run. He remarked, 'Nothing was completed, and confusion everywhere was immense. Had the Prussians known the weakness of Paris [on 19 September] they could have come right in ... But since then the city fortifications have become well established.'[18]

The glorious weather of September gave way to autumnal conditions in October. It became chilly and damp. Moltke commented:

> There was no lack of accommodation for the troops, for every village was deserted; but this made the difficulty of obtaining supplies all the greater. The fugitive inhabitants had driven off their cattle and destroyed their stores; there remained only the apparently inexhaustible wine-cellars. For the first few days all the food needed had to be drawn from the Commissariat trains, but ere long the cavalry succeeded in obtaining considerable supplies. High prices and good discipline secured a market.
>
> Only the troops in advanced positions had to bivouac or build huts, many within range of the hostile artillery, some even within rifle-shot of the enemy. Near St Cloud, for instance, no one could show himself without becoming a mark for the Chassepôts from behind the shutters of the houses opposite. The outposts here could only be relieved at night, and sometimes had to remain on duty two or three days at a time.[19]

It was not comfortable for the French soldiers manning the battlements, but they had some creature comforts. By early October it was evident that the Prussians had no intention of storming Paris and, by merely encircling the city, they denied Trochu the battle he relished. It was a stand-off. Trochu now placed his hopes on Gambetta and the new armies he was raising – officers or not. He also gave some thought to a foray in strength, a thrust into the Prussian line that might well bring a rich reward. However, he judged that the time was not yet ripe.

In the provinces the officer deficiency was not solved but, to de Freycinet, the simple expedient was to double the size of a company, thus reducing the officer deficiency by half. That was such an absurdly simplistic measure that, far from solving a problem, it made it worse. The US Federal Army, during the Civil War, had tried the same expedient – it did not work in the early 1860s and it did not work in 1870. With insufficient officers, discipline was eroded, and military efficiency was degraded. The mental and physical pressure on the few officers available had a deleterious effect on them as overwork took its toll. The capacity for these overlarge companies to manoeuvre was limited and could only be effected with 'ponderous slowness'.[20] This slowness made these French formations virtually sitting targets for artillery and small arms fire; it was a fatal battlefield weakness, soon to be exploited by a more agile foe.

Gambetta's decision to ignore the old system did have some benefits. One of these was his management of the officer problem. He issued a further decree on 13 October that swept away the long-established rules for commissions and promotions. He was able to commission retired NCOs returning to the colours and numerically, at least, this was a step in the right direction. He also was now able to promote young men on merit to general's rank without recourse to age or seniority.[21]

By decree, all troops who were not regular army, such as the *francs-tireurs*, the *GN mobilisées* and the *Mobiles*, were to be incorporated into an auxiliary army in which anyone of any background, experience or nationality could be appointed to hold any rank.[22] By this means foreigners such as Giuseppe Garibaldi or naval officers like Admirals Jaurès and Jauréguiberry were able to serve as French Army officers. The net was spread far and wide but, overall, the quality was indifferent. They do say that 'there are no bad soldiers, only bad officers'. Unfortunately, even outstandingly capable officers have their limitations and Gambetta had very, very few who fell into the outstandingly capable bracket to call on.

General Louis d'Aurelle de Paladines did not make his damning judgement on Gambetta until after the war. Perhaps it was just as well because in October 1870, after the loss of Orléans, Gambetta had appointed him to command the Army of the Loire. This was despite his often-voiced monarchist and Catholic beliefs, which as far as Gambetta was concerned were outweighed by his experience and ability.

In Paris there were fervent hopes that Gambetta's new armies would soon come to the rescue, because life was starting to become uncomfortable. There was dissension among the poorer people who had to bear the brunt of the shortages endemic in sieges – principally, food supply. Trochu was still the notional president, but he was unable to exercise authority beyond his walls. The functional president of France was Léon Gambetta, operating from Tours. Moltke was an interested observer of Gambetta's peregrinations and he made post-war judgement that the French:

> reserve store of 2,000 guns and 400,000 Chassepôts [this is an opinion not supported by the facts] assured the means of armament, and the

workshops of neutral England were ready and willing to fulfil commissions. Such resources for war, backed by the active patriotism of the nation, could maintain a prolonged resistance if a master will should inspire it with energy.

And such a will was disclosed in the person of Gambetta … in a Republic, a victorious general at the head of the Army would at once have become a dictator in his stead. M. de Freycinet, another civilian, served under Gambetta as a sort of Chief of the General Staff, and the energetic, but dilettante, commandership exercised by these gentlemen cost France very dear. Gambetta's rare energy and unrelenting determination availed, indeed, to induce the entire population to take up arms, but not to direct these hasty levies with comprehensive unity of purpose. Without giving them time to be trained into fitness for the field, with ruthless severity he despatched them into the field in utter inefficiency as they were called out, to attempt the execution of ill-digested plans against an enemy on whose firm solidity all their courage and devotion was inevitably wrecked. He prolonged the struggle at the cost of heavy sacrifices on both sides, without turning the balance in favour of France.[23]

Moltke knew a thing about soldiers and soldiering and that measured judgement of Gambetta is his military epitaph. Nevertheless, from early October 1870, the citizens of Paris rested all their hopes on Gambetta as they buckled down to siege conditions and contended with the worsening weather. Their increasingly squalid living conditions were as nothing compared to life in Metz, where Bazaine and his army were eating their way through their cavalry horses.

In Paris, Trochu was trying to juggle all the competing demands being made upon him. He was undeterred by Vinoy's abortive sally on 30 September and decided to try something similar again. On 13 October, Vinoy launched an attack on the villages of Clamart, Châtillon and Bagneux, all of which were on the forward slope of the Villacoublay plateau and within range of the French guns in the forts of Vanves and Montrouge, which could provide artillery support.

Vinoy was faced by the Bavarian II Corps, slightly less redoubtable opponents than a Prussian formation. Vinoy took both Clamart and Bagneux, and part of Châtillon. Then, having sustained 400 casualties, he withdrew, taking 200 Bavarian prisoners with him. These prisoners were extra mouths to feed and were, statistically, insignificant in the order of things. However, as a matter of principle, a besieged force taking prisoners flew in the face of common sense. This success, modest though it was, was celebrated in Paris by some.[24] Ducrot believed his side had had the better of the engagement.[25] However, it gave added impetus to the constant demands of the *GN* to be committed to battle. It craved the *sortie torrentiale*.

It fell to Ducrot to consider the future strategy. A breakout would only be of military value if it could widen the area of operations by linking up with Gambetta's forces. The site of any breakout would have to be carefully selected. To the west, the sinuous Seine with its triple bend appeared to present a major obstacle but, because the Prussians thought so too, it was the area most weakly defended.

An outline plan evolved. This was to engage 40,000 troops, who would cross the Seine onto the Gennevilliers peninsula. At this point, with the left flank protected by the Seine, the French force would drive on towards Rouen. A redoubt would be created and communication with Gambetta's force established by way of the sea.[26] This unlikely scenario became *L'plan Trochu*. It was the only plan, and Ducrot and his staff began to work through the myriad details that concern the movement of two army corps across a river and deep into enemy-held territory. The provision of transport, the resupply of food, ammunition, medical equipment and the evacuation of wounded had all to be catered for. It was a formidable task.

Ducrot decided that he needed to rehearse some elements of the operation. He intended to test the German defences, to take possession of the lower, western part of the Gennevilliers peninsula and build the morale and experience of his troops. The scale of this rehearsal was too small to win and hold ground, and too small to suffer great losses. The operation took place on 21 October and only one division of 8,000 men was employed (see map on page 195). Malmaison and Buzenval were taken, but on the defended ridge behind Buzenval, Prussian artillery was able to bring down sufficient fire to halt the advance and inflict casualties. Prussian infantry reserves came forward and, as the light faded, so too did French resolve. They withdrew, leaving behind 120 of their number as prisoners; 500 were dead or wounded and nothing material had been achieved. Despite this, Ducrot pronounced that he was content with the operation. His troops, even the *Mobiles*, had manoeuvred creditably, fought well and remained fairly steady under fire. He saw it all as a positive augury for the success of *L'plan Trochu*.[27] The implementation of *L'plan Trochu* was scheduled for the third week of November. Time enough to polish the plan and prepare the troops.

Towards the end of October, Brigadier Carey de Bellemare was in command of troops in the village of St Denis, a formidable redoubt that protected Paris on its northern face. Bellemare was a man whose personal ambition was not matched by his tactical ability. He was one of the many who criticised Trochu and was burning with a desire to take military action. On 27 October, he mounted a substantial fighting patrol of 250 *franc-tirailleurs* with orders to probe across open fields towards Le Bourget, a hamlet about 6 miles (10km) away (not shown on any maps).[28] This inconsequential place was currently a Prussian outpost.

Le Bourget was attacked and taken without difficulty; then it was rapidly reinforced. The architect of this operation hastened into Paris, where he spread the news of his conquest; his success was received with widespread celebration. Bellemare asked to see Trochu. When the brigadier was ushered in to see his president and commander, he made a series of demands, one of which was for artillery and another was his immediate promotion to major general.[29]

Trochu was having nothing of this nonsense. He was well aware that de Bellemare had created a deathtrap. Le Bourget provided no strategic or tactical advantages to the French; it now needed a line of logistic supply across ground dominated by Prussian artillery. The whole exercise would 'merely increase the death-roll for all'.[30] This view was shared with the Prussians, who had no pressing desire or need to hold Le Bourget. That said, conceding the village to the French was unacceptable and, after some dissension in Moltke's headquarters, it was decided to retake Le Bourget.

The assault on Le Bourget demonstrated a change in Prussian tactics when confronting entrenched troops armed with Chassepôts. The Prussian infantry recognised that the days of advancing in serried ranks, shoulder to shoulder, were gone. When facing breech-loading small arms there was a need to advance in very loose lines with wide space between individuals. By adopting this formation, the Prussians became the first exponents of the principle of 'fire and movement', in which one group moves while another provides fire onto the target. One hundred and fifty years later, that same principle is still universally applied, although it was forgotten in the trench warfare of the First World War – at enormous cost.

On the morning of 30 October, an artillery bombardment was opened on Le Bourget. It was accurate, and the 2,000 high explosive shells had a devastating effect. The infantry assault of 6,000 men that followed was ruthlessly effective. The fighting around the church of St Nicholas was as bitter as any in the war so far. There was prolonged house-to-house fighting and French reinforcements arrived, but they were too few and too late. The commander of a battalion of *Mobiles*, Major Ernest Barouche, shot himself rather than surrender. Nevertheless, the village changed hands. The French lost 1,200 men as prisoners, including several hundred dead. The Prussians had 477 casualties – all for a valueless, unimportant village.

The unbounded enthusiasm that had greeted the capture of Le Bourget was subsequently matched by a commensurate level of despair when it was lost.

This despair was further accentuated when news of the capitulation of the fortress of Metz was brought to Paris by Adolphe Thiers on 30 October. Moltke commented:

> This new disaster added to the dissatisfaction of the inhabitants of Paris. The revolutionary factions, which at all times lurk in the French capital, came ominously to the front.
>
> Highly coloured reports could no longer conceal utter lack of results; the authority of the Government was steadily on the wane. It was accused of incapacity, nay, of treason. Noisy mobs clamoured for arms, and even a part of the National Guard took part in the tumult. The Hôtel de Ville was surrounded by a throng shouting '*Vive la Commune!*' and though other troops dispersed these gatherings, the ringleaders, though well known, went unpunished.[31]

The events that led to the catastrophic loss of an army and its wider impact on the war, not least the Siege of Paris, merit close attention.

The fall of Metz

One of the ineradicable blots on the military history of France is the fall of Metz. It was an abject episode and the culmination of a brief three-month campaign. Historians have examined the conduct of Marshal Bazaine, the commander of the besieged fortress, seeking an explanation for the surrender of his army on 27 October 1870. His behaviour, intellect, leadership qualities, determination and political ambition have all been scrutinised – as have their bearing on the Siege of Paris and the ultimate outcome of the war.

Marshal Bazaine had retreated to the fortress after the Battle of Gravelotte on 18 August with his vast army intact. There had been an earnest hope in Paris that either de MacMahon and his Army of Châlons would fight their way to the city and relieve Metz, or that Bazaine would break out and meet de MacMahon. In Paris, encircled by Moltke's armies since 19 August, there was a presumption, among the uninformed, that two French armies would combine and march together to provide the salvation of Paris.

Bazaine's inadequate leadership had been exposed when he initiated the failed breakout to the east on 26 August and committed himself to a 60-mile (97km) odyssey across county to meet up with de MacMahon. Like so many French operations in this war, the staff work needed to coordinate the movement of tens of thousands of men and the provision of their equipment, food and ammunition was conspicuous by its absence. This breakout could expect to be harassed every inch of the way by the Prussian 2nd Army. Despite issuing orders for the breakout, Bazaine's obvious lack of enthusiasm for the operation drew adverse comment.

Moltke, later writing witheringly, said:

The whole affair of 26 August can only be regarded in the light of a parade manœuvre. Bazaine reported to the Minister of War that the scarcity of artillery ammunition made it 'impossible' to break through the hostile lines, unless an offensive operation from the outside 'should force the enemy to raise the investment'. Information as to the 'temper of the people' was earnestly requested.[32]

In the opinion of both Moltke and Bismarck there was no doubt that Bazaine was influenced, not wholly by military, but also by political considerations; his reluctance to leave Metz was indicative. Whilst besieged, Bazaine still commanded a considerable army in unimpaired condition, a political tool to be used at 'the given moment'. Moltke speculated that, 'at the head of the only French army not yet shattered, he might find himself in a position of greater power than any other man in the country'.[33]

In effect, the Prussian hierarchy saw Bazaine as a possible surrogate for Napoleon III with whom it could cobble together a workable armistice. They considered it 'not inconceivable that the Marshal, as the strongest power in the land, might be able to offer a price which should induce the enemy to grant him a passage [from Metz]'.[34] It was argued that, given Bazaine's freedom at the head of his army, would he not be the best person equipped to represent the Emperor and France in any negotiations and to ensure that French obligations arising from any armistice would be met in full? That was the Prussian view and at some stage Bazaine entertained similar thoughts. He was not politically aligned with Trochu and his self-appointed government, and he was not at one with Gambetta and his ilk. In early September 1870, Bazaine was one of the few Bonapartists with any power – albeit while besieged. There were, however, other Bonapartists with no power but a wealth of imagination.

In Metz, life was mundane and food and its unavailability were the source of discussion and anger. Sugar and coffee were now running low and, on 20 September, when the ration was reduced by a third, the deficiency was made up by substitution of *eau de vie*.[35] It was not popular.

At this point it is necessary to digress slightly and deal with the case of M. Edmond Régnier, who inserted himself into public affairs on 23 September.[36] This gentleman was a businessman and a devoted supporter of empire. He was a one-off but, briefly, he was at the centre of Franco/Prussian relations. Professor Sir Michael Howard wrote of him in terms that are uncompromising. He said of Régnier:

Yet there is something that commands respect about this man who had the energy, pertinacity and the self-confidence to gate-crash into the field of high diplomacy, like some member of the audience wandering onto the stage during a grand opera and boldly taking a hand ... He was convinced, with some reason, that Bismarck would prefer to negotiate with the Imperial régime rather than with the Council for National Defence and had therefore written, out of the blue, to the Empress in her exile in Hastings.[37]

In his letter to the Empress, Régnier suggested that she denounce the Government of National Defence and the Trochu government, place herself in the hands of the French fleet and then, rally to her cause loyalist members of the Army and the civilian population. Predictably, the Empress did not reply and declined to meet Régnier.

M. Régnier was not unduly discommoded by the rejection and decided that he would take his proposition to Napoleon III himself. However, to get to Napoleon he had to have the active support of Bismarck. Incredibly, Régnier persuaded the Prince Imperial (heir apparent) to pen his father a note on the back of a postcard of the Hastings sea front. Armed only with this document, Régnier sought an audience with the great Prussian statesman, who was, at that time, engaged in breaking the heart of Jules Favre (see chapter 9) over the terms for an armistice.

Bismarck met Régnier, heard him out and decided that he had nothing to lose. He *did* prefer to negotiate with the Imperial regime and Régnier 'gave him a second string to his bow'.[38] Régnier fleshed out his plan and asked for Bismarck's help in gaining access into the fortresses at Metz and Strasbourg (the latter did not fall until 28 September), where he could convince the respective commanders to capitulate, but in the name of the Emperor. This body of troops, released with its arms, would then overthrow the Government of National Defence and the Republic. It all sounded simple enough, if the personalities concerned cooperated and the constituent parts of the plan fell into place.

It was all rather unlikely, but nevertheless, Bismarck engineered a passage

Edmond Regnier (1822–86).

for his visitor through the lines of 2nd Army. Thus, on 23 September, using the postcard of Hastings as his only credential, Régnier entered Metz and asked to be taken to Bazaine.

Bazaine, in a parlous position, was unimpressed by Régnier and his plan. However, it filled a void because Bazaine had no plan of his own, other than to continue to tie up Prince Charles and his 2nd Army. Régnier suggested that it would be necessary for Bazaine to send an emissary to the Empress to assure her his army was in her support. General Canrobert, who was the first choice as the emissary, declined the mission and General Charles-Denis Bourbaki took his place.

That day, an anonymous soldier, certainly an officer, and probably of middle rank, wrote to Bazaine, delivered the letter to his door and slipped away. The letter, dated 23 September, was preserved in the French National Archive and one wonders why Bazaine did not destroy it because it read, damningly, as follows:

> You are aware of the rumours coursing through the army with regard to your inaction in the face of the enemy over the past twenty-two days … This inaction has ruined our cavalry and will soon ruin our artillery which will reduce the army to impotence. The tragedy at Sédan, and the army's continued ignorance as to the plans of its generals, makes it susceptible to the rumour that it is being prepared for delivery *pieds et poings* [feet and fists] to the enemy. And yet the enemy outside is inferior to us in every way; you must be aware of that fact. Surrender the army to the enemy when you have 130,000 elite troops in hand it is unthinkable.[39]

The letter did not have any discernible effect on Bazaine and on 25 September he bade Bourbaki farewell as, dressed in civilian clothes and wearing a Red Cross cap, he started out on the lengthy journey to England. Bourbaki was no fool and, while travelling, had ample time to review the situation. He soon realised that his mission had scant chance of success. While Bourbaki was en route, Bazaine launched the failed breakout of 26 August. Bourbaki knew the Empress well and, when eventually he reached her home in England, he was not overly surprised when she rejected the whole box of tricks. She said she would do nothing to hinder the Government of National Defence. Her refusal to be part of the exercise caused its immediate collapse. It might have all come to nothing, but Régnier had planted a seed in the mind of Marshal François Achille Bazaine – or perhaps in that of one of his senior officers?

Régnier had also inadvertently affected relations between the ruthless, political Bismarck and the soldierly Moltke, which had been strained for some time. The Régnier affair served to throw fuel on the fire. Moltke and Prince

Charles of 2nd Army shared the view that the fate of Bazaine and his army was a strictly military matter, and they were working towards a military solution. Bismarck, with the support of King Wilhelm, had muddied the waters and tied the hands of Moltke and Prince Charles in the process. On 29 September, as Bazaine and his men licked their wounds, Prince Charles sent a note to Bazaine advising him of the failure of Bourbaki's mission.

Régnier returned to the obscurity from which he had sprung. Bazaine had cause to regret ever having anything to do with Régnier because when he faced trial for treason after the war, Régnier gave evidence at the General Court Martial. Régnier was also called to account, but he fled to Switzerland, and was sentenced to death in absentia. He died in Ramsgate in 1886, at the age of 64.

In the beleaguered fortress a routine had been established and, day to day, the necessity of administration continued. Rations were issued, reports made, the sick were treated, dead were buried, fortifications strengthened, the horses fed but not groomed as they were intended for the knacker's yard. Drills were conducted half-heartedly by irritated, frustrated soldiers and, when necessary, disciplinary procedures were carried out. It was all morale-sappingly boring. Weapons that should have been cleaned were now neglected. The straw provided for bedding rotted and stank as many soldiers were afflicted with dysentery. Drinking helped to ameliorate the misery, but that led to a further degrading of discipline.

In a setting such as this, only high-grade leadership, from a charismatic commander, could maintain an army fit to fight. Bazaine was not that person. He laid great emphasis on administration to 'divert the minds of his subordinates from dangerous speculation'.[40] He issued daily bulletins that did nothing for morale, as he regularly described the 'invincible redoubts' of the Prussians. One French officer is recorded as expressing the view that his commanding general was 'deliberately demoralising the officers and frightening the men to make capitulation more palatable'.[41]

Foraging parties stole out of the fortress into no man's land to search for food from abandoned farms. Initially, these dangerous sorties were productive, but the besiegers also started to ransack the same properties and then razed them. The denizens of Metz began to starve.

Aware that he had to do something, but not sure what that might be, Bazaine called a conference with his corps commanders. This was unusual as it was his normal practice to consult no one. However, on 6 October, Bazaine suggested a breakout down the line of the Moselle River towards Thionville. The aim of the breakout was not identified. It was as if the breakout was an end in itself, something to do to counter the current idleness. General Grégoire Coffinières de Nordeck, the appointed garrison commander of

Metz, objected to Bazaine's plan on the basis that he already had 25,000 sick and wounded in his care and that the proposed breakout would probably generate a further 15,000 wounded, with no doctors, nurses or adequate supplies. He said he would need at least 20,000 fit men to remain with him to defend the fortress.

Bazaine took note of Coffinières's objections and adapted his plan. Instead of the original major operation, he decided on a large-scale raid to capture the recently gathered-in harvest, now stored in farms in the locale. This raid, dignified as the Battle of Bellevue, was initiated on 7 October and it did not go well. Although some farms and their produce were seized, the Prussian artillery rapidly came into action. It was sufficiently effective that the loading of wagons with grain, drawn by starving horses, was abandoned and the French withdrew into Metz. Prussian losses were higher than those of their adversary, but in the process the Prussians again frustrated a French advance, held the ground and most of the grain! The French lost 1,193 soldiers and 64 very valuable officers; the Prussians, 1,703 soldiers and 75 officers.

Some observers of Bazaine credit him with a political aptitude and cunning that belies his very obvious military failings. It is extraordinary that a man whose only discernible attribute was personal courage should have risen to the very top of the French Army. Bazaine was mediocre in every aspect of his military life. He was indecisive, logistically illiterate, lacking in imagination, and vastly overpromoted. It is argued that he did not have the Machiavellian political skills with which some credit him. At the Siege of Metz, his failings were writ large and acknowledged by his subordinates.

A siege, any siege, makes hard living for the besiegers and besieged alike – Metz was no different. The Prussian soldiers had no accommodation and about 40,000 of them were taken ill. The military hospitals were overflowing. It rained heavily and persistently, keeping dry was difficult, and drying wet clothes and boots impossible. Their logistic train was under pressure to sustain a force of almost 200,000 men now living in a muddy morass.

In the city, starvation started to show its hand and civil unrest led to rioting among civilians and ill-discipline among the military. Horses were being slaughtered to provide meat. Each horse that was slaughted reduced the cavalry or artillery capacity of the Army of the Rhine. Horsemeat is unpalatable, unless well salted. This fundamental item was in short supply and then, inevitably, stocks were exhausted. It was a minor crisis among many others. The civilian population of Metz struggled to maintain commercial life as best they could. Soldiers, tired of army rations, turned to the inns and hotels for food, but they too depended on horsemeat and the price rose to eighty times its normal amount. The cavalry and artillery horses were being slaughtered in large numbers and each corps was furnishing the abattoir with seventy-five horses per day.

Relations between the civilians and the military started to break down and the issue, the all-consuming issue, was food (no pun intended). General Coffinières accused his own army of eating food stocks intended for civilians and in response the military commanders counter-accused the civilians of hording supplies.[42] The atmosphere was ugly, and the gendarmerie had to be reinforced to maintain order. On 7 October, Coffinières reported to Bazaine that he had only sufficient flour to make bread, at the existing ration scale, for ten days. He added that, if the ration was reduced by two fifths, he could extend this to eighteen days. Typhus and smallpox had now taken root and malnutrition started to show in the faces of all in Metz.

On 10 October, after a welcome but brief period without rain, the weather had broken, and rain pelted down onto the camps, turning them into lakes of mud. As the rain came down, a council of war was called. It was no more than a meeting of the senior officers. The aim of the meeting was to consider their position and review the options open. Bazaine opened the meeting by stating that there was only sufficient food to allow resistance until 20 October. That stark fact coloured and limited the discussions. The findings of this 'council' were that, despite the hopeless military position, they should hold out for as long as possible as they were tying down two armies that might otherwise be fighting Gambetta's armies in the Loire region. Nevertheless, negotiations with the enemy should be opened *to secure an honourable settlement* (author's emphasis). The final option, if all else failed, was a further breakout.

Pursuing the 'honourable settlement', Bazaine revived and developed Régnier's previously abandoned philosophy. He signed a letter to Bismarck outlining his plan. He may have signed it and thereby taken ownership of the content, but the very high probability is that it was drafted and polished by his staff – a routine then, and now, in all military organisations.

Colonel Napoléon Boyer, a member of Bazaine's personal staff, was deputed to take the letter and enter into negotiations with Bismarck, now ensconced in Versailles. Boyer was granted safe passage and he put Bazaine's case to Bismarck, saying that 'the Army in Metz remained faithful to the Emperor and would have nothing to do with the republic of Parisian lawyers'.[43] That said, he went on to suggest that, if released from Metz, the Army of the Rhine would take no further part in the war. It would withdraw into southern France or even Algeria, and by so doing, permit the Prussians to focus their attention on Paris and bring the war to a speedy conclusion. Boyer explained that once the republic was defeated, the Prussians could hand France over to Bazaine and his army, which, reinforced by 140,000 French POWs, would have no difficulty in finishing off the 'demagogic anarchy'

A measure of the medical issues in Metz was the need to use unheated railway wagons as hospital wards for the sick and wounded, pictured here, on the esplanade. The snow indicates that this photograph may have been taken sometime after the fall of the fortress. (*L. Rouseet*)

of Gambetta, and would restore a conservative government.[44] This was a breathtaking concept that, if nothing else, showed innovative thinking – not Bazaine's forte.

Some might interpret Bazaine's second bite of the cherry, as presented by Boyer, as treachery. Was the GND a properly constituted Government of France, was it in control of France, and did Bazaine owe it his unqualified loyalty? This would be a matter for lawyers sometime in the future. There can be no doubt that Bazaine saw himself as a potential 'saviour' returning from exile to defeat the 'Red Revolution' and restore the Emperor to his throne.[45]

Bismarck and Moltke received Boyer and considered his offer, but both were well aware of the dreadful conditions in Metz. They saw no pressing need to cooperate because the military solution in Metz was just around the corner and that at Paris not too far away. On that basis, Boyer's words were treated with studied indifference. Boyer could not counter the Prussians' crushing assessment of the wider war and French prospects as he had no information, having been confined in Metz for weeks.

Boyer's mission had failed, and he returned to Metz on 17 October. The content of his letter and the bones of his negotiations became public knowledge and had a spectacular impact. The matter was widely reported in the German press but, inevitably, suppressed by the French. Internationally, the response to the Boyer mission was positive. This was because the intransigence of the Government of National Defence and its refusal or inability to hold elections had tested the patience of other European powers. The terms of an armistice offered by Bismarck to the National Council were not deemed too onerous, given that France had instigated the war.

Boyer briefed Bazaine and his senior officers, and two days later journeyed to Chislehurst to see Empress Eugénie. She had changed her position since the Régnier incident and declared that she would indeed assist but, shrewd woman that she always was, asked exactly what peace terms was she being asked to accept. Boyer ducked the issue, as did the Prussian Embassy, because no terms had been agreed. Eugénie was being asked to sign a blank cheque.[46] She did write to King Wilhelm, appealing to his 'Royal heart and soldierly generosity'. Her words fell on stony ground and, when Wilhelm replied, he was courteous but uncompromisingly blunt in his rejection of her appeal.

On that same day, 22 October, all food stocks were exhausted. The very few remaining horses gnawed at each other's manes and tails and the troops lay in the inadequate shelter of their bivouac tents. 'Some wandered round the fields in a hungry search for potatoes, which the Germans were too humane to interrupt; others in an ever-swelling stream presented themselves at the German outposts in a pathetic surrender which the Germans refused to accept.'[47] The Siege of Metz was causing human misery on an heroic scale.

Life within the fortress of Metz was unpleasant, but it was not much fun outside either. The Prussian troops were very uncomfortable, so much so that later some would describe their time in September-October 1870 Metz as 'the bleakest days of their lives'.[48]

The issues of meat had been reduced as supplies dried up, the consequence of an outbreak of 'cattle plague'. Tinned meat was the unattractive and tedious alternative. The army of Prince Charles was huge – about 200,000 men and their logistic support in all its forms was a major exercise. Not least of the support issues was medical. Even without firing a shot, men fell ill and died, others were bedridden. Throughout the period of the siege, 22,090 were ill with gastric flu and typhus, the latter a direct consequence of poor hygiene: 1,328 died from these maladies; 27,959 suffered from dysentery, and that claimed 829 victims. Local village houses were requisitioned to provide cover of sorts from the elements. The priority for this meagre accommodation was for the many who were wounded in the battle of the previous month but were too ill to be moved. The weather turned, and protracted periods of heavy rain made life for the besieging Prussians outside Metz even more miserable. By late October, just short of 40,000 Prussian soldiers were hospitalised.[49]

The city was massively fortified, and Moltke had realised, back in August, that he could not take it by storm. Accordingly, he employed the very oldest siege weapon, that of starvation. Success was close to hand. On 23 October, Bismarck wrote to Bazaine saying: 'The proposals that have reached us from

London are, in the present situation, absolutely unacceptable, and I declare to my great regret that I can see no further chance of reaching a result by political negotiations.'[50]

Time was running out for the starving people in Metz, and as Boyer was travelling to England seeking Eugénie's support, the Americans sent General Ambrose Burnside to try to create a mutually acceptable peace. However, Favre remained adamant and was prepared to yield absolutely nothing. His position was that 'there will be no armistice until the last German has been driven from French soil'.[51] That uncompromising position put an end to any meaningful discussions about an armistice and it spelled doom for the Army of the Rhine.

Bazaine now had no other option but capitulation, although he still had the opportunity to preserve his dignity and that of his army. Instead, he acted curiously and unprofessionally over several issues. During a lifetime in the French Army, he was imbued with the culture of that army. Nevertheless, he ordered that every regiment should surrender their colours to the Prussians. The colours are not mere flags. To a soldier, they are the physical embodiment of a regiment's soul and are always to be treated with great reverence and never surrendered. Bazaine's order was inexplicable, aberrational, and was received at first with complete disbelief and then with the blackest of anger. Commanding officers preferred to burn their colours rather than surrender them. Bazaine later claimed with some justification that the surrender of the colours was a prerequisite directed by Prince Frederick Charles. Nevertheless, this issue alone earned Bazaine the unbridled contempt of tens of thousands. A hundred and fifty years later, colours are not carried in battle but their importance, to those who have them, is unchanged.

Bazaine had over 600 guns and, instead of ordering them to be 'spiked', he directed that they be handed over to the enemy in working order despite the imprecations of many of his officers. This order, thought by some to be treasonous, sparked riots. Soldiers attacked the quarters of General Coffinières and, illogically, set a fire in the cathedral. The anger of the rank and file with their commander and his senior officers was palpable.

Amid this domestic turmoil, Prince Charles courteously offered Bazaine and his men the opportunity to surrender with full military honours. This would have entailed Bazaine parading his men and, with officers mounted (if they could find a horse) and bands playing, marching the army *with its arms* (author's emphasis) to the Prussian lines. With singular ill-grace Bazaine declined the offer. After the event he offered the excuse that the weather was inclement and further that the troops were not fit enough for such a parade. He averred that, if his men were in contact with Prussians while still armed, he could not answer for their actions.[52] 'It is hard to avoid the conclusion

The surrender of the Army of the Rhine at Metz, 27 October 1870.
(Conrad Freyberg, 1876)

that his real fears were for himself, the leader whom the troops had barely seen since the beginning of the siege and whose incompetence had betrayed them.'[53]

On 27 October, in cold driving rain, he surrendered his 173,000 men, 6,000 officers, including three Marshals of France (Le Boeuf, Canrobert and Bazaine), and their guns with the minimum of ceremony. Among the booty taken by the Prussians were 622 field guns, 876 fortress guns, 3 million rounds of gun ammunition, 8.27cwt (420,000kg) of gunpowder, 137,000 Chassepôts, 13 million cartridges, 72 *mitrailleuses* and 123,000 assorted other small arms.[54] For French soldiers, the most crushing loss was the fifty-three regimental colours from a total of eighty-four. It was the ultimate humiliation.

It was a very black, bleak day for France. The picture above probably attributes the event rather more grandeur than it deserves.

Bazaine continued to act selfishly and irresponsibly. He had managed to get his wife out of Metz and into Prussian care early on 27 October and, having gone through the formalities of surrender, he met the Metz paymaster and collected his salary for September and October as a Senator and a Marshal of France.[55] On 29 October he made his way, in the pre-dawn darkness, to the Prussian lines. It was unfortunate timing because he was not expected until later in the day. Prince Charles was still abed and could not receive him.

The Marshal took refuge in a small cottage near Fort Saint-Quentin but on his way there he was seen by some of his soldiers, who roundly abused and threw stones and putrefying rubbish at him. The downfall of Marshal Bazaine was complete. He had set a new benchmark for military failure.

The Prussians acted with commendable compassion and courtesy. Food was provided, and French officers were able to retain their swords. Inside the fortress the Prussians found about 20,000 wounded and sick men requiring immediate medical assistance.

It was a charnel house, a filthy house. Dead horses, unburied corpses and burnt or putrefying refuse were all in abundance to greet the German victors when they entered to seize their prize. Its contents and condition were a testament to the suffering the French had endured.

Meanwhile, Paris was in the grip of civil dissent and acute food shortages. Its only hope of salvation rested firmly in the hands of Gambetta and his faltering new armies.

Notes

1. Horne, p. 59.
2. Ibid.
3. Joubert de la Ferté, P., *The Third Service* (London, Thames & Hudson, 1955), p. 1.
4. *La Patrie en Danger*, 9 October 1870.
5. Howard, p. 240.
6. Reinach, J., *Dépêches, Circulaires, Décrets, Proclamations et Discours de Léon Gambetta*, 2 Vols. (Paris, 1886), Vol. I, pp. 41–5.
7. Bury, J.T.P., *Gambetta and National Defence* (Bath University), p. 136.
8. Wawro, p. 260.
9. Howard, p. 288.
10. PRO, FO, 27, 1817. Tours, 2 September 1870, Lyons to Granville.
11. PRO, FO, 42illy5, 97. Florence, 2 September 1870. A. Paget to Granville.
12. Howard, p. 247.
13. Ibid., p. 248.
14. War Correspondent, *Daily News* (London, October 1871), probably Labouchère.
15. Howard, p. 242.
16. d'Aurelle, de Paladines, *La Première Armée de la Loire* (2nd ed., Paris, 1872), p. 132.
17. *Guerre, La 1st Armée de la Loire*, Vol. 1: Docs, annexes 99–100.
18. Horne, p. 103.
19. *MMK*, p. 145.
20. Howard, p. 245.
21. Reinach, Vol. II, p. 9.
22. Ibid., p. 10.
23. *MMK*, p. 115.
24. D.T., Vol. III, (Ducrot), p. 99.
25. Trochu, I, pp. 320–34.
26. Howard, p. 333.
27. Ducrot, Vol. I, pp. 373–409.
28. Le Bourget has long since been swallowed up by an expanding Paris. It gives its name to the major airport close by.
29. Trochu, *Oeuvres posthumes*, Vol. I, p. 348.
30. Herisson, M., D'I., *Journal of a Staff Officer* (London, 1885), p. 187.
31. *MMK*, p. 156.
32. Ibid., pp. 103–104.
33. Ibid.
34. Ibid.

35. Andlau, Baron, d', *Metz: Campagne et Négociations* (Paris, 1871), pp. 182–3, 267.
36. Bazaine, A., *Épisodes*, p. 178.
37. Howard, p. 270.
38. Ibid.
39. SHAT, Lt 12, Metz, 23 September 1870, '*un member de l'armée*'.
40. Ibid, p. 267.
41. Matthias, A., *Meine Kriegserinnerungen* (Munich, 1912), p. 65.
42. Bazaine, A., *Épisodes*, pp. 261–2.
43. Busch, M., *Bismarck: Some secret pages of his history*, 2 Vols. (New York, 1898), Vol. 1., pp. 188–9.
44. Wawro, p. 245.
45. SHAT, Lt 12, Brussels, 5, 6, 22 and 30 October 1870. Tachard to Favre, London, 12 and 27 October 1870.
46. Howard, p. 279.
47. Kretschman, H. von, *Kriegsbriefe aus den jahren 1870–71*, ed. Lilly Braun (Stuttgart, 1904), pp. 110, 118, 144.
48. Fermer, *France at Bay*, p. 48.
49. *GGS*, Vol. 3, pp. 176–9, Vol. 5, p. 221.
50. D.T., Vol. IV, p. 268.
51. PRO, FO, 425,112. Tours, 31 October 1870, Lyons to Granville.
52. d'Andlau, *Metz*, p. 381.
53. Howard, p. 282.
54. *GGS*, Vol. 3, p. 201.
55. SHAT, Lt12, Brussels, 3 November 1870, Tachard to Favre.

Chapter Twelve

November: Coulmiers and *La Grande Sortie*

By the beginning of November 1870 there were 250,000 French soldiers in captivity, including four marshals, 140 generals and 10,000 officers. Parisians joked sardonically that 'at last Bazaine and de MacMahon have joined forces'.[1] Inevitably, the surrender of Metz was the subject of international comment and speculation. The British military attaché spoke for many, when he opined that 'such a military disaster as this was never heard of'.[2]

In Paris, on that day, the news that the relatively unimportant Le Bourget and the vitally important Metz had both fallen combined to produce a serious wave of anger and despair. Someone had to be blamed and the obvious target was President Trochu and his Government of National Defence. The fire-brands on the left, the Reds, were vociferous in their condemnation of authority and of President Trochu in particular. 'It was becoming painfully evident that Trochu's talents as a talker and writer, and his popularity as a pre-war critic of the army's failings did not translate into any real capacity for field command.'[3]

Adolph Thiers confirmed the fall of Metz when he arrived back in Paris from his peregrinations around Europe's capitals. He also brought further very bad news, reporting that no other nation was prepared to take any active steps to assist France, although the British did offer to mediate in any armistice negotiation. Thiers proposed to the GND that the Prussian terms be accepted. These included the cession of Alsace and the indemnity of 2 milliard francs. (A milliard was 1,000 million, a term now largely superseded by billion.)

The Reds judged this to be 'peace at any price', apparently unaware that France had no means of making any realistic counter-offer. Georges Clemenceau, the mayor of Montmartre, speaking for his constituents, claimed that to accept the Prussian terms 'would be committing treason'.[4] His view enjoyed wide support and clearly a storm was brewing.

The Chief of Police, Edmond Adam, went to see Trochu early on the morning of 30 October to express his fears. Trochu was the epitome of calm; 'We are a Government born of public opinion . . .' he said, 'consequently my dear Prefect, we only employ moral forces.' Adam was unconvinced and called upon ten battalions (say 5,000 men) of the *Garde Nationale* to stand to. Later, he called upon a further ten battalions, a measure of the gravity of the situation that was developing and worsening rapidly.

By midday, a mixed crowd of about 15,000 had gathered outside the Hôtel de Ville. It was noisy and well equipped with bugles and drums. There were constant chants of '*Vive la Commune*' and '*Pas d'armistice*'. Many of the crowd were *GN* members, some unarmed, but those with rifles carried them muzzle down, an indication that they were in sympathy with the mob.

The storm broke on the Monday afternoon of 31 October and it was nothing short of outright insurrection. The Red leadership was united only in a broad political view and was not, initially, present. Its absence gives validity to the view that, thus far, the unrest was spontaneous. It appears that the Red leaders were holding a council meeting in Belleville when they were belatedly advised of the unrest.

On receipt of the news it was proposed that the Belleville battalions of the *GN* should march on the Hôtel de Ville, overthrow Trochu and his ilk, seize the levers of power and form a new government to be led by Blanqui, Delescluze, Pyat, Flourens and Victor Hugo.[5] This was revolution, but the brew was a bit too strong for some and the Belleville battalions opted out. Undaunted, Flourens and other members of the embryonic 'new' government set off at the head of 400 of Flourens's *tirailleurs*. Meanwhile, in the square outside the Hôtel de Ville, although the mob was aimless there was the scent of violence in the air. Suddenly, a shot was fired. Who fired and at what was never established. Several more rounds followed, but at no discernible target. Nevertheless, the effect of this random fire was electric. The mob fell back from the Hôtel de Ville, but instant, wild speculation abounded about the source of the firing and its intent.

Trochu summoned all his ministers to meet at the Hôtel de Ville. He gave specific instructions to his Chief of Staff, General Isadore Schmitz, 'not to move either a man or a gun without my personal order in writing'.[6] Then Trochu showed great courage in the face of rising hostility. Dressed in his full uniform, decorated with the insignia of a *Grand Officier de la Légion d'Honneur*, he rode out with two aides from the Louvre to make his way to the Hôtel de Ville; the party was roundly abused and threatened on its journey. His subordinate ministers made their way to the meeting, all of them unescorted. Ernest Picard, the Finance Minister, complained, 'We are sticking our heads into a mouse-trap.' It was a prescient remark.

As the Government assembled, the mob was incensed at the sight of those it blamed for the parlous condition in which France now found itself. Their very presence fuelled the anger of the mob, which rushed the doors of the building and about 300 gained entry. The three companies of *Mobiles* providing domestic defence of the building were overrun and it was only the calming authoritive presence of Trochu that prevented bloodshed. He appeared on the first floor, at the head of the stairs, and ordered the *Mobiles* not to resist the mob. Then he returned to the conference room, locked the door, and left Étienne Arago, the 78-year-old mayor of Paris, to reason with the crowd, an excellent example of the folly of 'casting pearls before swine' (Matthew 7:6). Arago had no success because reasoned debate had long since fled.

Back in the conference room, the attendees considered the need to select a date for the long-promised election, which they saw as a readily available sop to appease the mob. No decision had been taken when the doors were thrust open. There was a burst of trumpets and a moment of absurd theatricality as a superbly uniformed Flourens, carrying a Turkish scimitar, appeared in the doorway. He was accompanied by the members of the 'new' government, formed earlier in the day at Belleville. Flourens, forever a poseur, jumped up on the conference table and strode about among the papers, upending inkwells, damaging the surface of the table. His spurs jangled at the chest height of Trochu and his governmental companions, who were stunned by this extraordinary individual issuing commands, amongst which was one for the immediate resignation of Trochu and his government. Jules Favre, speaking for the Government, calmly and courteously rejected the demand.

This rejection nonplussed Flourens, Blanqui, Delescluze, Pyat, Millière and all the other 'new' government ministers who had not anticipated resistance and had no Plan 'B' to counter it. A draft document authorising the arrest of Jules Favre was passed to Flourens to sign but he judged that the 'new' government was not strong enough to arrest a leading light with the status of Favre and so he declined to sign.

The 'Committee of Public Safety', as the insurgents now described themselves, set about mounting a straw poll, an ad hoc unofficial vote. The object was to measure public opinion or, more accurately, the opinion of the mob assembled outside the Hôtel de Ville. The process was ludicrous. Paper slips were hastily thrown into the mob and helpfully the names of Flourens and friends were already appended. Surprisingly, the mob, or at least the vociferous members of that mob, favoured Gustave Dorian. He had served as Minister of Public works since 4 September. Dorian, suitably flattered, nevertheless advised the 'Committee' that he could not accept office with them.

While all these political manoeuvres were being played out a vast Prussian army stood at the gates of Paris and latter-day historians can speculate on the likely result if that army had assaulted a leaderless city on 31 October. The probability is that Ducrot would have assumed overall control, have beaten

The scene in the Hôtel de Ville on 31 October to 1 November 1870, Gustave
Flourens astride the conference table on 31 October and issuing his demands to the
'Council of Regency and National Defence' (GND). On the left of the image,
Trochu is being led away by the 106th Battalion of the *Garde Nationale* on
1 November. (Cassell's Illustrated History of the Franco-German War, *London, 1899*)

off the Prussians and possibly superseded Trochu. However, unaware of the
internal strife, the Prussians did nothing.

The Committee of Public Safety, thwarted in its assumption of power,
started to lose its cohesion and its members split up and took post in separate
rooms. The exotically named Hippolyte-Prosper-Olivier Lissagaray, was
the 'official historian' of the Commune movement and, after the event, he
recorded with a measure of frustration and irritation that:

> each room had its own Government, its orators, its *tarentules* [tarantulas]
> … Thus, that day which could have revitalized the defence vanished in
> a puff of smoke. The incoherence of the *avant-garde* restored to the
> Government its virginity of September.

Blanqui, the elder and most radical leader of the Reds, would not have
Flourens on his list and Delescluze rejected Pyat. Blanqui set up his own
headquarters at the Prefecture of the Seine, which was close by. Here, Blanqui
sought to organise his own government, and to that end started to issue
orders to his followers.

The mob, which had been standing out in pouring rain for several hours, had been fortified by alcohol and, inexplicably, it now set about wrecking the Hôtel de Ville. The vandalism was mindless – but then, vandalism usually is. Captain d'Hérrisson, who witnessed the mayhem, commented:

> The mob brought with it its particular odour. The smell of its pipes and cigars contended with a stink as of wet dogs ... and of dried sweat which exhales from a mass of troops, especially when those troops are dirty and have only been partially washed by the rain.[7]

The outstanding individual during all these proceedings was Trochu. He stood an oasis of calm, dignity and resolve. His conduct on this day, which could so easily have turned into a bloodbath, was exemplary. He smoked a cigar and allowed a gentle smile to flit across his face. One observer said that he seemed to be enjoying the spectacle of the Red leadership falling apart before his eyes.

It was winter and darkness had enveloped Paris, the rain continued to fall and the mob, cold, soaked, dissatisfied and probably hungry, started to drift away. Trochu and his government were still confined in this siege within a siege. By early evening the Trochu government had already been prisoners for several hours and no attempt had been made to free them. Ducrot, by now aware of the situation, was inclined to take the Hôtel de Ville by force and summarily execute the insurgents. Subtlety was not Ducrot's strong suit. However, he was constrained by the orders Trochu's left with General Schmitz.

On the face of it the Reds appeared to have mounted a successful coup and Edmund Goncourt, who had witnessed it, was swift to judgement. He wrote, 'the Government has been overthrown and the Commune established ... It was all over. Today one could write *Finis Franciae* ... Civil war with starvation and bombardment, is that what tomorrow holds in store for us?'[8] Goncourt was not alone, and these dark thoughts were shared by many. The evening wore on and as it did so the tight cordon around the Hôtel de Ville slackened. Ernest Picard managed to slip out, undetected, and he set in train the release of his colleagues.

The leadership of the Paris police during the period August 1870 to March 1871 was chaotic and six men filled the post during that short, but vital, seven-month period in the history of the city.

Émile Piétri, a long-standing incumbent, had left Paris on the fall of Sédan and on 4 September was replaced by Émile de Kératry, who held office for only five weeks. Edmond Adam took up the reins and he was probably the hero of the extraordinary events of late October. In the midst of the insurrection Adam was confronted by the hardcore Red, Raoul Rigault, and told that he was going to replace him. Adam's deputy, Pouchet, calmly advised Rigault that 'only an hour previously he had had a similar order appointing someone else'.[9] He suggested that Rigault have a chat with Flourens to establish who was doing what. Rigault stormed out, not to return. Thereafter, seizing the moment, Adam headed a small team of *tirailleurs* from the Prefecture with the aim of capturing the Hôtel de Ville. His party gained access by way of its cellars and, with difficulty, avoided any exchange of gunfire.

The confrontation with the Committee that followed was potentially very dangerous but Adam, with great skill, tried to persuade the insurgents to evacuate the building. In these negotiations it emerged that Delescluze was the natural Red leader and his most capable protagonist was Gustave Dorian. By about 0230 hrs, it was agreed that, if released, the Government would not take reprisals against the dissidents. About half an hour later, the 'Council' and the Government left the building arm in arm – General Tamisier with Blanqui, then Dorian and Delescluze. It was surreal and only Flourens and Pyat were absent, having left for greener pastures sometime earlier.

Trochu and his government were released by loyal *GN* and *Mobile* troops, incredibly without any bloodshed.[10] The time was now right for the Government to assert itself. The chaotic incompetence of the Reds had been exposed; they had had the chance to seize control but failed to grasp the opportunity. The Red leaders, who were members of the *GN*, were, arguably, subject to military law and trial by court martial.

The next morning, 1 November, Adam was awakened by Ernest Picard who was insistent on knowing what steps Adam had taken to arrest Pyat, Blanqui, Delescluze, Flourens, Millière and a number of other, lesser lights in the Red firmament. Adam said that he had agreed 'no reprisals'. Picard was not satisfied with that answer and the rest of the day was spent arguing the value or otherwise of Adam's commitment. Like politicians the world over, a compromise position was established that only 'an armistice' had been agreed.

Adam was outraged and resigned on 1 November, after only three weeks of incumbency. He was replaced by Ernest Cresson, who held office for thirteen weeks, a lengthy tenure for this office. The importance of effective leadership of the police during a siege and its aftermath needs no emphasis. However, Albert Choppin (11 February–16 March 1871) and Louis Valentin (16 March–17 November 1871) were both, albeit briefly, in command of the function.

Opposition to Trochu was scattered to the winds and very soon after, on 3 November, a plebiscite was held seeking to measure the support for the Government. The result was staggering: 557,976 voted in support and only 62,638 voted against. The 9:1 split was a mandate 'to crush the insurrection and assume dictatorial power with a wide measure of public support – powers such as Gambetta had not hesitated to assume in Tours' only three weeks earlier.[11] However, those figures do not tell the whole story because the population of Paris was about 2 million, some of whom opted not to vote and others were disenfranchised. The political view of the balance of 1.3 million non-voters was a worrying unknown.

Despite the no reprisals agreement, twenty-two leading dissidents had been arrested and incarcerated in the Mazas prison. Sixteen battalion commanders of the *GN* were cashiered but not imprisoned and later all of them emerged as leaders of the Commune (more of that in Chapter 18).

The vengeful actions of Trochu's government were deplored even by right-wingers like the journalist Jules Claretie, who described the arrests as 'pitiful, useless, dangerous'.[12] The dishonourable actions of the Government polarised public opinion and bred a sense of dissatisfaction in some and stark betrayal in others. Ducrot, who wanted the blood of all the dissidents, given the choice, represented the far-right view.

The political clubs and the press continued to voice dissension and vitiate the *GN*. Privation, cold weather, despair and the widening gap between the social classes had briefly been set aside by the presence of a common enemy but now the rift between classes widened with every day that passed.[13]

Jules Claretie (1840–1913).

Adolphe Thiers manfully continued to seek the route to an armistice and, after another visit to Bismarck, returned, on 5 November, with the latest terms. The Prussians would agree to a ceasefire for long enough for a representative National Assembly to be elected. However, it would maintain its stranglehold over the city by denying any revictualling unless a fort was surrendered as compensation. The Chancellor also continued to demand the cession of all of Alsace, enormous reparations and now parts of Lorraine. Acting on Trochu's behalf, Ducrot, Theirs and Favre met. They could not agree; Ducrot was the hardliner. He said it was their *duty* to continue the war and he spoke of *national honour*. Thiers, a very tired man, commented, 'General, you talk like a soldier. That's all very well but you're not talking in political terms.'[14] When the trio met with government colleagues later that evening, Ducrot made his position clear; he said that the country should fight, 'if not to triumph, at least to succumb gloriously after having fought valiantly'.[15] It made no sense, but his audience applauded. It was brave, illogical and, to a point, admirable. Nevertheless, delaying an inevitable defeat would cost lives and treasure. However, despite the brutal reality of the situation, the Government of National Defence decided to continue the war and raise yet another new army to fight the Prussians.

Thiers always believed that if France had been able to accept Prussian terms in November 1870, she might not have lost Lorraine and might well have paid a smaller war indemnity.[16]

That decision having been taken, a factor in the hitherto uncoordinated French operations was Trochu's incapacity to communicate with anyone in a succinct, germane and timely manner. He had been asked by Favre, in mid-October, if he had briefed Gambetta on his intentions for the breakout planned for the following month in the north-west of the city and he admitted he had not, claiming that he entertained doubts about Gambetta's capacity to achieve any military success in the provinces.[17]

However, on 14 October he did brief Arthur Ranc on his intentions and asked him to pass them to Gambetta. Thereafter, Ranc left the city, by balloon, and joined Gambetta. Unfortunately, Ranc denied ever having been briefed by Trochu and certainly did not pass any instructions to Gambetta. The probability was the verbose Trochu concealed his wishes in excessive verbiage. Ranc then, and to his credit, organised a system that allowed Trochu to be kept abreast of Prussian strength and disposition around Paris. The need to communicate with Gambetta was evident and further messages were sent on 19, 23 and 25 October. By this time Gambetta had developed his own strategy and Trochu's wishes were ignored.

The major sortie from Paris was planned for 15 November. In outline, 100,000 men in three corps commanded by Ducrot were to make the principal strike: 70,000 men, the majority of them *Mobiles*, under 67-year-old General Joseph Vinoy were to carry out a diversionary role. In the absence of these two armies the city would be defended by 130,000 *Gardes Nationale*. This operation was a massive undertaking and the staff had to find and deploy mountains of ammunition, food and medical supplies.

The day before the breakout was to be launched, two unrelated events caused a delay. The first of these was the rise in level of the Seine and Marne after heavy rain – important because the rivers were central to the operational plan. The second was belated news from Orléans.

The Prussians were well aware that, in Paris, something was in the wind. However, on 9 November they were more than a little nonplussed when a

French army of 70,000 led by General d'Aurelle de Paladines roundly defeated a Bavarian army of 20,000 men at Coulmiers under the command of General Ludwig Freiherr von und zu der Tann-Rathsamhausen.

Coulmiers is a village about 15 miles (24km) west of Orléans and not of any particular importance, but it was here that d'Aurelle's army engaged Tann's numerically weaker force. Tann thought that his better trained and more manoeuvrable force would be more than a match for the inexperienced and poorly trained French. Tann's judgement was flawed, and the massive numerical advantage enjoyed by d'Aurelle and his very effective artillery was sufficient for the French to win a battle that was a slogging match. Tann eventually withdrew, having suffered 1,166 casualties and a further 1,000 taken as prisoners. French losses were about 1,500, but they held the ground and d'Aurelle moved on to retake Orléans and rest his men.

The Battle of Coulmiers, a rare victory, was a sop to French pride but little else. In the context of the war as a whole it was insignificant. It cost several hundred lives, but it had no material effect upon the Siege of Paris, and despite Gambetta's urging, the victory was not exploited. d'Aurelle was over-taken by a curious lethargy and for two weeks he and his army rested.

Gambetta, correctly, saw himself as having sole responsibility for national strategy – who else was there? Paris could only be relieved of siege conditions by a significant force, externally. That force, the only effective force, was in Orléans, some 70 miles (113km) from Paris. The overriding deficiency in French operations, post the investment, was communication. Trochu and his Council could communicate outward, albeit only by way of occasional balloon flights, but was not able to receive incoming communication other than by unreliable return pigeon post, the birds having first been ballooned out of the city.

Paris and Tours were pursuing two different strategies: Ducrot planned to exit the city with a large army and head north-west; Gambetta, on the other hand, planned to approach Paris from a diametrically opposite direction. Given the communication difficulty, this diversity was almost to be expected as Trochu and the GND had no inkling of the Battle of Coulmiers or its outcome.

In Paris, the result of the Battle of Coulmiers was delivered by Ernest Moll, a farmer, on 14 November. Moll was employed by the Prussians as a guide and a frequent 'line crosser'. The news was greeted with dispropor-tionate mass euphoria. There was widespread rejoicing and the ill-informed saw the victory as a harbinger of much good to come. That the new provincial armies could take on and beat the Germans was a major fillip to morale, but Trochu had no illusions and believed that the war would be decided in and around Paris. Nevertheless, the victory at Coulmiers had changed the situation. Now there was an army that could advance from the south-east and meeting it was clearly the best option. However, the Parisian Army was poised to strike in the north-west segment of the perimeter and had assembled its men and materiel accordingly. To the civilian members of GND it was just a simple matter of changing direction. The operational and logistic implications were enormous but conveniently ignored.

The operation planned for the next day was postponed. Earlier in November, Trochu sent an officer in a balloon flight with details of his proposed north-western sortie to Gambetta. The civilian took advice from General Charles-Denis Bourbaki, who was unimpressed with the plan. Trochu's request that Gambetta confine his operations to the lower Seine was firmly rejected. Instead, Gambetta decided that d'Aurelle would advance north from Orléans and suggested that Trochu's sortie should head south to meet this force.[18] On the face of it, this seems to have been a perfectly reasonable aspiration – if very difficult to achieve. Trochu, ever the realist, was assailed by the press, who misjudged the value of the victory at Coulmiers and indulged in a quality and quantity of rhetoric that served to mislead the population. It perceived the *sortie torrentielle* crashing through the Prussian lines and linking up with d'Aurelle's army around the Forest of Fontainebleau. Unfortunately, the members of Trochu's government subscribed to that same rose-tinted view.[19] Ducrot, the nominated commander of the operation, was not consulted, and he recorded his astonishment and indignance and said that they were 'not less than his embarrassment'.[20]

The earlier arrangements for the sortie had to be undone and rejigged. The breakout would now be directed at one of the most strongly defended sectors of the entire perimeter; 400 heavy guns, fifty-four pontoon bridge components and 80,000 men, organised into three corps with their supporting ammunition transport, had to be switched to a new start line across the city. Vinoy's army of 70,000 had similarly to be repositioned. Ducrot was not optimistic and:

> the only point at which he believed success was possible – or rather failure not totally inevitable – was to the east, in the loop of the Marne between Champigny and Brie, where both flanks of his army might rest on the river, with the St Maur peninsula on one side and Mont Avron on the other.[21] (See map on page 148. Champigny is bottom centre, Brie centre, north of Villiers.)

Ducrot's three corps were commanded by Generals Blanchard, Renault and Count Antoine-Achille d'Exéa-Doumerc (hereafter Exéa). Trochu held the latter in high regard and on 26 November he named him as the individual to command the Army in the event that Ducrot was killed or taken prisoner.

The operation, later to be called either the Battle of Champigny or Villiers, was to start on 29 November and would be mounted against an enemy fully prepared and alerted by an intensive bombardment from 26 November. The breakout point was readily identified by the Prussians, who could well see that the French aim was to link up with the Army of the Loire.

Vinoy's army had the task of creating a diversion on the left bank of the Seine advancing on Choisy-le-Roi and L'Hay. Its mission was to interceopt any Prussian reserves being brought in from the west.[22] Ducrot made the unusual decision to leave behind his logistic support. The men carried six days' supplies but no blankets. Any wagons accompanying the attacker would carry only ammunition. It was now winter, the weather was inclement and the temperature hovered around freezing point; those blankets would be sorely missed. Ducrot issued a vainglorious order of the day in which he said:

> As for myself I have made up my mind and I swear before you and before the entire nation: I shall only re-enter Paris dead or victorious. You may see me fall, but you will not see me yield ground.[23]

It was an ill-judged statement by any yardstick and, when Ducrot lived, returned to Paris defeated, he was constantly reminded of his folly. His new plan was to attack to the south-east and then over the Marne near to its confluence with the Seine; having broken through the ring he would then press on to the south-east and link up with Aurelle around Fontainebleau. Soldiers, from choice, avoid contested river crossings either in advance or withdrawal because it is an exercise fraught with a degree of danger that tests the very best of formations. Ducrot's plan called for very complicated bridging operations and they had only five days to prepare. It was inevitable that under such pressure there were compromises and omissions.

Surprise was not a factor in the forthcoming battle because in this operation there was a complete lack of security. The plan and its details were the subject of coffee house gossip. Thomas Bowles, always known as 'Tommy', was a journalist and later an MP who was present throughout the siege. He commented, 'I have had confided to me nothing less than General Trochu's plan and have witnessed the preparations for its execution.' Jules Claretie, the journalist and newspaper correspondent, noted the demolition of barricades at Nogent-sur-Marne 'so that artillery could pass'.[24] There was no attempt to mislead the Prussians, who had merely to observe the preparations.

Trochu procrastinated, as always, and although a decision had been taken on or about 15 November to redesign the breakout, he put off informing Gambetta of the new arrangements that would be initiated on 29 November. It was not until 24 November that he decided to send a message, and he entrusted the message to Leonard Bézier, who would be flown out in a balloon piloted by a man called Valéry Rolier. Their flight, the thirty-third, turned into such an epic journey that it merits a chapter of this book, but space does not permit. However, in brief, the balloon named *Ville de Orléans*, so called to celebrate the recent taking of that city, took off as darkness fell. The risk to balloonists from small arms fire in daylight was such that night flights were, by now, the norm.

The *Ville de Orléans* carried only the most primitive navigational aids and her course and speed were entirely dependent upon the wind. Some hours into the flight it was foggy, and the two men had no idea where they were. They heard sounds – they thought it might be of railway trains – and descended through cloud and fog to investigate. To their consternation they discovered it was the sea and they were dangerously low. The sea was the English Channel or the North Sea, they had no idea which. They tried to attract the attention of ships below them but without success and decided to ascend. However, to do so they had to jettison ballast and among that ballast was the 132lb (60kg) of despatches.

They rose into thick, freezing cloud and frost formed on them and their balloon. Bézier covered the cargo of carrier pigeons with his coat. They flew on without any reference point and out of sight of the ground. Eventually, after hours of discomfort and chilled to the bone, they descended. They found themselves above a world of pine trees and very deep snow. They both

Leonard Bézier and his pilot Valéry Rolier, in *Ville de Orléans*, just avoid disaster, probably in the North Sea.

jumped from the basket and the unweighted balloon with the unfortunate pigeons soared aloft and disappeared.

The two men stumbled around in an ice-covered wilderness for two days. They were found by some locals and discovered that they were in the middle of Norway at Lifjell, about 60 miles (97km) south-west of Oslo. They were taken to the city and feted. Their balloon was, by happy chance, recovered from the sea by fishermen who forwarded the remaining contents of the basket to the French Consul. Horne alleges that *Ville de Orléans* flew 900 miles (1,448km) in fifteen hours, an average speed of 60 miles per hour, which seems unlikely.[25] As the crow flies, Oslo is 824 miles (1,326km) from Paris and so the distance is not disputed, but the duration of the flight is problematic.

However, life had moved on. Gambetta eventually received Trochu's message on 30 November. Promptly, de Freycinet 'convened a council of war at Aurelles's headquarters somewhere between Châteaudun and Orléans and insisted that the entire Army of the Loire, 90,000 infantry, 5,600 cavalry and 260 guns, together with its vast logistic train should redirect itself towards Paris'.[26] Aurelle protested that the battle around Paris would have been decided long before he could get there. His political masters overruled him. The consequence was that *La Grande Sortie* was conducted without any external assistance.

In Paris there was a feeling of optimistic anticipation. The citizens had seen for themselves the mountains of equipment and had been aware of the overriding confidence of the soldiers. This looked like a win-win situation. Ambassador Washburne commented, 'Paris has never before been so tranquil, and never before has there been so little crime,' perhaps because the criminal fraternity were drilling with *GN* and the *Mobiles*, and this was conducted incessantly. On 26 November all the gates to the city were closed and there was an unseemly rush to get behind them. Washburne noted in his dairy that the American ambulance wagons had been ordered to stand by for an early start at 0600 hrs on the morrow.

A French artillery bombardment commenced during the night of 26/27 November as Prussian targets were softened up. The bombardment lasted until dawn on 29 November, at which time a very disturbed Ducrot made his way to Trochu's headquarters. It appeared that the level of the Marne was now so high as to prevent the launching of the operation. Prior to the investment back in September, all the bridges on the Marne had been demolished and so *La Grande Sortie* was going to depend on pontoon bridges for passage across the river and access to a bridgehead from which to attack to the targeted towns of Brie and Champigny.

The previous evening, 28 November, pontoons had been towed across the city and positioned at Charenton by 2300 hrs. The pontoons were then organised into a long train and were towed by the steam tug *Persévérance* from the Seine and along the recently opened Saint Maurice canal to the Marne at Joinville (see map on page 148, bottom left). At this point the Marne is always fast flowing and about 150 yards wide. The bridge at Joinville, like many others, had been 'blown'. But in this case the debris from two of the arches blocked the river and the current, through the remaining arch, was correspondingly forceful. In a perfect world the debris would have been cleared but it was not – just one of the failures in the short-term planning for the operation.

The remaining arch was navigable but *Persévérance* with her attendant pontoons could not force a passage against the powerful current. It tried a second time, got through the arch but, in the process, three of the pontoons were swamped and foundered. The night wore on, the tow was adjusted and at the third attempt the steam tug forced its way upriver. The sky was lightening, but it was clear that there was no chance of installing the pontoon bridge before dawn.

Ducrot was mortified as his plans had fallen badly at the first fence – well, bridge, to be more accurate. It was in a very agitated state of mind that he went to see Trochu. They considered abandoning *La Grande Sortie*. This was a realistic, blood-free, manageable, military option. Both men realised that the public relations exercise that had advertised a breakout at sometime had fed the hopes of Parisians. Abandoning the operation without a dead Prussian to show for their trouble would incite a riot. The likely behaviour of the mob was a factor that outweighed all the military considerations. The least damaging solution was to delay the main thrust for twenty-four hours, although Vinoy was to go ahead with his diversionary attack. The delay of the main force would give Moltke time to insert a Saxon division to bolster the understrength Würtemberger division and plug the critical gap between Neuilly-sur-Marne and Champigny. Vinoy, never a fan of Ducrot, realised that his diversion for an attack that had not taken place was inexplicable. He made his feelings known but got on with the job.

In Paris, news of the serious glitch with the pontoon bridge was kept from the public. Outside the Hôtel de Ville a notice was posted that advised that 'All General Ducrot's divisions have crossed the Marne'. This was premature. Nevertheless, on the basis of this misleading information, prices in the Bourse achieved their greatest gains since September. Goncourt recorded, 'an air of concentrated meditation. In the public vehicles no one speaks; everyone has retired within himself ... Any man who speaks, who suggests knowledge is besieged. The strain of the suspense is intolerable.'[27]

Outside the city walls Moltke had a clear view of Ducrot's intentions and he moved swiftly to counter them. The sector of his line that was to be

General Auguste Ducrot (1817–82), the commander of the French 2nd Army
and *La Grande Sortie*, photographed on 23 November 1870 for his family, prior
to the battle. (*L. Rousset*, Histoire Generale de la Guerre 1870–71, *2 vols., Paris, 1910*)

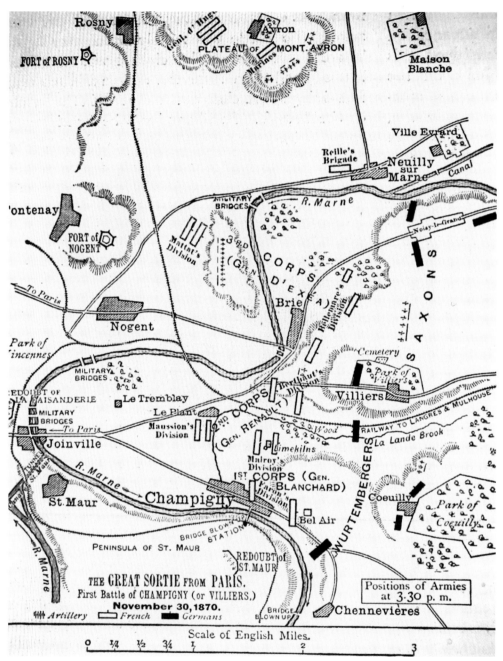

The disposition of forces at 1530 hrs, 30 November 1870. Note the high ground on the right of the map, all held by entrenched Prussians.

threatened was held by the weak Württemberg Division and he had instructed Albert, Crown Prince of Saxony, to reinforce it, as and when it was needed.[28] The twenty-four-hour delay played into Moltke's hands. He was able to observe the installation of new batteries on Mont Avron, and he could negate the now virtually pointless operations led by Vinoy, which cost the French 1,000 dead and wounded and 300 prisoners.[29]

Ducrot got his divisions across the Marne later on 29 November and established bridgeheads at Champigny and Brie. He held these two positions under the protective cover of intense artillery fire from Fort Nogent and guns in the St Maur peninsula. The most difficult part of the operation that followed was the attempt to take the high ground defended by the Württembergers and centred on the two parks of Coeuilly and Villiers.

Tommy Bowles had accompanied the first divisions across the Marne and took up a position on a hill just west of Créteil (see map on page 150 – Créteil is centre bottom), only 500 yards from the Prussian left wing. Behind him waiting in reserve was the 170th (Belleville) Battalion of the *GN*. Bowles wrote later in *Vanity Fair*, a magazine he had founded in 1868:

> I saw the French skirmishers dotted thickly along the flank of the hill at a distance of about 300 yards and, a short distance beyond, the Prussians firing on them from a wood. In a minute or two the fusillade began in earnest – a rolling, rattling, crackling fire which now and then rose to a continuous roar … I could see the Prussian barricade indicated by an incessant curtain of white smoke. Suddenly the smoke of the barricade cleared and was not renewed, and the instant after, I saw a swarm of men running rapidly and disappearing behind the barricade which was taken at the point of the bayonet.

This was clearly an early French success and Bowles went on to describe his panoramic view of the battlefield and said that about half an hour later, he 'took horse' and rode up to the captured Prussian barricade where he saw:

> a crowd of breathless men swarming around and through it [the barricade] and running to the shelter of a wall … Beyond I could see others running up and, as I foresaw confusion, I thought it best to return which I did, under a considerably increased accompaniment of balls.

On his return to Créteil, a place of safety, Bowles was questioned, and the most frequently asked question was, '*Nous battons en retraite n'est-ce-pas?*' ('We're retreating, aren't we?'). He wrote:

> the Belleville Battalion was there, and their remarks were not calculated to inspire confidence in their courage; '*nous sommes battus*' ['we're

beaten'] they said, looking with pale faces at one another, while some of them silently left the ranks and walked with a careless air to the rear.

Bowles's account is not typical of the French performance or attitudes. The owner of Château Coeuilly was alongside Ducrot and assisted in laying guns onto his property.

The *châtelaine* of Villiers stayed at home throughout the battle as shot and shell tore through her house. French artillery performed well and exacted a heavy toll among the defenders, even though they were well dug in. However, this was a battle for territory, and it fell to French infantry boots on the ground to deliver the prize. Three times with great courage and élan they 'charged', perhaps 'toiled' is more accurate, up the hills and each time they were repulsed with ghastly losses. They did not get to within 150 yards of

The area over which *La Grande Sortie* was fought.

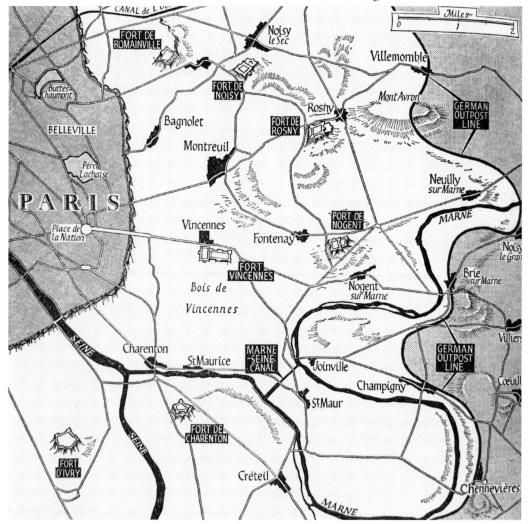

Château Coeuilly. The losses were akin to those suffered in 1914 – but then the tactics were the same.[30] Lacking in any tactical innovation such as the 'fire and movement' practised by the Prussians, they paid a very heavy price for employing the 'human wave' approach. Ducrot could not afford to deploy his troops 'in an open formation for fear that they might go to ground and become unmanageable'.[31] By remaining in 'close order' the French increased their vulnerability to rifle and artillery fire. Ducrot, mounted on a magnificent white charger, rode amongst his men assaulting Coeuilly. It was foolish perhaps but very courageous – he had no right to survive because he must have been a splendid target.

It was too late, but eventually a division commanded by de Bellemare, of Le Bourget fame, now forgiven and promoted to major general, was seen advancing from the bridgehead – but in the wrong direction. The division was aimed obliquely at Brie and not at Noisy-le-Grand. Brie was held by the French and did not want another 10,000 troops in an area already filled to capacity. By mid-afternoon it was evident that the planned flank attack on Villiers was not going to take place and, in fading winter light, the frontal attacks on the Villiers plateau continued, with a mounting butcher's bill to accompany it.

Ducrot realised that the day was lost; the obvious decision was to withdraw and cut his losses. However, like Trochu, he was only too aware of the probable anger of the Parisian mob just waiting to be uncorked. He was also hoist by his earlier absurd statements about being either victorious or dead – he was neither, and the loss of face was of epic proportions.

III Corps, led by General d'Exéa, had crossed the Marne at Neuilly with the objective of taking Noisy-le-Grand, but it had been delayed by a lack of pontoons. Ducrot was consumed by impatience and, during his wait for d'Exéa, he had ridden back and forth across the battlefield.

Bowles had returned to Créteil and the scene there was such that he felt the need to record:

> The pavement was covered with wounded men, generally half undressed, and lying there helplessly while one surgeon was doing his best to attend to them. In the middle of the Place a seething mob of soldiers of all arms, struggled and wrestled to get through the village without orders, without leaders without an idea what to do or whither to go, unless it were to avoid the Prussians. Every moment the mob increased, and with every moment the panic became greater and the struggle to get through fiercer. They fought with each other … Trampled even on their wounded comrades … It was not an army that was retreating, it was not even a respectable mob.[32]

This sad scene was replicated elsewhere and, as the French Army bled, night fell and with it came a deep frost. The decision not to take blankets was seen for its absurdity as freezing French soldiers huddled together in the darkness, dreading the morn.

In Paris, the Government clutched at straws and promulgated every perceived success. It made capital of the crossing of the Marne and the capture of Épinay-sur-Seine (to the north of Paris and of minor relevance). Two balloons were standing by, and when launched one was able to deliver to Gambetta all the good news. Unfortunately, and culpably, Gambetta misread Épinay-sur-Seine for Épinay-sur-Orge, a few miles south of Orly. He then piled errors on his original mistake and, assuming that Ducrot had broken out, he instructed his generals Aurelle and Chanzy to hasten to Fontainebleau. By so doing he split his forces – a serious error. He did not realise that Prince Charles and his army, now released from Metz, were heading towards the Army of the Loire.

The first day's fighting had cost the Prussians 2,091 dead and wounded; for the French it was more than double, at 5,236 the inevitable consequence of attacking an entrenched enemy at the top of a hill. There had been the early successes in Brie and Champigny, but the hillsides below Villiers and Coeuilly were now adorned with French dead and wounded; many of those wounded froze to death during the long night that followed. General Renault, commanding II Corps, was one of many who died of his wounds and the surgeon's attention.

The French Army had a well-established track record of medical incompetence and it added to that record over the period of this engagement. A French staff officer admitted to Felix Whitehurst, a British voluntary worker, that the management of the medical aspects 'beats the worst mess of the worst days of the Crimea'.[33] This really was a medical nadir.

The Prussians were amazed to observe French soldiers cutting flesh from dead horses and ignoring their wounded. The press were amazed too, as the illustration above shows.

On 1 December, a twenty-four-hour truce was agreed, during which the surviving wounded could be removed. Ducrot realised that, with his army short of ammunition and food, it was ill-prepared to resist any Prussian advance. He ordered his men to dig in and make ready their defensive positions. The day passed without any military activity. In Paris, the sight of a multitude of wounded men arriving from the battlefield had a sobering effect.

On 2 December, the Prussians, under Albert Crown Prince of Saxony, attacked. It was a misty, frosty morning and the poor visibility prevented the French batteries on Mont Avron and in the St Maur peninsula from providing support. Brie and Champigny were strongly contested and the latter almost

French soldiers stripping meat from dead horses. This image shows a camp scene, but the reality was that this activity also took place on the battlefield – an indication of the starvation conditions in Paris. (Illustrated London News)

fell. The mist cleared, the French guns spoke, the balance equalised, and the fighting went on for the remainder of the day. There was ample courage on both sides, hundreds died but, at day's end, the situation had changed little.[34]

Ducrot understood that his men were at the limits of their endurance; they had spent three freezing nights without cover or even a blanket. They had had no hot food, Ducrot could see for himself the condition of his men and he wrote that they were 'crouched on the frozen ground, exhausted and shivering, their bodies and souls enfeebled by weariness, suffering and lack of food'.[35] The mist reappeared and under its benign cover Ducrot's army withdrew, back across the Marne and into the relative safety of Paris. While this withdrawal was being conducted, Gambetta was able to get a despatch into Paris in which he announced the approach of his 120,000-man strong

Army of the Loire. It was not enough to alter Ducrot's decision; the three days had cost 12,000 casualties, including about 2,000 dead. The general was humbled and defeated. Ducrot reconsidered his position and later that day he urged Favre to sue for peace.[36]

Notes

1. Maurice, F., *The Franco German War 1870–71* (London, 1899), p. 290.
2. Wawro, p. 252.
3. Fermer, p. 74.
4. Horne, p. 107.
5. Ibid., p. 109.
6. Ibid.
7. d'Hérrisson, Comte, M., *Journal of a Staff officer during the Siege of Paris* (tr London, 1885).
8. Goncourt, E., *Journal*, 1870.
9. Horne, p. 117.
10. Mizla, P., *L'année terrible: La guerre Franco-Prussienne, Septembre 1870–Mars 1871* [2009] (Perrin, Paris,), pp. 206–13.
11. Howard, pp. 558–9.
12. Horne, p. 119.
13. Heylli, G. de., *Journal Siège de Paris*, 3 Vols. (Paris, 1871–74), Vol. II, pp. 593–625.
14. Favre, Vol. II, p. 25.
15. Ducrot, A.A., *Défense de Paris* (E. Dentu, 1876), Vol. II, pp. 72–7.
16. Thiers, M.L.A., *Notes et Souvenirs de M. Thiers 1870–73* (Paris, 1904), pp. 96, 101.
17. Horne, p. 141.
18. D.O., Vol. II, p. 278.
19. Trochu, Vol. I, p. 407–8.
20. Ducrot, A.A., *La Défense de Paris*, 4 Vols. (Paris, 1875–78), Vol. I, p. 109.
21. Howard, p. 342.
22. Ducrot, *La Défense*, pp. 135–45.
23. Ibid., pp. 156–7.
24. Horne, p. 144.
25. Ibid., p. 145.
26. Wawro, p. 274.
27. Goncourt, Journal, November 1870.
28. *MMK*, p. 403.
29. Vinoy, *Siège de Paris* (Paris, 1872), pp. 353–60.
30. Horne, p. 153.
31. Howard, p. 344.
32. Bowles's diary, quoted by Horne, p. 155.
33. Horne, p. 158.
34. Howard, p. 346.
35. Ducrot, *Défense de Paris*, Vol III, p. 63.
36. Favre, *Gouvernement de la Défense National*, Vol. II, p. 160.

Chapter Thirteen

December: Belfort, Amiens, Orléans

On 3 December, Jules Goncourt expressed a commonly held view when he wrote:

> the heights and depths of hope; this is what kills you. One believes oneself saved. Then one realises one is lost ... Today, the re-crossing of the Marne by Ducrot has thrown us back into the darkness of failure and despair.[1]

Goncourt had very good reason to feel despair because, after the investment of Paris on 19 September, the Prussian armies had enjoyed a lengthy run of successes against an increasingly disorganised opponent. Toul and Strasbourg both fell in late September and, during October, Artenay (10 October), Soissons (15 October), Malmaison (21 October), Metz (27 October), Le Bourget, again, (30 October) were all Prussian victories.

The Prussians had underscored the fall of Metz by the tightening of their grip on eastern France by taking the two small Lorraine towns of Schlettstadt

The Lion of Belfort, **commemorating the Siege of the City, 3 November 1870 to 15 February 1871.** (*Frederic Bartholdi, 1834–1904*)

and Breisach (south of Strasbourg). They had succumbed on 24 October and 9 November respectively.

Verdun fell that same day. On the south-east Rhine border with Prussia, Belfort had become the centre of *francs-tireurs* activity. These operated, effectively, in the rear of the XIV Corps, commanded by General von Werder, who was positioned around Vesoul, about 20 miles (32km) west of Belfort. The *francs-tireurs* were so successful that Trochu's Minister of War, General Adolphe Le Flô, had sent a brigade of regular infantry to provide a nucleus for operations.

The significance of both Strasbourg and Belfort, 77 miles (124km) apart, was their strategically important locations on the Franco-Prussian border. Belfort is in a gap between the southern Vosges Mountains and the Jura massif. It was in this border area, at the beginning of the war, that the French Army of the Rhine was heavily defeated in a series of battles, not least when Strasbourg fell on 28 September 1870.

Belfort was a fortified town with a garrison commanded by Colonel Pierre-Philippe Denfert-Rochereau, who set his men to work strengthening the defences around the city. He expanded those originally built by Sébastien Le Prestre de Vauban in the seventeenth century, when he realised that Belfort was a likely Prussian target. Werder's XIV Corps part invested the

Franc-tireurs sabotaging a railway line during the winter of 1870. This party is at least thirteen strong and so able to defend itself. The figure bottom centre appears to be a casualty. (*Alexandre Bloch, 1857–1919*)

city on 3 November, but the active resistance of the garrison of 15,000 men held back von Werder's force of 40,000 for 103 days and prevented a complete encirclement.

By early December, the Prussian forces extended south to Dijon, southwest to Orléans, and west to the English Channel at Dieppe (see the map on page 49). However, despite their strength they were not invulnerable. They had long lines of communications that were very susceptible to the *franc-tireurs*. These irregular troops were able to focus on the inadequate French railway system upon which the enemy logistic system depended. There were only three rail lines that crossed the Franco-German border, at Saarbrücken, Wissembourg and Strasbourg.[2]

The response of the Prussians to attacks by *franc-tireur*s was brutal. Extreme reprisals were the norm and villages such as Varice, Ourcelle and Albis were all burnt to the ground. Bismarck was well aware of atrocities being committed and went so far as to comment that there should be no 'laziness in killing'. This was a man who was the epitome of ruthlessness. He wanted his troops to fire on women and children scavenging for potatoes on the outskirts of Paris. He expected all the inhabitants of a village to be hanged if that village resisted Prussian 'exactions'.[3] Bismarck would have approved of Heinrich Himmler who, seventy years later, had a similar mindset.

In January 1871, a Prussian outpost near Toul was overrun by 400 *franc-tireurs*. In the counter-attack, the nearest village of Fontenoy-sur-Moselle was razed and, finding only 'a few citizen soldiers, the Prussians went on a killing spree spearing the inhabitants on bayonets and heaving them into the flames'.[4] Every war produces atrocities and war crimes are often not reported, the perpetrators are rarely named and almost always never punished. The Franco-Prussian War was no exception, with murderous behaviour on both sides. The French who, in the years that followed, sent French Jews to the gas chambers and were barbarous in Indochina and North Africa, would, in the short term, display appalling cruelty in the suppression of the Commune in early 1871.

'War', as someone once said, 'is hell'.

When Strasbourg fell, Prussian troops, employed in its siege, became available and the 1st Reserve Division reached Belfort on 3 November. The French defenders held out, under great pressure, until 15 February 1871. Although it was not a win, neither was it a defeat, and by that measurement, a rare French success.

Gambetta appreciated that his 'delegation' in Tours was vulnerable to the expanding Prussian advance and so, prudently on 8–9 November, he moved his operations 186 miles (300km) to Bordeaux – about as far as he could get from enemy activity, and 360 miles (580km) from Paris.

Coulmiers had offered the French brief respite from defeat but, on 2 December, Poupry (north of Orléans) was taken. A much more significant confrontation was at Amiens and that had fallen three days earlier, at the same time as Ducrot was launching his breakout. The battle for Amiens was a serious matter on a different scale to the operations mentioned above. The Prussians under Generals Edwin Manteuffel and August von Goeben out-numbered the French 43,000 to 25,000, and although they were the victors, they were unable to completely destroy the Army of the North commanded by the very junior Brigadier General Jean-Joseph Farre. Losses of the Prussians were seventy-six officers and 1,216 soldiers. French losses of 1,383 were in addition to about 1,000 either taken prisoner or deserted. Nevertheless, Farre preserved his army by withdrawing and Manteuffel did not pursue him. The Prussian general was directed by Moltke to move on Rouen and Le Havre. Rouen was taken, without a fight, on 5 December. Reviewing his progress at this point, Moltke commented:

> glancing back on the German successes during November and the general military position at the end of the month, we see the great sortie from Paris repulsed in the north, the menace to the investment of being hemmed in done away with by General von Manteuffel's victory at Amiens; in the east Thionville, Breisach, Verdun, and La Fère taken, Montmédy and Belfort surrounded; and in the south Prince Frederick Charles ready to attack the French army before Orléans.[5]

The effect of these multiple reverses suffered by the French was cumulative; each further reduced the possibility of Paris being relieved. It would not be too hyperbolic to suggest that each town lost was another nail in the coffin of French aspirations. These losses were, for the most part, not known to the Parisians. Accordingly, they had no immediate and discernible effect on their domestic life, but the failure of *La Grande Sortie* was a different matter. It was very close to home and it stunned the people of Paris when the very bad news was finally announced on 5 December.

There were recriminations in abundance and General Blanchard, who had commanded I Corps, had been sufficiently outraged by Ducrot's decision to retire that, to ameliorate his strong feelings, he sought to provoke a duel by alluding to Ducrot's ill-judged pronouncement before the battle. Blanchard said to his leader, 'I wish to know if your sword is as long as your tongue.' Ducrot, painfully aware of his failure, not only offered his resignation but asked to serve in the ranks.[6] Trochu briskly rejected the resignation and the unrealistic and the unacceptable offer to serve in the ranks was forgotten. The duel was not fought.

It was on that same day, 5 December, that Trochu received a courteous letter from Moltke advising him that the 2nd Army of Prince Charles and that of the Grand Duke Mecklenburg had overwhelmingly defeated the Army of the Loire, the result of which was the Prussian capture of Orléans. This was devasting news for Trochu. Bismarck was furious that Moltke had corresponded with Trochu and in saying so, further increased the distance between them.

Bismarck and Moltke had never had a warm relationship and they had grown further apart as the war progressed. Despite the overwhelming success of the Prussian armies, the two men did not share a philosophy.

> Moltke's principle was that the Emperor would call when he needed his advice. Only in war – and this led to his antagonism with Bismarck – did he claim to be the only advisor to the Emperor and the supreme warlord as long as operations were ongoing. He resisted, by all means, any interference by the politicians into the purely military sphere and the inclusion of political aspects into military considerations … He stood for the rule of the Prussian royal house and was against any notion of a republic, believing that, 'only soldiers are a cure for democracy'. He was also of the opinion that 'eternal peace is a dream … not even a beautiful one, and war is a part of God's order of the world'.[7]

Otto von Bismarck, on the other hand, realised that if the military leadership is concentrating only on the total defeat of the enemy, 'it will hardly be in a position to judge when the right time has come to initiate the transition from war to peace'.[8]

Personal relationships were a factor in the fall of Orléans, in this case, the relationship between General d'Aurelle and Charles de Freycinet, Gambetta's right-hand man. It had always been fraught because d'Aurelle, who held Gambetta in contempt, was also loath to take military instructions from a civilian such as de Freycinet. Nevertheless, although he had no military experience, de Freycinet was a skilful administrator who had enabled Gambetta to raise armies to continue the war. Arguably, he exceeded his brief by taking charge of strategy and involving himself in matters in which he had no expertise – as d'Aurelle told him. The personal friction between d'Aurelle and de Freycinet played a part in the loss of Orléans.

The battle had been fought in dreadful conditions. There was a snow covering and the temperature was down to $-7°C$. At 1600 hrs on 4 December, d'Aurelle had telegraphed to Gambetta his view that Orléans was indefensible and consequently he was withdrawing.

Gambetta and de Freycinet were furious. Both civilians had ordered the General to stand fast at Orléans and now de Freycinet reiterated the order.

He got a very dusty response from the old soldier, who said, 'I am on the spot and better able than you, to judge the situation.'[9] Later, d'Aurelle must have had second thoughts because he summoned all five of his corps, the XV, XVI, XVII, XVIII and XX, to the defence of the city. It was too late because the Prussians had already taken measures to block access, and the effective concentration of French forces was thwarted.

French soldiers, with only limited training, marched all night in the snow and razor-sharp wind and were exhausted. In some units the officers abandoned their soldiers, unforgivable behaviour that destroyed any commitment to the cause that the soldiers might have had. The Army started to disintegrate and d'Aurelle's order to evacuate Orléans accelerated the breakdown of discipline. Soldiers, with the

Charles de Freycinet (1828–1923), four times Prime Minister of France, from 1877 to 1882. (*Nadar*)

opportunity, took over private houses, ransacked wine cellars and abandoned their weapons. Those responding to the evacuation order made their way to the bridges over the Loire as an unregimented mob. An Irish doctor was an observer and he recorded:

> Most of them were without arms and all were limping along, evidently quite foot-sore while numbers were slightly wounded to judge from the bandages which they displayed round their heads, legs and arms. They looked more like a procession of invalids out for a walk than soldiers still capable of fighting. The poor fellows were dead beat and did not as much march, as shuffle along.[10]

The indiscipline, the pushing and shoving on the bridges, led to the deaths of those who fell into the river, so cold that it had ice floes floating on the surface. The bridges were blown when most, but by no means all, of d'Aurelle's men were across. The Prussians moved into the city having agreed not to shell Orléans if the French withdrew; the French accepted the offer with alacrity.

The battle of Orléans had lasted for two days, during which period the Prussians had suffered 1,747 casualties, of whom about 400 were killed. The French losses were very much greater: 20,000 in total, of whom 2,000 were killed or wounded. The balance were taken prisoner. Seventy-four guns and the usual mountain of small arms, ammunition and equipment were also seized.[11]

When news of the defeat of the Army of the Loire was promulgated it added to the gloom in Paris. The faint hopes for salvation were quashed and everyday life for Parisians became increasingly difficult. In December, temperatures dropped to −15°C (5°F), the Seine froze for three weeks and the streets were covered with snow. There were shortages of food, firewood, coal and medicine. The city was almost completely dark at night. The only communication with the outside world was by balloon, carrier pigeon, or letters packed in iron balls floated down the Seine. Rumours and conspiracy theories abounded.

The wealthy Parisians had made provision for a siege and had purchased their anticipated needs well in advance. For the well off, a restaurant service was still available, at a price. In this unequal society the hardship was borne by those less able to cope. Fresh vegetables became scarce and then the supply dried up, as did that of milk. Dogs, cats and rats were offered by butchers in the less affluent suburbs and people queued for these unattractive sources of protein. The onset of winter increased the use of fuel in its many forms and the cold days hastened a shortage. Life in Paris was grim, the bombast and enthusiasm for the war had evaporated and a new realism took their place. The prospects of relief were scant, winter had set in and the Prussian Army was at the gate.

'I can accept dogfish – but dog!'
French contemporary cartoon.
(*Ann Ronan Picture Library*)

Extreme poverty, starvation and despair are among the ingredients of civil disorder and criminality. Pillage became commonplace, offences of robbery increased. The streets of Paris, sometimes charming, were increasingly unsafe. To provide fuel for fires, property was invaded, and fences, trees and wooden buildings were taken. Anything that could be burned was. The police were overwhelmed and unable to maintain order. This served to inflame public opinion and, as is normal in such situations, the government of General Trochu was blamed.

Initially, food rationing was not imposed, although steps were taken to control food prices. The instruments to put this into effect were the mayors of the twenty arrondissements, but the unhappy result was that there were twenty different price regimes. The inequalities led to queues and higher prices. The poorest people could not afford food and for them the spectre of starvation was always present.

The plight of Paris and its people had caused a significant change in international opinion. Back in July, Britain had been sympathetically disposed towards Prussia and, when Queen Victoria was told of her son-in-law's (Crown Prince Frederick) victory over de MacMahon at Frœschwiller, she declared it to be 'wonderful news'.[12] However, as the Prussian juggernaut ground its way, inexorably, across north and eastern France, attitudes started to reverse. Crown Prince Frederick, who was politically aware, made an acute entry in his journal:

> The longer this struggle lasts, the better for the enemy and the worse for us. The public opinion of Europe has not remained unaffected by the spectacle. We are no longer looked upon as the innocent sufferers of wrong but rather as arrogant victors, no longer content with the conquest of the foe, but fain to bring about his utter ruin. No more do the French appear as a mendacious, contemptible nation but as the heroic-hearted people that against overwhelming odds is defending its dearest possessions in honourable fight … Bismarck has robbed us of our friends, the sympathies of the world and – our conscience.[13]

Gambetta's energetic efforts to raise, equip and train new armies attracted admiration and the curious British affection for the underdog was manifest. The *Illustrated London News* commented, with remarkable prescience:

> The war may or may not be over when Paris shall have capitulated … But it will not end in another sense, when the peace shall have been signed … It may be neither next year nor the year after, that the lessons of the last two months will bear fruit, but that they will bear it we have no doubt at all.[14]

Notwithstanding a swing in public sympathy, Gladstone and his Foreign Secretary Granville were firmly set upon a policy of neutrality. The sinking of five British colliers in the Seine, in December 1870, by Prussian troops could have impacted on this neutrality but Bismarck, ever the pragmatic politician, responded positively and apologetically. He instructed Count Bernstorff, his representative, saying:

> you are authorized to say to Lord Granville that we sincerely regret that our troops, in order to avert immediate danger, were obliged to seize ships which belonged to British subjects. We admit their claim to indemnification and shall pay to the owners the value of the ships, according to equitable estimation, without keeping them waiting for the decision of the question who is finally to indemnify them. Should it be proved that excesses have been committed which were not justified by the necessity of defence, we should regret it still more, and call the guilty persons to account.[15]

Russia took advantage of the French crisis. It was obliged by the Treaty of Paris, signed in 1856, to neutralise the Black Sea. The two powers that oversaw that treaty were Great Britain and France, but the latter was now a helpless and non-effective cypher. Bismarck played his cards with great skill. First, he worked to eliminate France from any renewed negotiations and then he exploited the British aim to retain good political relationships with both combatants and its wish not to fight with Russia. The Austrians were waiting on the sidelines, still smouldering over their recent defeat at the hands of Prussia, but not prepared to join the sinking French ship.

The search for rat meat. Contemporary French cartoon.

In Paris, the increasing, but distant, moral support of Great Britain did nothing to ameliorate the anti-British atmosphere. Frenchmen felt betrayed by Britain's neutrality. There were about 4,000 British nationals in Paris at this time, of whom about 800 were destitute.[16] Absurd although it might appear, these British citizens were at physical risk. There was a body of French opinion that felt strongly that Britain should be fighting on the French side – quite why that should be, in a war initiated by France without reference to any third party, was never a matter for debate.

On the other hand, the very positive, productive and compassionate behaviour of the American ambassador washed off on his fellow compatriots, who numbered only a few hundred. The French did not expect the USA to participate in the war – why should it, as it was 3,000 miles (4,800km) away? Its citizens had a much lower profile than the British and they were not viewed as useless mouths demanding to be fed. The two very significant pluses on the American side were first, Elithu Washburne, its splendid ambassador, and second, the American Ambulance, which made such a valuable contribution in supplementing the medical services, especially in the Paris-based military operations.

No matter what a resident's origins, hunger was ever-present for the majority. Trochu and his GND had, by early December, calculated that food stocks would last only one more month.[17] The price of fresh meat had been fixed by decree from the earliest days of the siege and meat rationing had followed in October. The stock of the most acceptable meat – beef, pork and mutton – was exhausted by late November and, at this stage, horses, donkeys and mules were incorporated into the Parisian diet. There were 45,000 of these beasts and they provided a daily meat ration of one ounce (30 grams) per head.[18] To put this in practical terms, it is about half a modern sausage.

The Government was loath to ration bread but had set prices in September. In order to endure a constant provision, it requisitioned all flour and cereals. There was wastage in the early days and, as stocks started to run out, on 11 December Jules Ferry made a proclamation. He forbade bakers from selling flour and ordered that flour be used only in bread. The public response was such that the following day, the Government issued assurances that 'bread will not be rationed'.[19]

In order to extend the stock of flour, all manner of other cereals was added. Among these were rice, wheat bran and rye. It did not make for an attractive product and was 'as disagreeable to the taste as it was unpleasant to the sight'.[20]

In a siege situation the overriding topic of conversation is always food and its availability. Paris was no exception. The more that hunger increased, the more obsessive the denizens of Paris became. Anything with a pulse was considered to be edible, but perhaps not palatable. Certainly dogs, cats, crows and sparrows found their way into the pot. There is a myth that Paris subsisted on rats. They *were* eaten and they were sold in butchers' shops, but the evidence is that in the majority of cases they were consumed by the wealthy acting out of 'bravado and dilettantism'.[21]

The meat shortage famously, and probably unnecessarily, led to the slaughter of the animals from the *Jardin d'Acclimatation*. Soon after, zebra, yak, buffalo, wapiti (a form of elk), camel and elephant made their appearance on smart menus cards. Although newsworthy, only a microscopically small proportion of the population savoured Elephant Consommé or Fillet of Camel. The menu card (below) does illustrate that the rich did not suffer hardship. Ernest Renan, the philologist, philosopher, biblical scholar and critic, with some of his literary friends went as far as presenting the restaurateur Paul Brébant with a gold medal for feeding them throughout the siege and 'not as if they were in a city of two million besieged souls'.[22]

The gap between the 'haves' and the 'have nots' was an unbridgeable chasm. Renan and those like him, able to commission gold medals, were in blissful ignorance of the seething cauldron of despair and anger being felt by the 471,754 working-class and lower middle-class people who were living in extreme poverty. The population of Paris at the time was 2,005,709.[23]

25 *décembre* 1870
99e *jour du siège*
—

HORS-D'ŒUVRE
Beurre - Radis - Tête d'âne farcie - Sardines

POTAGES
Purée de haricots rouges aux croûtons
Consommé d'éléphant

ENTRÉES
Goujons frits - Le chameau rôti à l'Anglaise
Le civet de Kangourou
Côtes d'ours rôties sauce poivrade

ROTS
Cuissot de loup, sauce chevreuil
Le chat flanqué de rats
Salade de cresson
La terrine d'antilope aux truffes
Cèpes à la bordelaise
Petits pois au beurre

ENTREMETS
Gâteau de riz aux confitures

DESSERT
Fromage de gruyère

VINS

PREMIER SERVICE	DEUXIÈME SERVICE
Xérès	Mouton Rothschild 1846
Latour Blanche 1861	Romanée Conti 1858
Ch. Palmer 1864	Bellenger frappé
	Grand porto 1827

Café et liqueurs

Café Voisin, G. Braquenas, 261, rue Saint-Honoré.

This Christmas Day menu card is of interest because it rather overplays the cooking and serving of zoo animals. The wine list is an indication of the level of the Café Voisin and the prices M. Braquenas probably charged.

The GND insisted that everything with food value was fully exploited and, to this end, requisitioned animal bones that were converted to gelatine, stock and a broth that proved to be highly unpopular.

As December wound to a close and a very unhappy Christmas beckoned, Trochu found his martial spirit. Trochu was beset on all sides but he had been bolstered by news that Major General Louis Faidherbe, commanding the recently reconstituted Army of the North, was proving to be a better general than many of his peers.[24] On 9 December, Faidherbe seized Ham on the Somme River, about 65 miles (105km) from Paris, and cut the rail link between Reims and Amiens. This caused serious alarm in the Prussian camp because now Faidherbe could advance on Amiens or attack the Prussian logistic base at Rheims.[25]

General Edwin von Manteuffel, commanding 1st Army, ordered General Graf von der Groeben to retake Ham. The latter decided that, despite Faidherbe's Army of the North being only 40,000 strong, he would *not* retake Ham but would withdraw from Amiens, and he did on 16 December – a career-inhibiting move by von der Groeben. Moltke was not best pleased and decided to control the situation personally, and he directed Manteuffel to concentrate his army on Beauvais because, from there, he could frustrate an approach, from any direction, on Paris. Faidherbe moved east with plans to interdict the Prussian lines of communication. His advance was barred by the fortress at La Fère and so he turned around and aimed for Amiens.[26] He quickly realised that the reoccupation of the city of Amiens was beyond him.

French soldiers manning trenches outside Paris in the winter of 1870/71.
Their misery is captured in this engraving, which is after a painting by
Alphonse de Neuville, who served in the *Garde Mobile*.

With the Prussian 1st Army fast approaching he decided to fight a defensive battle in the valley of the Hallue, a stream that did not merit the appellation 'river'. A bloody engagement was fought, and Faidherbe's Army of the North acquitted itself well. The battle was indecisive, but it was a moral victory for the French. On 24 December, Faidherbe moved to the security of Arras.

Meanwhile, in Paris, Trochu felt the need to lay the foundations for an advance by Ducrot's 2nd Army. He determined that, on 21 December, Le Bourget should be taken – again. This inconsequential village was currently held by about 750 men of the Prussian Guard. The assault, in a slowly clearing fog, by 5,200 men was stopped in its tracks by well-controlled rifle fire from loop-holed walls. One group did get into the centre of the village but then came under heavy 'friendly' artillery fire. The French withdrew having lost 635 men; Ducrot's 2nd Army had waited all day for the signal to advance – it never came. Elements of Ducrot's force did get involved but too late and in insufficient strength to affect the outcome. The battle was rejoined the next day and it was a replay of what had gone before. The French had a further 1,800 casualties, a number that by far exceeded the 519 Prussians. As the survivors struggled back behind the citadel walls a torrent of criticism and abuse was heaped on Trochu from the clubs and the Red press.

Trochu, bereft of ideas, called a council of war and the decision taken was that the French would sap towards Le Bourget. That is to say, they would dig trenches in no man's land and, from there, lay siege to Le Bourget. On the night of 21 December, the temperature was −15°C (5°F). The ground was rock-hard, so hard that entrenching tools broke, tent pegs could not be driven into the ground, all water froze solid, and the bread ration had to be portioned with axes. There was no fuel for fires and consequently, no hot food. Conditions were life-threatening. This was military nonsense but, as always, it was the soldier who suffered.

Outside the walls of Paris Moltke and his soldiers were no better off. They were possessors of a bleak wilderness that could offer not an item of succour. There was no foraging here and the logistic chain was placed under pressure as a result. The freezing weather made life even more uncomfortable for the besiegers.

On the morning of 22 December there were 980 cases of frostbite in the French lines.[27] Frostbite is a precursor to gangrene and death unless treated swiftly and professionally. Jules Favre and Jules Simon, both leading lights in the GND, made an excursion to the French lines and were stunned by what they saw. Both men were civilians and the sudden exposure to the military facts of life shocked them deeply. They could see for themselves the parlous condition of the soldiers struggling in the face of a ferocious, icy and unremitting wind and without adequate clothing. There was very scant provision of food. Favre recorded the response of Simon, who said, 'Moscow has come to the gates of Paris, which of us could have foreseen that we would be witnesses to such a dreadful scene?'[28]

The outcome of the latest Le Bourget debacle, when considered in association with the failed *Grande Sortie* and the loss of Amiens and Orléans, was that civilian confidence in the military was completely extinguished. On his return from the battlefield, Favre 'firmly declared that the Government must take back the control of military operation into its own hands'.[29]

That was all very well. However, *someone* had to command the soldiers, but who? That was the question. Trochu had no desire to cling to office but Ducrot could not succeed him. His defeatist attitude and his open hostility to the Liberal Republicans in the Government of National Defence made his appointment impossible. Vinoy was a possible 'runner' but he lacked the capacity for original thought, and that was the quality that was going to be needed. Despite the need to replace Trochu no one could be found to fill his boots and so, unwillingly, he soldiered on.

Outside the walls, Archibald Forbes, a correspondent of the *Daily News* and embedded with 103rd Regiment of Saxons, joined them as a guest for Christmas dinner. He was offered sardines, caviar, various kinds of *wurst*, boiled beef, macaroni and roast mutton – all rounded off with cheese, fresh butter and fruit. He noted sombrely that the Germans' diet was in vivid contrast to that of the French prisoners taken at Le Bourget, 'so ravenous with hunger that the men grubbed in the gutter after turnip tops and bones, and turned over dirt heaps in the search for stray crusts of bread'.[30]

Although Gambetta's armies toiled, they were in constant contact with their enemy. General Bourbaki commanded XV, XIII and XX Corps. He was under pressure from Gambetta to advance towards Paris, but Bourbaki resisted, saying his troops, thrashed at Orléans, needed to rest, regroup and re-equip. General Chanzy now commanded the newly designated 2nd Army of the Loire, and had 120,000 men, of whom only 75,000 were fit for operations. Chanzy was a confident man, aggressive, determined and efficient. He was blessed with the leadership qualities absent in so many of his peers. Moltke judged him to be 'probably the most capable of all the leaders who the Germans had to encounter'.[31]

In operations in early December he fought for four days at Beaugency; he inflicted 3,395 casualties but suffered 5,000.[32] Chanzy's operations were not helped by de Freycinet going over his head and giving orders direct to his divisional commanders. The ongoing conflict was costing thousands of lives on both sides but did nothing to alter the nub of the issue, which was the Siege of Paris.

The French situation was desperate and was exacerbated by the absence of any coordinated strategic plan. Charles de Freycinet, a self-confident civilian operating from Bordeaux, had apparently assumed the role of commander-in-chief. He had no understanding of the critical logistic vulnerability of the Germans and no coordinated attack on the German supply was initiated. Such an attack would not have been easy: Faidherbe was too far away, perhaps impossible for Chanzy and Bourbaki, but no more so than the oft-stated desire to relieve the sieges of Paris and Belfort. It was left to the *francs-tireurs* to do whatever damage they could to disrupt German logistics, but that was insufficient to affect the outcome.

Gambetta's armies were operating individually with mixed success. The entire operation should have been directed by a general – for example, d'Aurelle. Freycinet might then have been better employed seeing a big picture rather than fighting the detailed, divisional battle. A coordinated interruption in the Prussian supply system for, say, ten days would have major impact on the besieging force. History is full of 'what ifs'. This is one of them.

On the outskirts of Paris, just after Christmas, Moltke was assembling his artillery and he commented:

> two groups of battery emplacements were erected in spite of the severe frost on the western slope of the heights behind Raincy and Gagny, and on the left upland of the Marne Valley near Noisy le Grand, thus encompassing Mont Avron on two sides at a distance of 700–1,100 yards.[33]

As the new year dawned, 100 guns of the largest calibres stood ready to open fire on the south front of Paris. Bismarck was insistent that they be used, and soon.

Notes

1. Goncourt, Journal, 3 December 1870.
2. Howard, p. 375.
3. Dresden SKA, ZS, 158, 13 December 1870, quoted by Wawro, p. 179.
4. Horne, J. & Kramer, A., *German Atrocities 1914* (New Haven, USA, 2001), pp. 141–2.
5. *MMK*, p. 224.
6. Horne, p. 160.
7. Roth, G., 'Field Marshal von Moltke the Elder: His importance Then and Now', *Army History*, No. 23, Summer 1992).
8. Bismarck, O. von., *Erinnerung und Gedanke, die gesammelten Werke*, ed. Ritter, G. & Stadelmann, R., (Berlin, 1932).
9. d'Aurelle, pp. 314–13.
10. Ryan, C.E., *With an Ambulance during the Franco-Prussian War 1870–71* (London, 1896), p. 264.
11. *GGS*, Vol. 3, Appendix XCIII, p. 16.
12. Horne, p. 162.

13. Frederick III, War Diary, p. 240.
14. *ILN*, December 1870.
15. *Hansard*, Vol. 206, 23 May 1871.
16. Alan Herbert to Labouchère, quoted by Horne, p. 170.
17. Trochu, Vol. 1, p. 476.
18. Sarrepont, H. de, *Histoire de la Defense de Paris en 1870–71* (Paris,1872), pp. 221–33.
19. Heylli, G., *d'Journal du Siege de Paris*, Vol. 3, (Paris, 1871–74), pp. 81–2.
20. Evans, T.W., *History of the American Ambulance Established in Paris during the Siege of 1870–71* (London, 1872), p. 497.
21. Sarrepont, p. 173, quoted by Fermer, p. 127.
22. Duveau, G., *La Siège de Paris* (Paris, 1939), p. 118.
23. Larchey, L., *Mémorial illustré des deux sièges de Paris* (Paris, 1872), pp. 206, 222.
24. Faidherbe was a substantive colonel and an acting major general.
25. Bronsart, von S.P., *Geheimes Kriegstagebuch, 1870–71* (ed. Rassow, P. Bonn, 1954), p. 220.
26. Howard, p. 393.
27. Trochu, Vol. 1, p. 487.
28. Favre, Vol. 2, p. 197.
29. Ibid, p. 198, Howard, p. 360.
30. Forbes, A., *Daily News*, December 1870, Horne, p. 195.
31. *MMK*, p. 236.
32. *GGS*, Vol. 4, Appendix CVI, p. 33.
33. *MMK*, p. 264.

Chapter Fourteen

January: A New German Empire

As the new year of 1871 dawned, north and eastern France was filled with soldiers and many more who only looked like soldiers. In addition, there were tens of thousands of uniformed guerrillas. The defeat of French armies at Sédan and Metz had placed the military future of France into the amateur hands of Gambetta and de Freycinet. They were fortunate to have a handful of senior officers to command the new armies raised in unoccupied France.

By January 1871, French assets were divided into three armies. These were 2nd Army of the Loire, commanded by General Antoine Chanzy, the Army of the East, under Major General Charles-Denis Bourbaki, and the Army of the North, led by General Louis Faidherbe. In Paris there was a host of *Gardes Nationale* and *Gardes Mobile*, the organisation of which changed frequently.

On New Year's Day the siege of Mézières (now called Charleville-Mézières), close to the Belgian border and about 55 miles (89km) north-east of Rheims, was brought to an end. Its value to the French had been that it precluded the German use of the railway and impacted upon logistic support. The Germans kept it under observation until 19 December, when, after the fall of Montmédy, the 14th Division moved up before Mézières. The town was by no means a major facility, its defences were out of date and its garrison was only about 2,000 strong.

> Mézières stands on a mountain spur, surrounded on three sides by the Moselle, but it is hemmed by a ring of heights. The character of the defences, which had been strengthened by Vauban, with their numerous salient angles, was not calculated to resist modern long-range artillery. The place exposed an isolated rampart of masonry in a circumference of 2,160 to 3,250 yards, and although the long delay had been utilised in repairing the weak points by throwing up earthworks, a bombardment could not fail to be destructive to the defenders.
>
> When Verdun had surrendered, heavy siege guns were brought by rail from Clermont to a position close in front of the southern face of the fortress. The only hindrance to the erection of the batteries was the state of the soil, frozen to a depth of 20 inches; and at a quarter past eight on the morning of 31 December, sixty-eight siege guns and eight fieldpieces opened fire.

At first the fortress replied vigorously but, by the afternoon, its artillery was utterly silenced, and the white flag was hoisted next day. The garrison were taken prisoners; considerable stores and 132 guns fell into the hands of the besiegers. But the chief advantage gained (says Moltke) was the opening of a new line of railway to Paris.[1]

For the Prussians the new year had got off to a satisfying start and not just because of the capture of Mézières. That same day, 1 January 1871, the German Empire was born; now they were all Germans and united under King Wilhelm I. The King was not an enthusiast for empire, and he grumbled to Chancellor Bismarck, 'This is the end of Old Prussia.'[2] Nevertheless, the King accepted the imperial crown and the leadership of his diverse new realm.

This German Empire had not had an easy birth and the Reichstag had only voted for the measure on 10 December. The Empire was a complicated beast; it was composed of twenty-six separate states. It included four kingdoms, six grand-duchies, six duchies (until 1876), seven principalities, three Hanseatic cities and one imperial territory. Prussia was the dominant component with just short of 70 per cent of the population and territory.

King Wilhelm might have had reservations, but Bismarck had none as, for him, it was the achievement of a long-standing ambition. The formation of the German Empire had only come about after a great deal of horse-trading behind the scenes. Negotiations had taken three months and Bismarck had courted, wined and dined a long list of German princelings at Versailles. Each of the small German states had a price that had to be met before they would sign up to Bismarck's grand plan. Even then, not all were wildly enthusiastic about the proposed new arrangements.

The ceremony, on 18 January, was orchestrated by Bismarck and to some tastes it was excessively self-congratulatory. Prince Otto of Bavaria wrote to his brother and said, 'How infinitely and agonisingly painful I found the scene … It was all so cold, so proud, so glossy, so strutting and boastful and heartless and empty.'[3] The Palace of Versailles was and is a place of cultural and historical importance to the French and using it for the ceremony was a calculated affront that heaped further humiliation on France and the French.

In the German camp at Versailles, it should all have been sweetness and light. It was not. Quite the reverse, because 'all the German military and civil leaders were in a state of explosive irritation'.[4] King Wilhelm was unhappy at the slow progress of the war, the apparent reverse in German fortunes and the success of the French Army of the North led by Major General Louis Faidherbe. The success of General Bourbaki's Army of the East at Villersexel, on 9 January, would soon add to King Wilhelm's angst. The palace and its surrounds were filled with foreign dignitaries, military attachés, correspondents, staff officers and a host of princelings representing their part of the new German Empire. This host had to be wined and dined – adding to the logistic burden. The King's headquarters was a hotbed of gossip and intrigue.

Bismarck, who was the dominant personality, was in poor health. He was an heroic trencherman bordering on glutton and he suffered from gout. His work rate was unrelenting; he had been overworking and gave every indication of a man heading for physical collapse. It is little wonder that he was stressed as he tried to steer his ship of state through shoal waters. He was alert to the possibility of European intervention, unlikely though that was, in the war now so nearly won. He was increasingly caught up in a bitter feud with the General Staff as to who controlled state policy and where the line was drawn between the military and political.[5] As a consequence of this 'feud', relations between Moltke and Bismarck were glacial. The situation was exacerbated by Bismarck's constant, amateur interferences in military matters, which were the sole concern of General von Moltke who, in turn, made a specific point of *not* briefing Bismarck on operational issues. The relationship between these two men was so bad that King Wilhelm had had to intervene and draw demarcation lines of responsibility and authority.

Paul Bronsart wrote in his diary, 'God protect us from our friends! … He [Roon, Minister for War] appears to stand as a strategist on about the same level as Count Bismarck; but as a comedian he ranks immeasurably higher.' This from a lieutenant colonel on the Army General Staff. Bronsart was an active player in the personal relations in the War Ministry, as a biographer of Bismarck recounts:

> On 18 December 1870 Paul Bronsart von Schellendorf had put his career on the line to frustrate Bismarck's intervention in military matters. As he recorded in his war diary, he had been ordered by Eugen Theophil von Podbielski to provide Bismarck with the minutes of a Military Council and he decided to disobey orders, a court-martial offence. The whole entry records the agony of conscience of one of the most gifted of the 'demi-gods', a lieutenant colonel, a Division Chief in the General Staff, 'for me the hardest day of the entire campaign'. He had received an order from the King, approved by the Chief of the General Staff, General Count Moltke and handed to him by Lieutenant General Podbielski, Quartermaster General of the entire army. As he records the moment of his decision:
>
>> if a man with the ambitious thirst for power like Count Bismarck were once to be admitted, there would be nothing more to be done … I thought about it for ten minutes; the habit of obedience got me through the address and then it failed me, and the feeling of duty,

and the need to be disobedient even to the King, won the upper hand even at the sacrifice of my own person.

He reported to Podbielski that he could not carry out the order in good conscience and submitted his resignation letter at the same time. Podbielski at first flew into a rage and questioned Bronsart's sanity. Then in the face of this act of moral courage by a senior staff officer, he consulted Moltke, who revoked the order and told the King of his decision. Bismarck never got access to the Military Council minutes. Bronsart joins von Werther as two examples of unusual civil courage in the face of Bismarck's increasing dictatorial attitude. Bronsart concludes the entry by averring that if he had done as he was bidden:

> then Count Bismarck would sit in the saddle. He knows very well how to ride, as he once said about Germany. Where this ride would have taken us is not in doubt.[6]

It was not only Moltke who was at odds with Bismarck, the antipathy extended further down the chain of command. The uniformed element of the headquarters 'resented the very presence of this civilian masquerading, in his reservist uniform, as an officer'.[7] Bronsart commented acidly that 'the wearing of a cuirassier's greatcoat was no aid to military understanding'.[8]

Bismarck was well aware that he was being 'cut out of the loop'; he complained, with some justification, that even the newspapers got more information than was provided to him. The Chancellor and the War Minister, Roon, were concerned about the domestic pressure generated by Moltke's demands. Bronsart was unsympathetic, writing, 'People seem generally to have forgotten in the victory celebrations we are at war and they must learn to put up with its exigencies.'[9]

Relations between Moltke and General Albrecht Count von Roon were also poor as Roon struggled to meet Moltke's demands for men and materiel. Roon had served under Moltke in the war against Austria and Moltke had no qualms about browbeating his erstwhile subordinate – even though he was the Minister for War.

The weather conditions were extreme but, notwithstanding the abject misery of enduring, let alone fighting, the French Army of the North moved, on 2 January, to relieve the besieged town of Péronne. It clashed with the German VIII Corps just outside the village of Bapaume. Faidherbe was a skilful and resourceful commander, a substantive colonel and an acting major general. His soldiers admired and trusted him but that could not compensate for the logistic weakness and the training deficiency of his men.

The Battle of Bapaume was indecisive but Faidherbe was unaware that he had actually outfought the Germans, who were 'outnumbered, weary and short of ammunition'.[10] The casualties suffered by both sides were similar – however, a sign of the times was the desertion by some of the *GN*. While Faidherbe was giving orders to abandon Bapaume his opponent Lieutenant General August von Goeben was doing something similar. The Germans withdrew and the investment of Péronne was lifted – but not for long.

Back in Paris, the aftermath of the recent fighting was to be seen in the base hospitals. The wounded were tended by untrained nurses and there was a dearth of doctors. The twin killers of French soldiers were septicaemia and gangrene. Juliette Lambert visited one hospital and reported that she was disturbed by the terrible cries of the wounded, having limbs amputated in the Palais de l'Industrie. She was shocked to see 'one of our great surgeons weep in telling me that, in his hospital, he had not saved a single amputation case'.[11] Most hospitals had a death shed into which those with septicaemia were sent to die. Tommy Bowles underscored the horror of these hospitals, writing that the wounded were:

> packed three, four and five in each of the little rooms. Ventilation cannot be said to be imperfect, for there is none; and the dead, as many as fifty at

| Colonel, acting Major General Louis Faidherbe (1818–89). | Tommy Gibson Bowles (1842–1922). |

a time are placed, packed like sardines, in the centre of a gallery into which the rooms open. The stench is something terrible and only last night a French gentleman said to me, 'to be taken there is death'.[12]

The only bright spot on the medical scene, which was akin to that of the Crimean War, was the presence and professional skill of Dr John Swinburne, the chief surgeon of the American Ambulance. Henry Du Pré Labouchère wrote:

the ambulance, which is considered the best, is the American. The wounded are under canvas, the tents are not cold, and yet the ventilation is admirable ... It is the dream of every French soldier, if he is wounded, to be taken to this ambulance'.[13]

Dr Swinburne's results seemed to be miraculous. 'Whereas four out of five died in the purulent confines of the Grand Hotel, four out of five of Swinburne's amputation cases survived.'[14] It is little wonder that Americans were popular in Paris.

However, most people were still hungry and, whilst young girls sold themselves for a crust of bread, Henry Markheim recalled eating roast beef in a restaurant, on 20 December, and being assured by the proprietor that there was a further week's supply of beef in his cellar.[15]

Bismarck had been disproportionately aggrieved by Moltke's courteous letter to Trochu concerning the fall of Orléans. He chose to make it a major issue and, as a result, in some circles his mental health was being questioned, albeit behind closed doors. Others, not least Ducrot, Favre and Picard, interpreted the letter as an overture for peace. Trochu did not agree that it opened the door to negotiations. The reality was that Bismarck was thirsting for more French blood and was pressing Moltke to open a bombardment on Paris to force its surrender and an early end to the war.

General Karl Graf von Blumenthal, who had excelled in his role of Chief of Staff to Crown Prince Frederick in 3rd Army, was recognised as being second, only to Moltke, in experience and ability. He contended that a swift French surrender would leave the French armies of the 'East', 'North' and 'Loire' undefeated and would allow France to renew the war at its convenience. Blumenthal and Moltke believed that the remaining French forces would have to be destroyed first, and when that was achieved, Paris would be starved into surrender.

Notes

1. *MMK*, p. 258.
2. Pflanze, O., *The Rise and Fall of the Second Empire* (Princetown, 1990), Vol. 1, pp. 499–500.
3. Wawro, p. 182.

4. Howard, p. 349.

5. Fermer, D., p. 145.

6. Steinberg, J., *Bismarck: A Life* (Oxford University Press, 2011), pp. 300–301.

7. Howard, p. 350.

8. Bronsart, p. 281.

9. Ibid., p. 279–80.

10. Ibid., p. 397.

11. Horne, p. 174.

12. Tommy Bowles, quoted by Horne, p. 174.

13. *Daily News*, 11 November 1870: Seltzer, G., *The American Ambulance in Paris, 1870–1871* (University of Carolina).

14. Horne, p. 175.

15. Markheim, H.W.G., *Inside Paris During the Siege* (London, Macmillan, 1871).

Chapter Fifteen

January: Bombardment – Ethics and Practicality

It is necessary at this point to divert from the chronological and consider one specific issue that became, in effect, the political football that divided the German high command in the latter part of this war. It had been the major topic of debate since the investment of Paris on 19 September.

Bismarck favoured the shelling of Paris as soon and as heavily as possible in order to bring a swift end to the war, and he said so, loudly and often. 'To shell or not to shell' became the philosophical battlefield for the next three months. The bombardment of a civilian target is an ethical issue that arises generation on generation. On the one hand it could be argued that total war has no boundaries and any enemy asset is a legitimate target. The counter-argument is that it is uncivilised, unnecessary and inefficient. It does not destroy civilian morale; rather, it hardens resolve. Examples of that phenomenon are the blitzes of London, Coventry and Bristol, the Allied air campaign against Germany and the bombing of North Vietnam by the USA. All of those events lay far in the future, but Moltke was a shrewd practitioner of war and, perhaps, he intuitively perceived the likely effect.

German public opinion was strongly in favour of a bombardment. Its soldiers saw it as reasonable, to strike against enemy fortifications. However, public opinion and especially Bismarck preferred a general attack on the civil population as an act of national revenge for past misdeeds. Bismarck fed this attitude and enlisted the support of the German press.[1] He identified the Crown Prince as an opponent and even went so far as to suggest that the Crown Prince and his British wife Victoria were complicit in an anti-bombardment position.

Crown Prince Frederick was a capable and successful soldier who had commanded 3rd Army with skill. He was a convinced anglophile and his wife Victoria was a daughter of Queen Victoria. Crown Prince Frederick did not support a bombardment of the city and he wrote in his diary, 'All persons in authority, I at the head of them, are at one in this, that we must use every endeavour to force Paris to surrender by hunger alone.'[2] He was most concerned about civilian casualties and especially children. He was, by most measurements, a compassionate, Christian gentleman. He was all of the things that Bismarck was not. Bismarck viewed the heir to the throne as hostile.

> The Crown Prince and Princess shared the outlook of the Progressive Party and Bismarck was haunted by the fear that, should the old Emperor die, and he was now in his seventies, they would call on one of the Progressive leaders to become Chancellor. He sought to guard against such a turn by keeping the Crown Prince from a position of any influence and by using foul means as well as fair to make him unpopular.[3]

Bismarck was a ruthless man and he played a shrewd political card when he raised the possibility of some form of neutral intervention in the war. He advanced a bizarre theory that the forthcoming meeting of European powers in London presented a danger. The meeting was to discuss the Russian denunciation of the Black Sea clauses of the Treaty of Paris, held in March 1856, after the Crimean War. Bismarck asserted that the meeting would increase the likelihood of an intervention. However, he did not say how, by whom and for what purpose. Based on his theory, the fall of Paris was not a military matter, it was a political issue to be managed by politicians, and who better than himself? He believed that the longer the war dragged on the greater the danger. He wrote, 'Political considerations make an acceleration of this bombardment of the forts very desirable.'[4] He specified 'forts' but, in effect, he meant the city.

King Wilhelm was convinced by Bismarck's argument and he expressed support. He was also dissatisfied to learn that the build-up of ammunition was slow, and sufficiently so that a bombardment could not commence until the new year. He sent Moltke a summary of his views. Bronsart drafted the General's response. It did not duck the issue and 'robust' would be an understatement. It was just short of insubordinate.

The General made clear his irritation with 'military ignoramuses who sit behind green tables'. He explained:

> The question when the artillery attack on Paris should or can begin can only be decided on the basis of the military situation. Political motives can only find consideration in so far as they do not demand anything militarily inadmissible or impossible.

To begin the bombardment prematurely was inadmissible and to speed the collection of materiel was impossible. He commented that he had only one railway line and that terminated 15 miles (24km) short of the siege park. From there, ammunition had to be downloaded from the train and reloaded into carts. They then were hauled, slowly, along icy, snow-covered tracks to the siege park at Villacoublay, just south and east of Versailles.

This, he said, was the cause of the delay. He finished by reiterating his view that bombardment was an expensive and inefficient weapon, to be used only if hunger failed.[5]

Moltke did not believe that a bombardment was impossible or useless, but he insisted that it was not to be carried out without appropriate preparations – the possibility was that hunger would intervene before those preparations were made and the 500 rounds per gun had been assembled.

When Paris was first invested Moltke had set in train the provision of siege artillery, but at that time, over three months past, neither he nor Roon thought it likely that the guns would be needed. The siege park had been established but siege ammunition was just one of the multitude of items to be transported along the single railway line.

Bronsart had noted that the bombardment of Strasbourg had wasted ammunition and alienated the population but did not advance capitulation by a single day.[6] He was firmly on side with his boss on this issue. The argument rolled on but, until Moltke had his stockpile of ammunition, it was all academic. However, it had been agreed that, as a precursor to any city bombardment, an experimental attack would be made on the French position at Fort Avron.[7] 'Experimental' is a strange word to be used in this context. The destructive power and efficiency of the German artillery had been demonstrated time and again in this war. An 'experiment' would do no more than confirm what everyone already knew. Perhaps 'experiment' was just a diplomatic face-saver. King Wilhelm was now taking a close personal interest in bombardment matters and made it clear that he would not countenance any technical problems as an excuse for further delay.[8]

Unaware of the brisk Germanic debate about the fate of Paris, the GND was now in tatters, Trochu's authority wafer-thin. He was quite prepared to resign; he had never wanted the job in the first place. But who could replace him? Not Ducrot, whose defeatist attitude and monarchist sympathies made him ill-suited to any form of office. Politically, Vinoy, as a former imperial senator, was equally unacceptable. He was also an unobjective optimist and he was sure that a thrust against the German encirclement would succeed. 'Where?' enquired Ducrot acidly. There were no other evident candidates and so Trochu hung on to the job, by default.

Mont Avron was commanded by Colonel Stoffel, the former military attaché in Berlin (see map on page 150, top right). The mount had been taken by the French in *La Grande Sortie*, but now it had no strategic value. It made no sense to retain it, as it lay outside the line of defensive forts. It was isolated from Fort Rosny by a deep ravine, and its resupply could be interdicted by artillery fire. The defences were poor and were exposed to the Germans on the north, east and south. Despite the decision to garrison Mont Avron, the

French did little to improve its defences. In January, the ground was frozen solid, and digging was a fruitless exercise for Stoffel's half-starved men, so they did not bother. They were to pay a high price. The Prussian preparations could be seen and heard as Moltke moved up seventy-six Krupp guns that fired a 56lb shell. They opened fire on 27 December and kept up the barrage for two days.

> At 0830 on the morning of 27 December, those seventy-six guns opened fire. A heavy snowstorm interfered with accurate aim and prevented any observation of the execution done. ... But the batteries had fired more effectually than had been supposed. The artillery strike was devastating, and the frozen ground enhanced the lethality of Prussian fire. The shallow French trenches provided scant cover and the horror of an artillery bombardment broke the nerve of many young, barely trained soldiers. They streamed to the rear where they spread disaffection among the civilians they encountered. The clear weather of 28 December allowed of greater precision; the Prussian fire proved most telling, making fearful havoc in the numerous and exposed French infantry garrison. Mont Avron was silenced, and only the forts kept up a feeble fire. General Trochu, who was present in person, ordered the abandonment of the position, which was so effectually accomplished in the night by the energetic commander, Colonel Stoffel, that only one disabled gun was left behind.
>
> On 29 December the French fire was silent, and the hill was found deserted. The Germans had no intention of continuing to occupy the position. Their batteries now turned their fire on the forts, which suffered severely, and on the earthworks near Bondy.[9] [Moltke refers here to 'Germans' but until 1 January 1871 they were still technically 'Prussians'.]

The Prussian gunners having switched targets took on the more substantial forts, one of which was Fort Issy, which attracted the close attention of twenty-eight guns. It was one of the six forts built to defend Paris from the south-west (see map on page 195, central). A similar weight of firepower was focused on Fort Vanves and eighteen German guns targeted Fort Montrouge.[10]

The forts now under attack were well equipped. Issy had ninety guns, Vanves eighty-four and Montrouge fifty-two. Fort Valérien had no less than 106. This formidable array of artillery replied promptly, and in kind, to the Prussian batteries. Over a period of several hours the greater accuracy of the Prussian gunners altered the balance and, by 1400 hrs, Issy had stopped returning fire. In Vanves, nine of its guns had been dismounted and it had suffered thirty casualties.[11] Only Montrouge stayed in the fight, and then not for long.

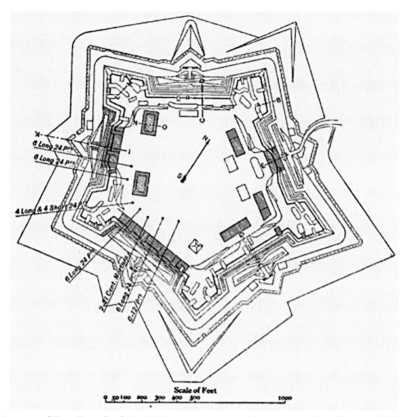

This map of Fort Issy, built in 1840, serves to provide a view of its all-round defence capability, but able, in 1871, to resist a German artillery attack on its walls.

The perimeter forts were all substantial installations, stone built, capacious and with ample accommodation for a large garrison. The effect of the Prussian fire on Issy was considerable: 220mm guns firing from the Châtillon heights wreaked havoc among Issy's batteries. Guns were dismounted and men blown to pieces. In half a day, Issy was silenced. Despite the awesome firepower unleashed upon them, none of the walls of the forts were breached although the ramparts were badly damaged and many of the facilities within the walls, like barrack accommodation, were destroyed. At Issy, despite the torrent of fire it had undergone, incredibly there had been only ninety-eight casualties, of whom eighteen were killed from a garrison of 1,900. Prussian casualties were slight. As for the Prussian gunners, the whole operation had the air of an exercise.

Fort Issy was on the heights overlooking Issy-les-Moulineaux but it was the product of an earlier age when any advance in artillery capability was neither considered nor planned for. Accordingly, it was too close to the city walls to be effective. What had happed to Issy was now wrought on Vanves and Montrouge. The latter responded with commendable spirit, but it was overwhelmed and when its guns were silenced it had no further means of retaliation. Vanves had a garrison of 1,730 and suffered only twenty casualties.

The attackers employed, to great effect, Chassepôts captured previously. Their fire was so accurate that the French were obliged to abandon their ramparts. The Prussian outposts took possession of the trenches of Clamart, and in the course of the night reversed them to face the French positions.

The 'rapidity of this success surprised the Germans themselves and made most of the sceptics think again about the efficacy [*sic*] of bombardment.'[12] The Crown Prince in particular confessed himself converted and admitted that 'bombardment may perhaps lead to important results'.[13]

Moltke and Blumenthal also changed their minds because Prince Charles and his 2nd Army had, thus far, been unable to eliminate Gambetta forces in the provinces that were being more than a mere irritant. The generals realised that perhaps bombardment should be tried.

The King was 'champing at the bit' and he bypassed Moltke to direct General Hohrenlohe to commence firing on 4 January. Fog delayed the start

Fort Issy, whose walls resisted German artillery in 1871 but which succumbed to urban sprawl later.

and the first rounds were fired on 5 January. Before the city could be attacked all the southern forts had to be silenced and this the Germans set about. They employed not only the heavy Krupp guns but also a 'low-trajectory Rampart gun'. This weapon fired a 20mm shell and was employed almost like a rifle; it was lethal out to about 1,500 yards. Its effect was to prevent repair work to the ramparts of its target. The targeting of the southern forts was successful because the French had no effective answer to German artillery superiority.

Moltke, the consummate professional, having started the bombardment applied himself to its efficient management. He directed fire into the city and the first of many shells burst in rue Lalande on the left bank. The shelling was entirely arbitrary and had no specific targets. The inhabitants of Montparnasse cemetery were shelled, some were moved from their repose, but, of course, they reported no injuries. A correspondent commented:

> Not content with directing their projectiles against the forts and ramparts of the city, the enemy began, on the night of 6 January, to fire volleys of shells against the defenceless quarters of Paris inhabited by women, children and non-combatants, and has continued this practice.
>
> On 7 January, the Germans likewise unmasked batteries which spread death and destruction through the districts of Vauvres, Montrouge, Montparnasse, the Pantheon, Luxembourg, and Jardin des Plantes; the churches of St Sulpice, St Étienne-du-Mont, the Panthéon and the Sorbonne; the Polytechnic School; the hospitals of the Val-de-Grâce, filled with wounded soldiers; of the Pitie de la Charité, and Le Salpêtrière, filled with sick of all ages, were shattered with shot and shell, in violation of the Geneva Convention. The line from the Point du Jour at Auteuil to the Jardin des Plantes presents a series of most harrowing devastations.
>
> Shops blown up, the houses in many of the upper storeys pierced by the passage of shells; the transport of the wounded to the ambulances; the sight of the mutilated dead; the hurried passage of terror-stricken families presented a series of heartrending pictures of the cruelties and iniquities of war overwhelming the old, the sick, and the feeble, tender women and children. Mothers have been killed with their children in their arms; fathers on their doorsteps; children at play or asleep in the dormitories of boarding schools, the sick and the wounded in the refuges.
>
> No wonder, then, that the spirit of exasperation against their merciless enemies has rapidly ripened into an intensity of hatred which the influence of many years alone will modify. The leaders of the German nation in their hour of triumph have neglected nothing to ensure the prospect of a war of extermination, into which the struggle has degenerated.[14]

An estimated 60,000 shells were fired into Paris at a rate of 300 to 400 per day. The deaths caused by the bombardment are a subject of speculation. Some sources (such as the one above) suggest that 400 deaths were caused by the initial bombardment. Others believe that it was far fewer. Whatever the number, in the hard, cruel world of military logistics, it was a very expensive operation with scant return. It was remarkable how many of the un-aimed shells fell onto open ground, killed no one and caused only nominal damage. Nevertheless, the earlier concerns of Crown Prince Frederick about civilian deaths were fully justified because women and children fell victim to German high explosives. On 11 January, a funeral was held for six small children all killed by the same shell. The anger of Parisians turned to hate and Tommy Bowles wrote: 'It might perhaps have been expected that the God-fearing and laws-of-war-respecting Prussians would have followed the ordinary usage in such cases and given notice before bombarding a city full of defenceless people.'

There is a 'sameness' in the reports by witnesses to the early shelling. It is an amalgam of shock, outrage and despair. For example, Goncourt wrote:

> The shells have begun falling in the rue Boileau ... Tomorrow no doubt, they will be falling here; and even if they do not kill me, they will destroy everything I still love in life ... On every doorstep, women and children stand half frightened, half inquisitive.[15]

The German guns were operating at a range of 7,500 yards, a distance without precedent. From this range the strike was bound to be entirely random although hits on the Salpêtrière Hospital and the Odéon Theatre, which was being used as a hospital, gave rise to a suggestion that the Germans were targeting medical facilities. This was fallacious. German shells also struck the Church of St-Sulpice and the domes of the Panthéon and the Invalides. The shelling was entirely random and so was the killing. Nevertheless, the injection of fear into the population drove perhaps 20,000 people to vacate their homes on the left bank. They became refugees in their home city. Having left their arrondissement, their food provision faltered and could cease until they had re-established themselves elsewhere. Their care, albeit cursory, added to the burden of Trochu and his GND.

The Germans were damned for bombarding Paris but what were their other options, starvation having been rejected? Felix Whitehurst commented:

> Like a door, a city must be *ouvert ou fermèe*. If it is an open city, the law of nations says you must not fire on it, only summon it, and then take it by an attack. If it is a fortified city, behind forts, you may bombard it when and how you can.[16]

Any infantry assault on the Paris defensive wall would be very costly and unlikely to succeed unless the wall had been breached. Taking Fort Issy as an example of defensive walls, it survived a lengthy bombardment and its construction was not dissimilar to those of the city. Unpalatable as it is, the Germans had two options only and they were starvation or bombardment. Despite this, the strong international criticism of the bombardment ran off Bismarck's back, like water off the duck of proverb. It is curious but the shelling provided a distraction from the unutterable tedium of the siege.

It became a spectator sport.

The American ambassador commented: 'The carelessness and nonchalance of the Parisians in all this business is wonderful . . . Ladies and gentlemen now make excursions to the Point de Jour to see the shells fall.'[17] Washburne's observations were reiterated by Labouchère, who cheerfully reported that he too had left his hotel, 'to see for myself what truth there was that we are being bombarded'.[18]

After the first shock had waned life went on much as usual. Doors were left unlocked so that passers-by could take refuge and buckets of water were kept at the ready. Most national treasures, normally resident in the Louvre, had been moved out of the war zone. The Venus de Milo had been encased in wood and secreted in a cellar.

From the Germans' perspective the bombardment was not having the anticipated effect. Roon had accepted Herr Krupp's offer to provide the giant siege guns exhibited at the Great Exposition of 1867, but inexplicably they were never delivered. Not that Moltke was short of weaponry; unfortunately, what he had was not doing the job. In order to achieve the range, additional charges were being used, and the effect was to cause excessive wear of the tubes. In extreme cases, the gun blew up to the detriment of its crew.[19] The German gunners were subject to counter-battery fire and 'several hundred' were killed. Ambassador Washburne, having been under fire for ten days, writing of the bombardment recorded: 'it had not so far had the effect of hastening a surrender. On the other hand, it apparently had made the people firmer and more determined.'[20] Shades of London and Hamburg seven decades later. At the end of the siege and when an appraisal of the shelling could be made, it was concluded that only 97 people were killed, 278 wounded and 1,400 buildings damaged or destroyed.[21]

Notes

1. Howard, p. 355.
2. Frederick III, War Diary, pp. 165, 169.
3. Balfour, M., *The Kaiser and his Times* (Boston, Houghton Mifflin, 1964), p. 70.
4. Bismarck, O.E. von, *Bismarck, die Gesammelten Werke*, 15 vols. (London, 1898), Vol. VI, No. 1933, p. 602.

5. Moltke to King Wilhelm I, 30 November 1870: *MMK*, p. 417.
6. Bronsart, p. 109.
7. Howard, p. 356.
8. Busch, W., *Das Deutsche Grosse Hauptquartier und die Bekämpfung von Paris im Feldzuge 1870–71* (Stuttgart, 1905), pp. 248, 251.
9. *MMK*, p. 265.
10. Ibid., p. 352.
11. Ibid.
12. Howard, p. 357.
13. Frederick III, War Diary, p. 247.
14. *Manchester Guardian*, 18 January 1871.
15. Goncourt, E. & J., de, Journal, 1851–95.
16. Whitehurst, F.M., *The Siege of Paris*, 2 Vols. (London, Tinsley Bros, 1875).
17. Horne, p. 215: It was the first gateway to Paris located on the right bank, downstream of the Seine.
18. Ibid.
19. *GGS*, II, p. 369.
20. Horne, p. 217.
21. Sheppard, N., *Enfermé Dans Paris: Journal Du Siège Du 2 Septembre 1870 Au 28 Janvier 1871* (Dijon, Darantière, 1877).

Chapter Sixteen

January: Chanzy, Faidherbe, Bourbaki and Armistice

Although Paris was standing up well to the shelling, its population, especially the poor, was exhibiting all the signs of deprivation; this was not causing death by starvation but exacerbating a miscellany of other ills. The bitter cold and lack of fuel were additional, life-limiting factors. The population could do nothing about the food, shelling or the unremitting cold; 'it was sinking into a drab grumbling apathy.'[1] An analysis of deaths in Paris shows the accelerating losses due to 'respiratory ailments' during the siege.

Cause	1st week (19–26 Sept)	10th week	18th week (14–21 Jan)
Smallpox	158	386	380
Typhoid	45	103	375
Respiratory Ailments	123	170	1,084
Total all causes (incl. above)	1,266	1,927	4,444[2]

These figures include a disproportionate number of infants who were deprived of milk, a balanced diet and warmth. Deprivation also swept away the old, ailing and those unable to buy the food they needed. That said, Professor Nathan Shepherd, who conducted a study into mortality during the siege, could only identify six people who expired 'apparently from want of food'. He did conclude that 4,800 deaths were 'hastened by want of food or bad food'.[3] Moltke was aware of the domestic circumstances in Paris and wrote:

> Since the return of Monsieur Thiers from his diplomatic tour, it was certain that no mediatory interposition [intervention?] by any foreign power could be expected. The distress of the capital had become more and more severe. Scarcity and high prices had long borne heavily on its population; provisions were exhausted, and even the stores of the garrison had been seriously encroached on. Fuel was lacking in the lasting cold, and petroleum was an inefficient substitute for gas.[4]

On 9 January, General August von Werder's XIV Corps encountered General Charles-Denis Bourbaki's Army of the East at Villersexel on the Ognon River

Battle of Villersexel, 9 January 1871. (*Alphonse de Neuville, 1835–1885*)

and, in the opening moves, the Germans had the advantage, but the French held on in the village and a counter-attack proved to be successful. The fighting was intense and continued all day and into the night. Although French losses exceeded those of its adversary it was Werder who withdrew 14 miles (23km). This was an expensive but rare French victory. German losses were 438 killed or wounded and 140 captured. The French had 654 dead and wounded and 700 captured.[5] Bourbaki's aim now was to relieve the siege of Belfort. In the bigger picture, the victory at Villersexel was offset by the surrender of Péronne the next day.

Moltke responded to the resolution of Gambetta's forces by forming a new army, the Army of the South. It was to be commanded by General Edwin von Manteuffel, currently commanding 1st Army, who had been thwarted by Faidherbe. Manteuffel's aim was to obstruct Bourbaki and maintain the investment of Belfort. First he had to assemble his army, composed of XIV, VII and II Corps, and in the rugged country of the Vosges Mountains, in extreme conditions, this was a test of generalship.

Werder, having withdrawn, now positioned his corps along the east bank of the frozen Lisaine River and by so doing closed the roads that gave vehicular access to Belfort. This defensive position was about 13 miles long (20km) and well served by recently laid telegraph wires that provided Werder with communication along the length of his front. Numerically the two sides were mismatched; his corps of 45,000 men was half the size of the Army of the East. Werder was apprehensive and considered abandoning Belfort. However, despite the odds, he decided to stay put. Soon after, Moltke sent his orders to hold his position.[6]

In Paris, it was difficult, for many, to understand why, with 400,000 men under arms, Trochu and his acolytes were doing nothing positive to confront the enemy. There were the usual calls for a *sortie torrentielle* but where was it to be launched, who was to lead it, and what was to be the aim? Moltke, although he was not a witness, wrote:

> there was a large class of people in Paris who were, but little affected by the general distress. Numbers of civilians had been armed for the defence of their country and were fed and well paid by the authorities, without having too much to do in return. They were joined by all the dubious social elements, which found their reckoning in the disorganized situation ... Already some popular gatherings had been dispersed only by force of arms, and even a part of the National Guard was not free from mutinous tendencies. The revolutionary clubs, too, supported by the press, clamoured for further enterprises, even a sortie *en masse* of all the inhabitants of Paris. Thus, the feeble Government, dependent as it was on popular favour alone, was under pressure from the impossible demands of an ignorant mob on the one hand, and, on the other, the inexorable force of actual facts.[7]

That is an accurate summation. The pressure on Trochu to mount another sortie was intense. He was also hoist with his unwise declaration of 6 January that 'the Governor of Paris will not capitulate'. The 'Reds', as vociferous as ever, called for the replacement of the Government by what they termed a 'commune'. Gambetta sent a report that exaggerated the success of Bourbaki and foresaw his cutting of German supply lines, at some unspecified time in the future. This misleadingly optimistic report influenced what was to follow.

General Antoine Chanzy had commanded XVI Corps in the Army of the Loire in its victory at Coulmiers, where he had demonstrated tactical skill and personal courage. He was appointed to command 2nd Army of the Loire and in early January 1871 he was one of Gambetta's last hopes. Moltke saw Chanzy as a serious threat to his lines of communication and ordered his 2nd Army to move west between Vendome and Chartres to confront him.

Chanzy withdrew to Le Mans. En route, thousands of his soldiers deserted, and those who did not made their tortured way over difficult terrain without paved roads. 'The country it had to traverse was close and hilly, the fields small, the hedges high and impenetrable, the lanes twisting and sunk between high banks.'[8]

Major General Antoine Chanzy (1823–83).

There had been a brief thaw and tracks turned to quagmires as Chanzy's exhausted, unfed, and ill-equipped army centred itself on Le Mans and dug in. Chanzy planned to fight a defensive battle and to retain control over the town. Le Mans was strategically important as it was a railway junction and controlled the lines west to Nantes and Brest. These railway lines offered a line for withdrawal if required. However, Chanzy was not defensively minded, and he submitted plans to Bourbaki for new concentric attacks on Paris. Both Gambetta and de Freycinet urged restraint until the two new corps, being raised at Cherbourg and Vierzon, could join him.

The confrontation between Chanzy's Army of the Loire and the German 2nd Army, composed of four corps, XIII, X, II, and IX, took place on 11–12 January, by which time it was snowing again. The French had started with a numerical superiority, having 100,000 men and opposed by only 73,000. However, as on so many previous occasions, it was not about numbers, it was resolve, commitment, training, junior leadership and logistic strength that counted most. The agile, well-rehearsed German Army outflanked the French and carried the day. The arithmetic tells the story. The Germans had 3,650 casualties, of whom about a quarter were killed. The French losses were huge: 6,200 killed and wounded, 18,000 captured, but, critically, 20,000 deserted.[9] The loss of seventeen guns is insignificant against that backcloth. This defeat ended French resistance in the west as Chanzy retreated to Alençon, 107 miles (172km) west of Paris. The 2nd Army of Prince Charles was in no condition to pursue the Army of the Loire and stopped to lick its wounds.

It was on 15 January that the Government first made mention of 'surrender'. However, fear of civil revolt was the single factor that shaped government action – or inaction. The clubs demanded a *sortie torrentielle* on the basis that there were masses of 'soldiers' available to take the fight to the enemy, but they had no other ambition except fight – not the basis for any military action. In an effort to quell dissent and disorder Trochu agreed a plan, created by General Schmitz, to break out in the west towards Buzenval. There was the unstated aim of perhaps linking up with General Antoine Chanzy and his 2nd Army of the Loire. However, Chanzy, defeated at Le Mans, had moved to Alençon, not in retreat, 'but to be in a position to advance again on Paris'. It was only in compliance with Gambetta's instructions that, on 13 January, he altered the direction of his march to fall back on Laval, a town about 57 miles (92km) south and west of Alençon.[10]

Chanzy was sick and exhausted and his 2nd Army of the Loire, really now no more than a mutinous mob, was in disarray. Chanzy was not well placed but he was not beaten, and he started to plan his next move. Gambetta visited and he harangued Chanzy's officers to greater efforts, but with no discernible effect, and Chanzy would play no further part in the war.

Mesmerising speaker though Gambetta was, his rhetoric no longer had the ability to inspire and motivate. He left for Lille and delivered another speech, but Dr Armand Testelin, the Defence Commissioner for the four most northerly departments, made quite clear his view when he told Gambetta that 'the mass of the nation is going to hold the Republic and yourself responsible for our material disasters and will prostrate itself at the feet of the first-comer who will give peace'.[11]

On 17 January, the conference on the Black Sea and the extant treaty arrangements from the Crimean War opened in London. Articles XI–XIII of the 1856 Peace of Paris restricted Russian access to the Turkish Straits and forced a demilitarisation of the Black Sea. The Tsar, Alexander II, although defeated in the Crimean War, was loath to accept the reality that defeat engenders penalties. For fifteen years he had sought to find an excuse or an opportunity to renege on his treaty commitment. Alexander decided to turn the Franco-Prussian War to his advantage and in October 1870, his Foreign Minister, Alexander Gorchakov, announced that Russia would no longer comply with the treaty conditions. The French, represented by Favre, had no national government, its capital was under siege and the Black Sea was the very least of its problems. Favre was in no position to take a strong line with Russia. Britain, the other signatory to the Treaty of Paris, could either go to war with Russia over the issue or find a compromise.[12] It most emphatically did not want a war with Russia and accordingly acceded to Russian pressure in the Treaty of London in March 1871.

Many French hopes now centred on Major General Charles-Denis Bour-baki and his Army of the East, which was intent on lifting the siege of Belfort. Buoyed by his success at Villersexel on 9 January, he was brought back to earth, a week later, at Lisaine where, despite massive numerical advantage, he was repulsed in a three-day battle by General August von Werder and his XIV Corps. The French suffered 6,000 to 8,000 casualties, of whom at least

 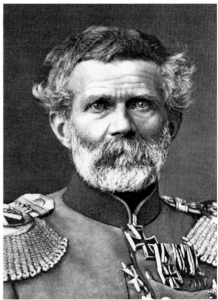

The two German generals who destroyed French military ambitions in the east and who accelerated the end of the war: General August von Werder (1808–87) and *Generalfeldmarschall* Edwin von Manteuffel (1809–85).

Major General Charles-Denis Bourbaki (1816–97).

1,500 were killed; the opposition recorded merely 1,646 killed and wounded. It was a stunning victory by von Werder and this reverse made the relief of Belfort impossible. On 14 January, General Edwin von Manteuffel, with his Army of the South, started to move into a position from which he could administer the *coup de grace*.

The German 'tactic of dispersing to move and concentrating to fight' presented the staff of the Army of the East with situations that were beyond them.[13] The flexible German Army was too much for Bourbaki and he was driven to retreat east, towards the border. On 14 January, Charles de Freycinet had told the commander of the Army of the North that he was to attempt to draw German troops to him from Paris and by so doing assist in the anticipated sortie to be made by the Army of Paris in a few days' time.

The day of 19 January marked two significant events. The first was that bread rationing was introduced in Paris, a significant indicator of the rapidly fading well-being of the city. It was also the day that the Army of Paris was to break out in the west of the city, and its first objective was to be Buzenval (shown on the map as Bouzenval). Trochu and his associates had included all the mayors of arrondissements in the decision-making although there was little expectation of the sortie being successful. 'Trochu's staff regarded the operation as a necessary bloodletting to cure the fever of the clubs.'[14] The probability is that members of the Government in Paris thought that another heavy defeat would prepare the population for the predictable surrender.

> The government had 400,000 National Guard; it had trained them and armed them insufficiently to be of any military value, but just enough to constitute the most revolutionary threat the nineteenth century had yet seen.[15]

The plan was for the Army of Paris to advance, at 0600 hrs, under the guns of Mont-Valérien across the Gennevilliers peninsula in three columns: Vinoy on the left, against Montretout, de Bellemare towards Buzenval and Ducrot on the right towards Malmaison. That all seems to be straightforward, but with its extraordinary capacity for calamity and fiasco the Army excelled itself. The start was delayed because Ducrot failed to meet the timetable. He was late, having had to lead his men 8 miles (13km) across country he must have known well, but over which he clearly had not carried out a recent reconnaissance.

The attacks eventually went in without Ducrot and initially there were some minor successes. Vinoy's Zouaves acquitted themselves well and took Montretout. They then pressed on to St-Cloud. Similar success was enjoyed by de Bellemare but, without Ducrot's support on the right, he was obliged to halt.

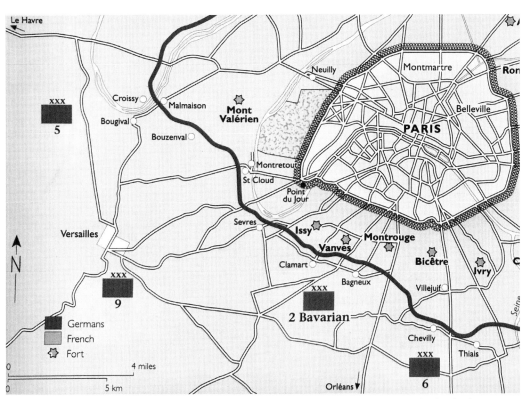

The Battle of Buzenval – the ground over which the Army of Paris made the final sortie and which heralded the end of the war. (*Badsey*)

The Germans were sufficiently concerned that in Versailles, as a precaution, they were packing wagons and preparing to leave. King Wilhelm made his way to the aqueduct at Marly, where he and his court watched the battle unfold – not without anxiety. The *Gardes Nationale* was performing well and rather better than expected despite the heavy going, although the recent thaw had turned the ground into a morass and made swift movement impossible.

By early afternoon the Germans' artillery, with well-coordinated fire, halted the French columns in their tracks, and they lost the initiative they had enjoyed up to this point. Ducrot made an appearance and, as was his wont, mounted on his white charger paraded ahead of his troops. He was, as ever, extraordinarily lucky and was untouched by shot or shell. The display was all very well, but it did nothing to benefit the French cause. An incident, noted by several, was recorded:

> The most painful scene during the battle was the sight of a French soldier felled by French bullets. He was a private in the 119th battalion and refused to advance. His commander remonstrated ... the private shot him. General de Bellemare who was near ordered that the soldier be killed at once. A file was drawn up and fired upon him; he fell and was supposed to be dead. Some *brancardiers* [stretcher-bearers] passing by,

thinking he had been wounded in the battle, placed him on a stretcher. It was then discovered that he was still alive. A soldier went up to finish him off, but his gun misfired. He was handed another and blew out the wretched man's brains.[16]

The attack had lost all momentum and it was stalled along its front. Trochu, demonstrating his ample courage, rode to Montretout to inject some backbone in the faltering national guardsmen. He was very exposed and set a fine example, but no one responded to his encouragement. The lack of training, esprit and commitment among *GN* and *Mobiles* became painfully evident as they refused further action; Ducrot characteristically went to one battalion to encourage them, shouting, '*En avant!*' The soldiers responded with a cry of '*Vive la République*', but no one stirred. The battlefield was static and bitterly cold. As night fell, French wounded lay unattended, men went hungry. The aggressive spirit of the *GN* had completely evaporated in the face of the professional soldiers who opposed them. Trochu, watching, realised that, much as he had anticipated, the Battle of Buzenval had gone against him and he ordered a general withdrawal.

The withdrawal was not well ordered, and the infantry had to struggle to get through the jam of supply wagons, gun limbers and ambulances. All roads were choked. Unit cohesion disappeared and the Army of Paris degenerated into a heaving, aimless mob. Ducrot conceded that that mob had inflicted just 700 casualties on the Germans. French losses were 4,000 killed and wounded. Considering the size of the French force its losses were modest – perhaps an indicator of the deficient martial prowess and enthusiasm of the *GN*.[17] Moltke commented on the abortive sortie, writing:

> The French attack of 19 January was wrecked even before it had reached the main position of the defenders. The reserves in readiness on the German side had not needed to be brought into action. The V Corps alone had driven back an enemy of four times its own strength. It lost 40 officers and 570 men; the loss of the French in killed and wounded was 145 officers and 3,423 men, besides 44 officers and 458 men taken prisoners.[18]
>
> When the fog lifted at about eleven o'clock on the morning of the 20th, their long columns were seen retreating on Paris across the peninsula of Gennevilliers.

The ignominious retreat behind the city walls had a severe and deleterious effect. Ducrot, who bore some responsibility for the failure, recorded:

> Hardly was the word retreat pronounced than in the rear areas on the left the debacle began … Everything broke up, everything went … On

the roads the muddle was terrifying … Across the open country the *Garde Nationale* were taking to their heels in every direction … Soldiers wandering, lost, searched for their company, their officers.[19]

Concurrently with the Parisian sortie, Faidherbe's Army of the North had been operating in the area west of Saint-Quentin. Its aim, as directed by de Freycinet on 14 January, was to make a major diversion. However, the conditions were dreadful, the ground was covered in mud and slush, and the available roads were very narrow and inhibited swift movement. The morale in Army of the North was fragile at best and worsening hourly as the supply system broke down. Cold, wet and hungry, this was an army ill-prepared for confrontation with an agile, experienced and well-led adversary.

General August von Goeben (1816–80).

Faidherbe was at a disadvantage when, on 19 January, General August von Goeben and his 1st Army attacked. The sides were numerically dissimilar, von Goeben being outnumbered by 40,000 to 33,000. However, as had been the case so many times before, superior training, better junior leadership and tenacity all combined to provide a crushing German victory. German casualties were 2,400 and the French 3,384 with a further 12,000 captured.[20] The Army of the North withdrew towards Le Cateau and Cambrai. Faidherbe realised that his army was no longer viable, and he deployed his survivors among the forts north of Paris. They played no further part in the war.

In Paris, Trochu was considering the option. The first was to request a two-day armistice in order to clear the battlefield; the second was to hasten a permanent armistice. Jules Favre was incensed by Trochu's acceptance of defeat and called for his dismissal and a renewal of offensive operations. It was in this emotional, fevered and divisive atmosphere that a despatch was received from Count Jean-Baptiste Chaudordy, the *chargé d'affaires* in Bordeaux. He advised that 'a crushing defeat had been inflicted at Le Mans, 10,000 men were lost as prisoners and there was now no force capable of marching to the relief of Paris'.[21] The news was several days old but even Favre accepted the inevitable and a surrender was openly discussed in the streets. The writing was now firmly on the wall and, looking a little ahead, King Wilhelm ruled, on 20 January, that Bismarck would lead any German delegation in armistice negotiations.

Not all the members of GND were as pragmatic as Favre and there was a lobby for *others* to continue fighting. These GND members enjoyed the support of all the mayors. It made no military sense at all but, nevertheless, this non-combatant group insisted that the *GN* be given another opportunity to fight. Based on nothing except emotion, they were confident that victory was at hand.[22] The arrogant self-belief of these people flew in the face of reason. Trochu declined to resign as he had previously said that 'the Governor of Paris would never surrender' and he could not break his word. The solution to that issue was for him to vacate the appointment of Governor of Paris and remain as President of the Council. Washburne wrote: 'Trochu is dethroned, having remained long enough to injure the cause.' He added that he had 'proved himself the weakest and most incompetent man ever entrusted with such great affairs'. The consensus was not in Trochu's favour and his loss of office was generally approved. There was a view that if Vinoy or Ducrot had had Trochu's role, public affairs would have been better managed. Conversely, it is argued that neither of these senior officers had the imagination, capability or political savvy to do the job.

The leadership of all French armies was offered to Ducrot – who, to date, had lost every engagement in which he had participated. He declined. Vinoy, the former imperial senator and anti-republican, was the only other viable candidate and when he was offered the job, much to general surprise, he accepted it. His role was to contain the anticipated explosion of public anger and probable rioting that would follow the announcement of the surrender. Vinoy's assumption of command, even before any announcement, coincided with towering rage in Belleville at the pointless sacrifice of its *GN*. Goncourt observed shrewdly that Vinoy's appointment was a case of 'changing of doctors when the invalid was on the point of death'.[23]

On 22 January, an armed group of men presented itself at the Mazas Prison and demanded that the governor release Flourens and several others who had been imprisoned after the events of 31 October. The governor, ill-advisedly and with extraordinary lack of backbone, allowed a small deputation to enter the prison to discuss the matter. Once inside, the deputation seized control of the gates and allowed the rest of the armed party access. Soon thereafter, they left in triumph with their revolutionary comrades. Flourens prudently made himself scarce and made only a brief appearance at the party held in the *Mairie* of the 20th arrondissement.

The following day was of very great significance. It was the first time, during this war, that Frenchmen shot and killed other Frenchmen for political motives. It was to be the catalyst for much more bloodletting in the near future. On 23 January, the 'Red' leadership marched to the Hôtel de Ville leading a group of vociferous protesters. The demonstration started peacefully enough and, in an attempt to quell disorder before it started, Gustave Chaudey, a minor official, came out of the building to advise the crowd that there were no members of the GND present. He added that the building was defended by well-armed *Mobiles*. Chaudey's advice was ignored and several hours later, at about 1500 hrs, a large contingent of *GN* arrived. Unfortunately, they were headed by deeply committed 'Reds' such as Eugène Razoua, Benôit Malon, Louise Michel dressed as a man, the deranged Theophile Sapia and the eccentric Jules Allix. The crowd was noisy, broadly hostile, but not violent.

Then someone fired a single shot. Who fired the shot was never established but the crowd panicked and a group of *GN*, encouraged by Sapia, fired on the Hôtel de Ville. From this point it was downhill all the way. Fire was returned by the *Mobiles* defending the Hôtel de Ville, and the shooting went on for about thirty minutes. Vinoy sent armed reinforcements and when calm was restored, the *GN* had left the scene. Five people were dead and eighteen wounded. Among the dead was Theophile Sapia.

Gustave Chaudey (1817–71).

Gustave Chaudey was later accused of ordering the *Mobiles* to open fire although no evidence was ever produced to substantiate the accusation. Nevertheless, he was executed on 23 May 1871 in an extra-judicial killing.

This incident was not as politically dangerous as had been the uprising on 31 October and the most eminent 'Red' leadership was not present. Delescluze, Blanqui, Pyat and Flourens were all elsewhere, perhaps for the better. Vinoy took the strong action that his predecessor should have taken months before. First, he ordered the closure of *Le Combat* and *Le Réveil*, then he closed the clubs that were hotbeds of revolution, and finally he indicted Delescluze and

Pyat to answer to a military tribunal, although Pyat, as was his practice, had disappeared.

It was evident to Vinoy and the GND that no time should be lost in establishing an armistice and, on 23 January, a ceasefire having been arranged, Jules Favre, accompanied by Captain Hérrisson, left Paris carrying a note for Bismarck. They were not received warmly and when Favre mentioned his pride in the French resistance during the siege, Bismarck grunted, 'Ah! you are proud of your resistance? Well, sir let me tell you that if M. Trochu were a German general I would have him shot tonight ...'[24]

That night the two Frenchmen dined with Bismarck and he commented on their appetites. The negotiations were one-sided, and a sticking point was whether or not the *GN* could hang on to its arms. Favre met Bismarck on three successive days, 25–27 January, and in the discussions Favre maintained that France would need three regular divisions to keep order. Moltke, in response, said he could have only two and that the *GN* would have to be disarmed. Favre became agitated and protested that to disarm the *Garde Nationale* 'would lead to civil war'. Bismarck was unmoved and replied, 'You are being foolish. Sooner or later, you will have to bring reason to the National Guard, and you gain nothing by waiting.' Then he added, 'Provoke an uprising while you still have an Army to suppress it.'[25]

Despite his apparently brutal opinions Bismarck was, in fact, remarkably flexible. He agreed that the Parisian garrison should not be sent as prisoners to Germany. Clearly and reasonably, he did not want to import hundreds of thousands of probably hostile, hungry young men into his country where their management would be a major economic and logistical burden. He did, however, insist on the future staging of a token German parade in the city. He agreed to the most politically stable battalions of the *GN* retaining their arms. Quite how this was to be accomplished was left undecided. Bismarck had been also negotiating with the Empress – she was a useful second string to his political bow. However, he agreed to abandon his dealing with her if he could come to terms with the GND, as represented by Jules Favre.

The terms on offer were that Alsace and a large portion of Lorraine were to be ceded to Germany, reparations of 200 million francs were to be paid, and the perimeter forts were all to be surrendered and their guns thrown over the ramparts. No German troops would enter Paris during the period of the armistice, which would last until 19 February. By then the French were expected to have held an election and formed an assembly to meet in Bordeaux that represented the whole of France and was a body with whom the Germans could cooperate. Bismarck finally played something of an ace when he agreed to revictual the city, and he even agreed to permit Paris to fire the final shot of the siege – symbolic, pointless, but something important to

Favre. Favre signed the armistice agreement with a heavy heart and forebodings of what might follow.

Whilst Jules Favre toiled in his dealings with Bismarck, at the same time in the east, Bourbaki and his Army of the East were facing a bleak future. Manteuffel had closed in and had reached Dôle, on the Doubs River, about 30 miles (48km) from the Swiss border. It was Manteuffel's plan to pin his enemy against that border and he acted successfully with Werder to cut the communications of the Army of the East with the rest of France. At Dôle, the German force had cut most road and rail links, leaving only the road and rail to Lons-le-Saunier and Lyons. Once they too were cut, Bourbaki would have to take to the hills in the midst of a very bitter winter.[26]

The capture of Dôle had thwarted an ambitious plan created by de Freycinet that had called for Bourbaki to circumnavigate Besançon, there to collect supplies and move on towards Auxerre and Troyes to join forces with Faidherbe. When Bourbaki arrived at Besançon the *Intendent* (quartermaster) of the Army said he had no instruction to stock up there. This was an excellent example of de Freycinet's ignorance of military logistics and their absolute criticality.

Bourbaki had not only to contend with the brilliance of Werder but also the malevolent de Freycinet, who had concluded some weeks before that 'Bourbaki is not the man the situation requires'.[27] He was probably right. Bourbaki was no strategist and he never came to terms with his ineffective staff. He displayed 'a listless almost masochistic fatalism, reminiscent of Bazaine's attitude at Metz'.[28] He was also a pragmatist and made it clear that he favoured an armistice – and the sooner the better.

Freycinet wanted to replace Bourbaki with a recently promoted Major General Jean-Baptiste Billot, who was commanding XVIII Corps. Gambetta did not agree and so de Freycinet had inserted, into Bourbaki's headquarters, a representative in the form of August de Serres. He was a young man of some thirty summers, had no military background but was equipped with a surfeit of self-confidence. Like his master de Freycinet, Serres saw military strategy as a simple matter of drawing large arrows on maps. He was logistically illiterate and the cuckoo in Bourbaki's nest.

The unavailability of supplies at Besançon sealed the fate of the Army of the East. de Freycinet bombarded Bourbaki with instructions and advice with no conception of the situation on the ground, nor feeling for the men. Bourbaki knew that his soldiers had reached the end of their corporate tether. They were not going to stand and fight and were quite incapable of meeting de Freycinet's demands. For the men of the French Army, personal survival was now the aim. Convoys and trains were pillaged by starving men. All villages and hamlets were ransacked for food. The soldiers' boots had long since disintegrated and their feet were bound in ice-caked rags. Bourbaki decided to move towards Pontarlier and when he told de Freycinet, the civilian was dumbfounded. He signalled, saying:

> haven't you made a mistake about the name? Do you really mean Pontarlier, near Switzerland? If that is really your objective have you envisaged the consequences? What will you live on? You will certainly die of hunger. You will be forced to capitulate or cross into Switzerland … at all costs you must break out.[29]

Freycinet was correct but he was far distanced from reality when asking 'What will you live on?' He may have assumed the responsibility for grand strategy but clearly did not understand the less attractive elements of commanding an army and especially the tedious but vital business of supply, in modern terms 'logistics'. Seventy years later, a highly capable German general commented: 'An adequate supply system … the essential conditions for any army to be able to stand successfully the strains of battle. Before the fighting proper, the battle is fought and decided by the Quartermasters.'[30]

On 26 January, Bourbaki offered command of the Army to General Billot, who declined, just as he had done several days earlier when Bourbaki had discussed with his generals a move to Pontarlier. As the Army of the East marched south towards the small town, Bourbaki returned to Besançon to write his orders. That done, he went to his bedroom and shot himself in the head, unable to face the abject humiliation that he faced.[31] His suicide attempt was unsuccessful. There cannot be many would-be suicides who fail in this way. The humiliation was complete. He survived and lived for a further twenty-six years. The remnants of the Army of the East – about 85,000 men – sought refuge in Switzerland, where they were interned – and fed.

Immediately after the battle on the Lisaine, fought on 15–17 January, Manteuffel had been able to supplement the forces investing Belfort to twenty-seven battalions, six squadrons, six field batteries, twenty-four companies of fortress artillery, and six companies of fortress pioneers – 17,602 infantry, 4,699 artillerymen, and 1,166 pioneers, in all 23,467 men, with 707 horses and 34 field guns. The place was invested on the north and west by only a few battalions, and the main force was assembled to the south and east.

At a distance of 150 years one might wonder why the Germans put such value on Belfort with the war about to reach its finale. The town's only significance was that it was French, a fortress, and located on the border. It had played no part in the war in the east other than to tie up the force besieging it. It may well be that Bismarck had Belfort in his sights as part of the reparation package.

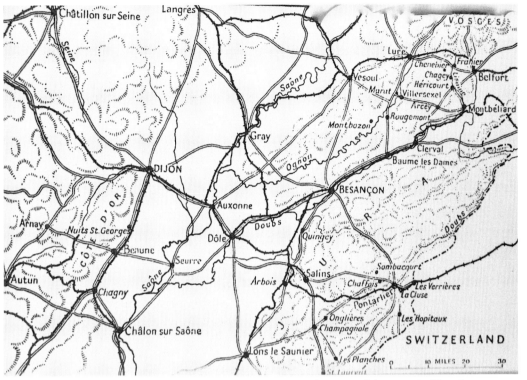

This map shows the site of the demise of the French Army of the East. Belfort, its original objective, is at top right. Freycinet's alarm at the Army's withdrawal to Pontarlier (bottom right) can be readily understood when the proximity of the Swiss border is seen to be so close.

The armistice and its terms were greeted in Paris with anger and disbelief, this despite the Government's attempts to dress the news in a halo of undeserved corporate heroism. It alleged that 'the enemy is the first to render homage to the moral energy and to the courage of which the entire Parisian population has just given an example'.[32] The press was not convinced and *Le Soir*'s headlines read, 'France is dead; Vive la France'. *Rappel* said ominously and accurately that 'it is not an armistice, it is capitulation'.

At Fort Issy the garrison that had endured the full weight of German artillery paraded in front of their colonel. He told his officers to retain their arms but instructed his men to lay theirs down. Then he led the parade from the fort, watched by the curious Germans who were to take possession. This scene was replayed around the city perimeter. This was the most compelling and, for some, upsetting manifestation that the siege – 130 days long – was over. The armistice was to last only until 19 February, by which time France would have a new government.

In the German camp, Bismarck, the Wilhelm-appointed negotiator, scored points over his military by making it clear that the final agreement with the French would be a 'convention' and not a 'capitulation'. This is mere semantics, but it was designed to irritate Moltke, who insisted on 'surrender'. As far as Bismarck was concerned this military rose would smell as sweet by any other name. The unvarnished fact of life was that the French had been utterly defeated, and they knew it.

One of the terms of the armistice was that both sides should withdraw 6 miles (10km) from a military demarcation line. However, only the Germans knew where the front line was positioned. Moltke was not a man to make concessions and, in some cases, French troops 'had to withdraw from positions securely held'.[33] The ceasefire arrangements around Paris did not apply in the provinces and Favre was ill-supplied with information. He knew that Belfort still held out and hoped Bourbaki and his Army of the North might yet deliver a victory. This might then enhance the French negotiating position but, in fact, the Army of the North was already beaten, starving and crossing into Switzerland.

Gambetta was in complete ignorance of Favre's negotiations and their outcome. When rumours reached Bordeaux the delegation there issued a reasonable and mild statement, saying, 'We cannot believe that negotiations of this kind could have been undertaken without the Delegation being previously notified.' Gambetta did not leave it there and he told Jules Favre that any negotiations settled by Paris with the Germans would not be binding in the provinces.[34] The message took until 2 February to reach Favre, by which time the deed was signed. Gambetta had no option but acquiesce to the Paris position and he put in place arrangements for elections on 8 February.

The war was concluded and there was time to count the cost. French losses were 138,871 killed and died of wounds, 143,000 were wounded, but the crippling figure, is the number of French prisoners taken. Moltke provided the statistics of prisoners:

	Officers	Soldiers
In Germany	11,860	371,981
In Paris	7,456	241,686
Disarmed in Switzerland	2,192	88,381
Total	21,508	702,048[35]

French military casualties, including *GN*, during the siege were 28,450, of whom less that 4,000 were killed. During the siege there were 6,251 deaths from all causes and only six of these were attributed by Professor Shephard to 'want of food'.[36]

German casualties were 44,700 killed, 89,732 wounded, 10,129 missing or captured. The great difference between French and German dead is the indicator of the vast mismatch between the two sides.

Notes

1. Police report, 5 January 1871, *DT* ,Vol. V, ii, p. 159.
2. Sheppard, N., *Enfermé Dans Paris* and quoted by Horne, p. 221.
3. Ibid.
4. *MMK*, p. 263.
5. *GGS*, Vol. IV, Appendix CXLI p. 182.
6. *GGS*, Vol. IV, Appendix CLI, p. 176.
7. *MMK*, p. 264.
8. Howard, p. 388.
9. Howard, p. 402, asserts that desertions amounted to 50,000. To this author that seems to be excessive.
10. Ibid., p. 408.
11. D.O., I, p. 505.
12. Fitzmaurice, E.P., *Life of Lord Granville* (London, 1905), Vol. II, p. 73.
13. Howard, p. 423.
14. Ibid., p. 364.
15. Horne, p. 229.
16. Labouchère, H., *Diary of the Besieged Resident in Paris*.
17. Ducrot, Vol. IV, p. 188.
18. *MMK*, p. 360.
19. Ducrot, A.A., *Défense de Paris*, Vol. IV, pp. 159–88.
20. *GGS*, Vol. IV, p. 296.
21. Howard, p. 368.
22. Favre, pp. 340–2.
23. Goncourt, Journal, 22 January 1871.
24. Horne, p. 239.
25. Favre, Vol II, pp. 382–6.
26. Wartensleben, H.L., von Graf, *Operations of the Southern Army in January and February 1871* (London, 1872), p. 41.
27. Freycinet to Gambetta, 24, December 1870. *Assemblée National Enquêt ...* Vol. II, *Expedition de l'Est*, p. 535, quoted by Fermer, p. 174.
28. Howard, p. 422.
29. D.T. III, pp. 355, 377, 433. Freycinet, C., *Guerre en Province* (Paris, 1871), pp. 263–6.
30. Rommel, FM E., quoted by Field Marshal Lord Wavell, *Soldiers and Soldiering* (London, Jonathan Cape, 1953).
31. Eichthal, L., *Le General Bourbaki* (Paris, 1885), pp. 336–54: Fermer, p. 186.
32. Horne, p. 242.
33. Freycinet, p. 320.
34. D.T., Vol. V, ii, p. 305.
35. *MMK*, p .409.
36. Horne, p. 244.

Chapter Seventeen

February: Election, Peace, Reparations – The Gathering Storm

The guns had fallen silent and, in Paris, the clarion calls for further military action by the vociferous Reds, from the safety of their clubs, died away. The Siege of Paris was at an end. Many histories of the period cease at this point. However, it is suggested that although the physical siege of Paris by the Germans was at an end, as a direct consequence, a siege of a different complexion would now be initiated by a proportion of the citizenry. On that basis, this story is unfinished.

The effects of the German siege were about to manifest themselves in an explosion of anger and extreme violence, brought about by a combination of vast political differences, inept communication, uncompromising postures, incompetent leadership and, *possibly*, a form of collective psychosis, although the weight of medical opinion is unconvinced in this case. It is, however, acknowledged that the mind is a complex and powerful thing that can be affected by outside forces – both real and imagined.

In Bordeaux and Versailles there were those opposed to the probable terms of the armistice, but they were not in a position to thwart its imposition. Moltke accepted that the 'convention' was political, but he also was not satisfied with the terms, believing them to be too moderate, a view widely held in Germany where extermination of the French state had been the desired aim.

Bismarck found himself as lord of all he surveyed. The war had lasted only a scant seven months and the nation that he and most other Europeans had always looked to as the fount of all things social, political, cultural, diplomatic and military lay in ruins at his feet. Bismarck could afford to be generous, even sympathetic, but in his dealings with Adolphe Thiers, he was brusque and uncompromising. He humiliated Thiers, a man he could have cultivated to their mutual advantage. There was a fear that France might initiate a war of revenge but, as the sole republic in Europe, without a functioning government, without allies and its army in shreds, it did not pose a realistic risk to anyone. In addition, France was too busy meeting the terms of the 'convention'.

The German armies were no longer confronted by armed Frenchmen but by a brutal winter, a strained logistic chain and, at home, a domestic population tired of making sacrifices to provide for the Army. Gambetta set about organising the election, but he fully intended to renew hostilities at the first opportunity thereafter, having taken no cognisance of the defeat and dispersal of his three armies. He had still to have news of the fate of his Army of the East. Gambetta was distraught when the fate of Bourbaki's army finally reached him. It was with great reluctance that he accepted the inevitable consequence.

Under the French electoral system, established by the Second Republic back in 1849, a candidate could stand for any number of seats. Under this unusual arrangement, when the results of the election were announced, Thiers was elected in twenty-six constituencies and Gambetta in ten. Jules Simon, General Adolphe Le Flô, Ernest Picard and Jules Favre – all of the now defunct Government of National Defence – offered themselves for election and, to the disgust of people like Jules Goncourt, were elected. The results demonstrated an overwhelming vote for 'Peace'. There were 768 seats; and those won by candidates with conservative, Catholic and monarchist leanings were in an overwhelming majority. Only 150 Republicans won a seat and they were divided between the 'moderates' like Jules Favre and the 'Reds' of the extreme left. Of the latter, only twenty won seats of the forty-three available in Parisian constituencies.

The voters of Paris were predominantly monarchist. However, not everyone who had a vote exercised it, and others were not enfranchised. The political scene was volatile. In the short time frame of five months, French

The defeated Army of the East, protected by a small rearguard, crossed into Switzerland on 1–3 February 1871. It was required to surrender its arms and was interned until mid-March.

(P. Neri (Foto) Édouard Castres (Panorama) – tableau du muse de Lucerne)

government had swung from the stable monarchy of 31 August 1870 to a broadly liberal Republic, and now, on 8 February, back to a right-wing, monarchist-favouring administration. Horne observed succinctly that 'the Empire was blamed for having started the war, the Republic for having prolonged and lost it'.[1]

Many Frenchmen subscribed to the view of the Revolutionary Danton, who famously alleged, '*Paris, c'est la France.*' However, and notwithstanding the emotion encapsulated in that statement, in 1871, 80 per cent of the population lived in rural communities and the 2 million Parisians were an insignificant minority in national terms.

The election result came as a shock to the Reds although some of the leading lights such as Louis Delescluze, Félix Pyat and Jean-Baptiste Millière had been elected. There were others with leftist Republican sympathies like Léon Gambetta, Henri Rochefort, Georges Clemenceau and Victor Hugo, but by any yardstick, democratic elections did not work for those determined 'to serve the masses' – whether they wanted it or not. *La Rappel* commented bleakly: 'It is no longer an army you are facing … It is no longer Germany … It is more. It is monarchy, it is despotism.'[2]

During February 1871, whilst national elections were putting France on the road to normality, a potentially dangerous alternative was being formed solely for the governance of Paris. Under the terms of the armistice, the *Garde Nationale* were not to be disarmed and it had an estimated strength of 260 battalions, each of about 1,500 men. This body was politically very alert and from 15 to 24 February, 500 representatives held a meeting and elected thirty-eight of its number to form the *Comité Central de la Garde Nationale*. (This is not to be confused with *Comité Central* of the twenty, extreme left, arrondissements that formed in September 1870.)

The first action taken by this Central Committee was to reject the authority of General d'Aurelle de Paladines, the commander of the *GN*, recently appointed by Adolphe Thiers. In addition, it refused to accept General Vinoy as Military Governor of Paris.[3] This was civil disobedience of the most extreme nature. Clearly, at sometime in the near future, there would be a confrontation over the issue of who governed France in general and Paris in particular.

On a brighter note, food was starting to flow into Paris from Great Britain and the USA. Accordingly, the stock of British people rose with the import of food. 'Many blessings are invoked on English people for their generous charity in this crisis of need,' and previous hostility was put aside.[4] Although, by the second week of February, when restaurants were in full swing, the provision of food to the poor and needy was inefficient.

Unfortunately, as the siege slipped into the background and life for Parisians returned close to normal, a widespread malady was diagnosed. It was 'obsidional fever', a mental condition allegedly brought about by a combination of anxiety, humiliation, boredom and deprivation. The vast mood swings generated by good news followed by very bad news added to the mix. The mental health of Parisians was exemplified by 'spy-mania, mistrust, and defiance of authority, hollow verbosity stemming from a need for self-assurance and fear created persecution that identified "enemies" such as Freemasons, Jews, and Jesuits'.[5] It was suggested that:

> from one day to the next these Parisians so gay, so carefree … have become Spartans, grave, sober, ready to look death in the face without constraint and without effort they have entered into the epic … Paris will not succumb; but in spite of her heroism is reduced to burying herself beneath her own ruins.[6]

This obsidional fever was not an illusion; but references to it are scant and only Horne among the leading historians of the war makes mention of it. Almost as an afterthought, in a summary of public health conditions, one academic commented:

> The poor sanitary conditions were favourable for the spread of epidemic disease that included smallpox and typhoid fever, besides hospital infections that caused increased mortality among operated patients, the newly born, and the injured. All factors together, plus the famine made the poor begin to die *en masse*. Consequently, military and civil were decimated by cold and hunger, and especially epidemics, including smallpox that struck all of France. Besides, it happened *the so-called 'obsidional fever' that was considered a collective psychosis striking a besieged population that had allegedly pushed the Communards to excesses in their behaviour.*[7] [Direct quote but author's emphasis.]

Life had changed and the frisson of living under siege had gone, to be replaced by what? Jules Goncourt observed that there was one aspect of siege life that almost made you love it. 'The continual flutter of a war that surrounds you, that almost touches you, of being brushed by death, of one's heart always beating a little fast; this has a certain sweetness.'[8] The atmosphere generated by siege conditions evaporated. Paris was now quiet, devoid of any form of excitement; it was dull and boring. The streets were filled with depressed, anxious, destitute people walking aimlessly, window shopping. There was a vacuum waiting to be filled. Two million people had spent four months preparing to kill Germans and almost 400,000 of these were fully armed and had relished the imminent prospect; now all that repressed violence had no outlet.

The newly elected 'Assembly' of France, at Bordeaux, had first to select its leader. On 17 February, it picked the best qualified in 73-year-old Louis Adolphe Thiers (known as Adolphe). He was a politician to his bootstraps, with five decades of experience in public affairs. He was described as being 'a small, white-haired, gnome-like figure with a bespectacled and owlish face of a sallow tint'.[9] He might not have been a prepossessing figure but he more than compensated by having a quick mind, enormous intellectual depth and the capacity to pursue political aims ruthlessly.

He was a distinguished historian and his magnificent work *Histoire de la Révolution Française*, first published in 1823

Louis Adolphe Thiers (1797–1877).

when he was only 26, made his name and his fortune. It was a massive academic achievement, running eventually to ten volumes. It was reprinted four times.

The first task facing Thiers, aided by Jules Favre, was to conclude the negotiations with Bismarck. They met Bismarck over a period of three days and suffered indignity at the hands of the German. Although Thiers was reduced to tears, he managed to lower the cash reparations from 6 billion francs to 5 billion. He also retained Belfort and Nancy as French possessions, but he lost Alsace and a large part of Lorraine. The cities of Metz and Strasbourg passed into German hands. The loss of Alsace and Lorraine was a very sharp stone in the French shoe for the next forty years as it involved the loss of 5,791 square miles (15,000km^2) of territory and 1.6 million inhabitants. The people, who were but pawns in this arrangement, were predictably outraged and 128,000 – about 8.5 per cent of the population – promptly 'emigrated' to France, followed over the years by many more.[10]

The atmosphere in Paris was a cause for concern. Goncourt recorded in his Journal that something, difficult to define, was abroad in the city. He wrote, 'something sombre and unquiet ... Upon the physiognomy of Paris ... Impossible to describe the ambient sadness which surrounds you; Paris is under the most terrible of apprehensions, apprehensions of the unknown.'[11] The malaise, whether it was obsidional fever or not, was fed by a mass march-past of the *GN*, on 26 February, which paraded with its bands and with its regimental colours draped in black. An estimated 300,000 people were on the streets and emotions ran high after hearing several provocative speeches that were fiercely republican in sentiment. The crowd was inflamed and suddenly a shout went up: 'A spy!' The unfortunate individual, so arbitrarily identified, was a man called Vincenzoni. He was alleged to be an undercover policeman, but that has never been confirmed.

Vincenzoni was hauled into view, beaten and kicked; then dragged to the banks of the Seine. There was a call for him to be drowned. Vincenzoni asked to be allowed to shoot himself but the crowd were in no mood for that and were intent on a more protracted, painful death. The victim was bound hand and foot and, 'like parcel', carried across the deck of several barges moored at Quai Henry IV. Here, ruthlessly, he was cast into the freezing waters of the Seine. The Seine would not accept poor Vincenzoni; he bobbed to the surface and was thrown up onto the shore. At this point, some merciless individuals started to stone the helpless man. This grotesque behaviour went on for 'not less than two hours, until the victim was finally drowned. This frightful murder was witnessed by several thousand, unprotesting, Parisian men and women.'[12] This was a despicable lynching and all of those present

The lynching of Vincenzoni, 26 February 1871.

were complicit in the murder. Four years later, just one of the perpetrators was tried and shot.

That same day, 26 February, a group of dissidents, by force, gained entry to the prison at Sainte-Pélagie Prison and demanded the release of Lieutenant Paul-Antoine Brunel. This young man of 30 had been jailed for his actions in ordering his men of 107th Battalion of the *GN* to take control of magazines and telegraph stations just before the armistice. Brunel was an active participant in the uprising of 31 October 1870 and a staunch opponent of the new Assembly. He would play a part in the events of the near future.

Following Brunel's release the *GN* became increasingly aggressive and proprietorial. It was on the basis that much of the artillery in the city had been bought with public subscriptions that the *GN* believed ownership of the cannons was theirs. Late on 26 February, and feeding off the raised emotions of the crowd, the *GN* determined to salvage the guns, allegedly to stop them falling into German hands. This was spurious because the Germans had shown not the least interest in seizing French guns – theirs were far superior. Nevertheless, the *GN* located 245 cannons from across the city's various gun parks. They concentrated this hardware at the base of the hill of Montmartre and then laboriously hauled 171 guns up the single, very steep, access road to Montmartre and placed the balance of seventy-four in Belleville. This was a huge physical effort, but it was not treasonous, nor even illegal. The men who grunted and sweated to move the guns sang the *Marseillaise* and, if asked, all would have claimed, vehemently, to be patriots. The rationale for the movement of the guns is obscure – however, if nothing else, it was an effective demonstration of the power of the *GN*.

Georges Clemenceau, a friend of several of the revolutionaries and the mayor of Montmartre, made every effort to find a solution and he suggested that ownership of the guns could be shared between what was still the community and the Assembly. This was an unacceptable compromise as far as Thiers was concerned. It was his intention to apply the authority of the elected Assembly over Paris as soon as was practical. The guns were less important than what they represented.[13]

In 1870, the Montmartre hill had not been developed and, equipped with the guns, it became a formidable redoubt. However, there was no question of anybody attacking Montmartre and so the installation of 171 artillery pieces was purposeless as a military exercise. From the top of the hill there were magnificent views of Hausman's Paris, the only possible target, which lay at its feet. Amongst the *GN* involved in the requisitioning of the guns, morale was high and there was an expectancy that further measures against the Assembly would soon follow.

The best 'recruiting sergeant' for the new *Comité Central de la Garde Nationale* was, without a doubt, Adolphe Thiers. The measures put in place by the Assembly, under his leadership, were the incentive for more members of the *GN* to gravitate to the *Comité Central*. When the siege was lifted, many of the more right-wing battalions had disbanded as their members were free to conduct their affairs outside of Paris. The armistice terms were put to the Assembly in Bordeaux on 28 February for ratification. It gave rise to anger, despair and any number of emotional speeches but, nevertheless, the Assembly voted, by 546 to 107 with 23 abstentions, to accept the terms. There were a number of resignations in protest. Léon Gambetta and all the deputies from Alsace and Lorraine walked out, accompanied by six Reds, including Henri Rochefort and Félix Pyat, and soon after by Victor Hugo. There was a social and cultural chasm dividing the Parisian and provincial deputies. Jules Grosjean spoke for the ceded provinces, saying:

> Handed over to foreign dominion in contempt of all justice and by an odious abuse of force, we … declare null and void a pact which disposes of us without our consent … Your brothers of Alsace and Lorraine separated at this moment from the common family, will conserve a filial affection for France … until the day when she returns to take her place.[14]

It is remarkable that Grosjean was so measured. His words were promulgated in 1970 by, presumably, a family member. Certainly, someone of the same name.

Thiers had not only to cope with the raw emotions generated by the peace settlement but, much closer to home, he had also to grasp the nettle of the *Garde Nationale*, which, correctly, he saw as a serious problem. He started to take measures to reduce its latent power. His appointment of General Louis d'Aurelle de Paladines to overall command of the *Garde Nationale* vice, General Jacques Clément-Thomas, had already misfired as he had picked the wrong man for a very sensitive appointment. This was, not least, for d'Aurelle's Bonapartist views and his inability to lift the Siege of Paris. Irrational perhaps – but emotion never rests on rational thought. However, leadership in any field is dependent entirely upon the good will and acquiescence of the led. General d'Aurelle had neither of these. He compounded the problem because he did not read the situation very well. His announcement that he 'had the intention to repress with energy all that could impair tranquillity' was seen as the threat it clearly was. He summoned all his battalion commanders to a meeting but, of the 260, only a derisory thirty turned up – a very clear indicator of the strength of the dissident faction of the *GN*. d'Aurelle was only notionally in command.

Unfortunately, when Adolphe Thiers and Jules Favre had been negotiating with Bismarck only a few weeks before, they had agreed that the French regular army would be reduced to one division – 12,000 men – but had managed to retain a fully armed *GN*. Accordingly, the *GN* was the most powerful force in France, but not under government control. The *Garde Nationale* saw itself as the guardian of republicanism, facing a government with strong Bonapartist affections. By early March, only about sixty of the 260 *GN* battalions could be counted on to defend 'order', as Thiers defined it.[15]

Notes

1. Horne, p. 255.
2. *La Rappel*, Paris, 8 February 1871.
3. Milza, p. 45.
4. Gibson, W., *Paris during the Commune* [1895] (Trieste Publishing, 2017), p. 104.
5. Horne, p. 251.
6. Jellinek, F., *The Paris Commune of 1871* [1930] (reprinted by Hesperides Press, 2013).
7. da Mota Gomes, M., France's *'année terrible'* of the Franco-Prussian War and Paris Commune, 150 years ago, and some remarkable neurologists at the time. Revista Brasileira de Neurologia, 2019.
8. Goncourt, Journal, February 1871.
9. Horne, p. 257.
10. Poidevin, R. & Bariéty, J., *Les relations Franco-Allemandes 1815–1975* (Paris, 1977), p. 103.
11. Merriman, J., *Massacre* [2014] (Yale University Press, 2016), p. 35.
12. Ibid. *See also* Horne, p. 267.
13. Milza, P., *L'année terrible: La Commune Mars–Juin 1871* (Paris, Perrin, 2009), pp. 8–9.
14. Grosjean, E., *Belfort: la sentinelle de la liberté 1870–1871* (Colmar, 1970), pp. 247–8.
15. Simon, J., *The Government of M. Thiers* (New York, 1879), p. 291.

Chapter Eighteen

March: Rise of the Commune

On 1 March, the German Army exercised its right to march through Paris, as per the armistice agreement. 'At 0800 hrs, a lieutenant and six troopers of the 14th Hussars rode up to the Étoile, jumped their horses over the chains and other obstructions that Parisians had placed around the Arc de Triomphe and continued insouciantly through the sacred edifice.'[1] Parisians were stunned and surprised; it heralded the start of 'The March'.

Only four years previously, 30,000 French troops had paraded in honour of King Wilhelm I and Tsar Alexander II. Now the victors of Wissembourg, Spicheren, Frœschwiller, Strasbourg, Metz, Sédan, and Orléans, led by King Wilhelm I, goose-stepped through the streets of Paris as conquerors. It was a most impressive parade – as it was intended to be. When the parade was dismissed, the German soldiers strolled through the city. Some were barracked but they were not attacked. A British correspondent observed, 'there was a gala look about the place which was revolting under the circumstances.'[2] For two days the German Army occupied Paris and the occupation heaped more humiliation on France and the French.

On 3 March, the Germans departed by the same route by which they had exercised their right. As soon as they had left, Parisians set about disinfecting the streets that had been trodden by German boots. Symbolic, perhaps, but the stain on national honour could not be erased. It would fester as generations of Frenchmen hungered for redress. After the Germans had left, French troops thronged Paris awaiting demobilisation: 'soldiers wandered about ... their uniforms sullied dishevelled, without weapons, some of them stopping passers-by, asking for money.'[3]

Adolphe Thiers, well-educated and balanced individual though he was, now associated himself with one legally and several politically doubtful decisions. Paris and its inhabitants were in a fragile and unstable state. What was needed was a leader who could bring an empathic, thoughtful approach to its multiple problems. Thiers was, demonstrably, not the person to provide that style of leadership. He was proving not to be the steady hand on the tiller that had been expected. He was authoritative, single-minded and seemingly unaware of the mindset of the citizens of Paris. He was misreading the situation and it was to have dire consequences. Although the guns still stood mute on

Montmartre hill, Adolphe Thiers had not forgotten that they represented what he saw, with some justification, as civil disobedience.

The National Assembly ended the moratorium on items deposited at the Municipal Pawnshop on 3 March. The result of that was that goods deposited there could now be sold if not redeemed – but redeemed with what? Those who had pawned their livelihoods did not have the cash to buy them back. It was a remarkably insensitive measure and the benefits, for anyone, are difficult to discern. The London *Times* commented: '2,300 poor wretches had pawned their mattresses and starving seamstresses had pawned 1,500 pairs of scissors ... How many necessities to existence were stored away in these cruel galleries? ... Starvation!' This apparently straightforward minor piece of legislation had a significant social effect in that it badly damaged the standing of Thiers and his government.

Given the volatility of the domestic scene, Adolphe Thiers made matters worse, on 7 March, when he ended the moratorium on the payment of bills of exchange. These were promissory notes previously issued that had now to be paid on demand – again, with what? An adjunct was that interest was to be paid for non-payment. The immediate effect was that '150,000 Parisian business-men of modest means defaulted on payment'.[4] The Government applied salt to the corporate wound when it ended the moratorium on delayed rent payments – non-payment meant immediate eviction. We must presume that Thiers and his colleagues reasoned that, now Paris was no longer under threat, the *Garde Nationale* had lost its *raison d'être* and, on that basis, it should no longer be paid. That was a perfectly reasonable position to take but, given the circumstances in Paris, was it wise? Perhaps not, and finally, in its apparent unending quest to lose friends and alienate its people, the Assembly voted to cease the daily payment of 1.50 francs to members of the *Garde Nationale*. At a stroke the Assembly had provided some of its armed opposition with what they would judge to be a *casus belli*. This income was all that most of these men had to live on – now they were destitute. Thiers, and the Assembly he led, had unwittingly put a match to a social fuse.

It was significant that when the assembly voted on 10 March, by 427 to 154, to leave Bordeaux it opted to take up residence in Versailles, an indicator that the Assembly did, at least, recognise the volatility of Paris. Thiers said, 'Honesty would not allow me to promise the Assembly complete safety in Paris.'[5] The British ambassador, Lord Lyon, now returned to his parish, reported to the Foreign Secretary Lord Granville, writing:

> the majority of the Assembly, which is decidedly anti-Republican, hardly expects to establish a Government to its tastes, without some actual fighting with the Reds in Paris and other large towns. It therefore does

not at all like the idea of moving the Assembly to Paris ... I cannot help thinking that the sooner the Government settles in the capital and has its fight (if fight there really must be) with the mob over, the better.[6]

The understandable decision to eschew Paris in favour of Versailles sent all the wrong messages. It indicated an inability to cope with local conditions and mistrust in the citizenry. In short it was a weak solution that ducked the issue and exacerbated the situation. On 11 March the Government banned six newspapers that were demonstrably and vociferously left wing. At the same time, the miscreants of the uprising of 31 October 1870, Blanqui, Flourens and two others, were sentenced to death in absentia – a grotesque travesty of justice.

Demonstrations vilifying the Assembly were, by now, a commonplace, everyday event in Paris. It fell to General Joseph Vinoy and his meagre force of 12,000 soldiers and 3,000 gendarmes to keep order. Vinoy was not a man who would seek a compromise and his description of the demonstrators as 'the lowest of the low' was in line with his view that they were 'guilty agitators, intent on pillage and sowing disorder'.[7] The situation got worse and the US ambassador advised Washington that 'the insurrectionists of Paris are gaining in power and strength every hour'.[8]

The pace of life was accelerating, and Adolphe Thiers decided that the issue of the guns and their removal would have to be addressed. There was no immediate military need for this to be done. The guns did not threaten anyone, although they had the capacity to do so at sometime in the future. However, there was an economic factor also to be considered because local businessmen had argued to Thiers that the *GN*, by its very presence, was inhibiting normal commercial intercourse.

The earlier removal of the guns to Montmartre and Belleville had been no more than a demonstration of the power of the *GN* at the time, but it was a dire affront to the pride of the regular army. Vinoy mounted an operation on 8 March to recover the guns but it failed in the face of an implacable barrier of *Garde Nationale*. The Army, with complete lack of resolve, backed off. Many of the local citizens stood firmly behind the *GN* in this, and their participation in any exercise had to be factored in. Georges Clemenceau, the mayor of Montmartre, was aware of the rising temperature on his streets and he strove to find a compromise position. He proposed once again that perhaps the ownership of the guns could be divided. Thiers rejected the suggestion out of hand. The guns were of little practical importance, but it was what they represented that was critical.

That same day, 8 March, Émile Duval, a member of the *Comité Central*, raised the stakes by burning down an army barracks in the rue de Grenelles.

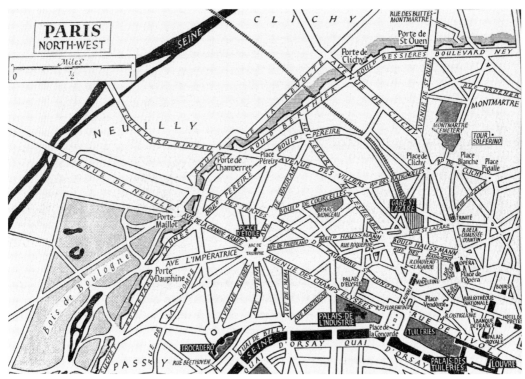

Montmartre (top right) was the site of the outbreak of civil disobedience on 18 March. (*Horne*)

This was a serious crime by any yardstick, and it could not be permitted to go unpunished. A week later, Adolphe Thiers told Vinoy to try again to capture the guns. Vinoy did not share his plans with the mayors of the arrondissements, who had previously tried to negotiate a peaceful handover of the guns. The mayors could and should have been key players in the operation.

The Vinoy plan was to seize the guns very early in the morning of 17 March and before the local residents were awake. It would be necessary to haul the guns down very narrow cobbled streets, but it would be impossible to do this quietly. General d'Aurelle called upon the commanders of about thirty-five of his most conservative battalions and warned them for duty the next morning. At 0430 hrs on 17 March, 3,000 gendarmes and about 12,000 regular soldiers were in place. The top of Montmartre hill was swiftly occupied but, in the process, one *GN*, a Guardsman Turpin, was wounded. Some 4,000 men under General de Susbielle had established a firm base at Place Pigalle. Belleville was occupied and at the base of the hill there were sufficient men to control the local neighbourhood. What could possibly go wrong?

The weather was awful: it was raining and very cold. Then the French Army, already with an heroic and unenviable track record for incompetence, plumbed the deepest depths of crass ineptitude. It was discovered that the 2,000 horses required to haul the guns were missing, as were the harnesses to

The guns, located on the high ground of Montmartre, which were at the centre of events on 17 March 1870.

make them up into gun teams. This was a situation bordering on farce. Someone, somewhere, should have had the task of managing the horse commitment. Perhaps someone had been given the job, but he had failed – abjectly and miserably. Later, Adolphe Thiers said of the operation with masterly and massive understatement, 'it lacked the ardent vigilance which makes affairs of war succeed'.[9]

The guns were all in the possession of the Army, but they did not have the means of moving them and dawn was approaching. Louise Michel, known as the 'Red Virgin', was treating Turpin's wound when she abandoned the task, escaped, and ran down the hill, raising the alarm as she went. Dawn broke and, as it did so, the Montmartre 'Vigilance Committee' was assembling its multitude of supporters. The streets filled; the crowds hemmed in the soldiers sitting with their captured guns. Church bells were rung as an alarm signal and more people flooded onto the streets. There was still no sign of any horses.

It was an impasse.

All over the city large hostile crowds, supplemented by battalions of armed *Garde Nationale*, confronted Vinoy's troops. Barriers were being erected to prevent the passage of the guns, should by any chance the horses ever arrive. It would take cool heads and sound judgement to bring this emotion-charged situation to a peaceful conclusion. One such was Dr Georges Clemenceau. He suggested to Brigadier General Claude Lecomte, who was commanding the troops at the hilltop, to allow the wounded Guardsman Turpin to go to hospital. Lecomte refused and this goaded the already furious mob into paroxysms of rage. The soldiers were under threat and Lecomte ordered his men to shoot into the crowd. They refused.

A non-commissioned officer stepped from the ranks and bellowed over the tumult, 'Turn up your rifle butts.' Some the soldiers of the 88th Regiment reversed their rifles, indicating that they were at one with the mob.[10] Lecomte had lost control of the situation and further attempts to rally his soldiers fell on deaf ears. Suddenly he was pulled from the saddle of his horse and was enveloped by the crowd.

Horses had finally arrived at the hilltop although by what route is unclear. Soldiers, still responding to army discipline, hitched them to guns and started on the seemingly impossible journey down the hill through tightly packed crowds. 'The waves of people engulfed everything, surging over the cannon-mounts, over the ammunition wagons, under the wheels, under the horses' hooves.'[11] The horses were agitated, difficult to control in the confined street, their traces were cut, and the guns were loose. It was clear that the operation to recover the guns had failed. The scene was repeated elsewhere and ominously, soldiers who had abandoned the guns started to fraternise. They 'were the object of frenetic ovations from the crowd'.[12]

Lecomte, beaten and abused, was bundled away and taken to a *Garde Nationale* post located in a dance hall called the Château-Rouge. Captain Meyer was in charge there and Clemenceau arrived and made it clear to Meyer that he was responsible for the safety of the general. Soon after, the deputy mayor, a man called Théophile Ferré, and a hard-left Red, counter-manded Clemenceau's instructions and in accordance with the wishes of the Vigilance Committee, moved Lecomte to a *GN* post at rue des Rosiers, in a pleasant suburb. Despite constant threats to his life, Lecomte arrived at rue des Rosiers at 1430 hrs, the time that Vinoy had called off the operation and Thiers ordered the immediate evacuation of all government officials and troops.

At 1600 hrs, Lecomte was joined in captivity by General Jacques Léon Clément-Thomas, a former commander of the *Garde Nationale* who had been recognised in a Paris street, apprehended and hurried to rue des Rosiers. Thomas was retired and had no part to play in the day's operations. However, the mob were now out of control and thirsty for blood. There was a vociferous demand for the death of both generals. A *GN* officer called for a vote – everyone present condemned the two men.

They were promptly murdered.

It emerged that Thomas had faced his death with great courage and said to his captors, 'Kill me! You won't prevent me from calling you cowards and assassins.'[13] At a subsequent post-mortem it was discovered that several of the

Brigadier General Claude Lecomte
(1817–71).

General Jacques Léon Clément-Thomas
(1809–71).

Theophile Ferré (1845–71).

bullets had been fired from Chassepôts – a weapon never issued to the *GN*. Lecomte had been killed by his own men.

The squalid murder of the two men was dressed up and made to look like a formal execution, after some sort of quasi-judicial hearing. Several weeks later, as part of that myth, it was re-enacted for the camera, as in the photograph below. The killing of the generals revealed a disgusting mindset amongst the mob. The bodies were mutilated, and further shots were fired into them. Some urinated on the cadavers.

Doctor Guyon, who examined the bodies shortly afterwards, found forty balls in the body of Clément-Thomas and nine balls in the back of Lecomte.[14] Clemenceau arrived, but too late. He was distressed and recorded:

> the mob which filled the courtyard burst into the street in the grip of some kind of frenzy. Amongst them were chasseurs, soldiers of the line, National Guards, women and children. All were shrieking like wild beasts without realising what they were doing. I observed then that pathological phenomenon which might be called blood lust. A breath of madness seemed to have passed over this mob ... Men were dancing about and jostling each other in a kind of savage fury. It was one of those extraordinary nervous outbursts, so frequent in the middle ages, which still occur amongst masses of human beings under the stress of some primaeval emotion.[15]

Clemenceau's account needs no further amplification. At this distance one might speculate that Paris was suffering a symptom of that obsidional fever mentioned on pages 209–10. Whatever the cause, the result was clear to see. There had been an insurrection. Guardsmen answering to Émile Duval had occupied the Panthéon and the Prefecture of Police, Eugène Varlin, led 1,500 guardsmen into the so-called *beaux quartiers* and controlled Place Vendôme, where the *GN* had its headquarters. Red flags were everywhere and, significantly, one flew over the Hôtel de Ville. Vinoy's foray to recover the guns had provided the trigger for mass insurrection and revolution. No one was more surprised at the turn of events than the revolutionaries themselves.

Foreign observers were appalled by what they had witnessed and one questioned:

> Wherever is Paris and where too is France drifting? ... A strong government has proved feeble in the hour of danger and has abandoned a city of 2,000,000 inhabitants and untold wealth to mob rule. And, worst of all, the representatives of the opulence, the intelligence, the energy, and the common sense of what the French vaingloriously style the capital of civilisation have not intervened.[16]

The staged photograph of the bogus execution of Generals Lecomte and Thomas,
17 March 1871. In reality, their murder was not quite so dignified.

*　　*　　*

It is the business of military historians to chronicle death and destruction
and, as neutral observers, select their words with care. Violent death can be
described in several ways. These range from, *accidental*, *shot* and *killed*, to the
more emotive *executed*, *slaughtered*, *butchered*, *assassinated*, *liquidated*, *massacred*
and *murdered*. Whichever word the historian selects is primarily an indicator
as to the circumstances; however, it can reflect his/her feelings on the matter.
In this case, there can be no doubt that the demise of the two generals was
murder. There were many more to come.

By mid-morning on 18 March, it was clear that the mobs controlled the
streets and any government ministers trying to do business were at risk and
were beating a hasty retreat. General Adolphe Le Flô, the Minister for War,
had no illusions and he calculated that not more than 6,000 of the 400,000
Garde Nationale could be relied upon. The recovery of the artillery was now a
matter of no consequence; it had been overtaken by events. The preservation
of life was the overriding priority and, to that end, the complete withdrawal to
Versailles was the only viable option. Simon, Favre and Picard contested the
decision made by Adolphe Thiers, but he was adamant and argued that 'the
moral contagion of the insurrection would spread to the regular army, which
would lose no time in abandoning us'.

Moltke observed the activity in Paris and had no doubt that his soldiers could easily have put a speedy end to the matter. However, he rightly questioned, what government could allow its rights to be vindicated by foreign bayonets? He wrote:

> The German Commanders consequently limited themselves to forbidding, at least within their own districts, any movement of disturbance, and to preventing all further ingress into Paris from outside. The disarmament operations which had commenced were interrupted; the troops of the 3rd Army were drawn closer to the forts, and the outposts were replaced along the line of demarcation, whereon 200,000 men could now be collected within two days.
>
>   The authorities in Paris were also warned that any attempt to arm the fronts facing the Germans would be followed by the immediate bombardment of the city. The insurgents, however, were fully occupied in destroying and burning, and in executing their commanders in the interior of Paris. They did not turn against their foreign enemy, but against the Government chosen by the nation, and prepared for an attack on Versailles.[17]

The German Army clearly had no intention of getting involved in domestic French affairs, but it remained close by and a very formidable force on French soil composed of:

Infantry   464,221 men with 1,674 guns
Cavalry   55,562 horses

Troops in garrison:

  Infantry   105,272 men with 68 guns
  Cavalry   5,681 horses

Total   630,736 men and 1,742 guns

Reserve forces remaining in Germany:

  3,288 officers
  204,684 men
  26,603 horses

The revolutionaries occupied all the key locations and buildings in Paris, but they had neither a coordinated plan nor any form of central leadership until Paul-Antoine Brunel seized the initiative. This capable young man mustered a group of *Garde Nationale* and they surrounded the 120th Regiment in Prince Eugène barracks. He imprisoned the officers, disarmed the soldiers and incorporated into his force soldiers who were prepared to turn their coats in his favour.

Brunel went from strength to strength and moved on, gathering adherents along the way. He confronted the Napoleon Barracks, which was linked to the Hôtel de Ville by its secret tunnel. This was the tunnel that loyal troops had used during the insurrection of 31 October. There was a brief exchange of fire outside the barracks, resulting in the wounding of three people. The regular soldiers defending the barracks did not resist and came out, with hands up, shouting, '*Vive la République!*'[18]

The evacuation of all government officials from Paris left the city devoid of any form of civil management. This triggered an exodus by the socially mobile, middle and upper classes. Communication with the provinces was cut and Paris was isolated. Throughout France there was a republican faction, almost all of it centred on the large cities. Representatives from Lyon, Bordeaux, Rouen and Marseille met the Central Committee to hear its side of the events of the 18th but the location of this meeting is unknown. Within weeks there was insurgency in Narbonne (23–28 March), Saint-Étienne (22 March), and Le Creusot (24–27 March).[19] Limoges was one of only two cities in which there was a violent confrontation. Although a commune was not declared, nevertheless, from 3 to 5 April, revolutionary *Garde Nationale* soldiers blockaded the city hall, mortally wounded an army colonel, briefly preventing a regular army unit from being sent to Paris to fight the Commune, before being themselves disarmed by the Army.[20] The other city in which violence erupted was Marseilles. However, the mob frenzy seen in Paris was unique to that city. The majority of the country was shocked by the events of 17 March and its immediate consequences.

Despite the political turmoil, once the mobs had dispersed, life returned to relative normality. The shops were open for business and cafés and restaurants served their usual customers. There was considerable change in the *Garde Nationale* because most of the more conservative membership had set their military duties aside. Those with strong republican leanings soldiered on for their soon-to-be-stopped 1.5 francs per day. Paul Vignon, a wealthy lawyer and former guardsman, opined:

> a kind of fever had come over ordinary Parisians. The Franco-Prussian War had wrenched them from their normal occupations and they now seemed to believe that no leaders were necessary in a world of total equality without a ruling class and in which any kind of luxury to which he was accustomed would be a stigma.[21]

Raoul Rigault had been unaware of the disturbances on 17 March as he had slept late, but when he realised what was happening he hurried to the Prefecture of Police, determined to take control there. He was somewhat discommoded to discover that Émile Duval had beaten him to the punch and was already ensconced. Although Rigault brushed Duval aside, they worked together and set to, signing orders for the release of 'political' prisoners. Among the most fervent dissidents there was an ambition to march in strength on Versailles. However, cooler heads on Central Committee advised patience.

Edward Moreau, a 27-year-old maker of artificial flowers and a member of the *Comité*, emerged briefly as a leader; he headed the element that formulated the demands of what was soon to be called the Commune. The requirements of the Commune were exacting. It demanded of Thiers's government that:

- All Parisians were to have the right to elect mayors of each of its twenty arrondissements
- The Prefecture of Police be abolished
- The Army in Versailles not be deployed in Paris
- The *Garde Nationale* have the right to elect its own officers
- The moratorium on the payment of rents be re-installed
- The National Assembly to proclaim, officially, the Republic.

Émile Eudes, 'for the avoidance of doubt', as lawyers say, made a proclamation of his own. He said, 'there is no other government than that of the people and this is the best one. Centralised authority no longer exists.' Clearly there was little or no room for compromise. Attitudes hardened on both sides. Despite the allegation that there was no 'centralised authority', the Central Committee was just that. On 20 March it published the *Journel Officiel de la Commune*, which was a propaganda document written in trenchant terms and congratulating the participants in the insurrection. The word 'commune' had been used previously but with the publication of this newspaper it became officialised and the insurrectionists took pride in the appellation communards.

The day after the tumult was a Sunday. It was a lovely spring day and Parisians enjoyed the change in the weather. It was noted by the diarist Gibson, on 20 March, that:

> Paris could hardly be said to be agitated yesterday, as it was on Saturday, for all the population of the city, the National Guards included, seemed to be giving themselves up to enjoyment, the people promenading as usual on Sunday and the national Guards marching down the middle of the streets. Indeed, all had a complete holiday air.[22]

The *Comité Central* found itself in control of the city but was quite unprepared for the responsibilities that came with that. Initially it did take one decision, and that was to appoint a failed naval officer called Charles Lullier to command of the *Garde Nationale*. He was an incredibly bad choice; a hopeless drunk he sincerely believed himself to be a great writer, a great politician

Charles Lullier (1838–91), commander, very briefly, of the *Garde Nationale*, 1871.

and a soldier of genius. He had convinced many good people that he was the world's first swordsman, and perhaps he was convinced of it himself.[23] In his new role he reinforced the Hôtel de Ville to an absurd degree but what he did not do was occupy the abandoned Mont-Valérien, which dominated the western edge of the city and was a key factor in the defence of both Paris and Versailles. Several days later, Vinoy's troops re-occupied the fortress: a prime opportunity missed by the Commune.

In the Hôtel de Ville the revolutionaries were variously exultant, astonished, appalled and in awe of what had been achieved. The *Comité* had no plan and no idea how it was to fill the administrative vacuum left by the elected but rejected Assembly. The debate raged: Brunel wanted an immediate attack on Versailles, Louise Michel suggested that the priority was the assassination of Adolphe Thiers. Louis Blanc cut to the quick when he said sombrely, 'You are insurgents against an Assembly most freely elected.' This was the very crux of the situation. On the face of it there was no room for manoeuvre or negotiation.

In the *Comité Central* the most pressing topic was the murder of the two generals and how the incident should be presented. None of the *Comité* had been present and so had not participated in the atrocity. Nevertheless, it recognised that there was a public relations exercise to be resolved. *Le Rappel*, speaking on its own account, expressed 'grief' but pointed out that it was the mob who were responsible and not the *Garde Nationale*. The *Journal Officiel de la Commune* then published an editorial that fed the fire, declaring: 'That frightful crime accomplished under the eyes of the *Comité Central* gave the measure of the horrors with which Paris would be menaced if the savage agitators who troubled the city and dishonoured France, should triumph.'

This editorial was a career-inhibiting move by the editor. He and his entire management team were immediately sacked and replaced by others more likely to toe the line. Further editorials followed with a different message; they cleared the *Comité* of any responsibility for the deaths. The *Journal* went on to describe the demise of the generals as executions, 'according to the laws of war'. It did not quote which law applied in this case.

The *Comité* made a serious strategic mistake in associating itself with this position and across France there was widespread revulsion at the behaviour of Parisians, and the *Comité* in particular. Jules Goncourt noted in his diary that he experienced 'a sensation of weariness at being French'. Jules Favre made clear the Assembly position when he said bluntly, 'One does not negotiate with assassins.'[24]

As soon as the Government withdrew from Paris the only legal, democratically elected body was the mayors of the arrondissements. Adolphe Thiers instructed them to act as his proxies and to find some way to conciliation, unlikely as that might seem. However, he was not in a hurry because he needed time to rebuild the Army. The mayors covered the whole political spectrum and even the conservative mayors were aggrieved by Thiers's arbitrary decision to vacate Paris.

On 19 March, with the blood in the streets hardly dry, the mayors met with the *Comité Central*, at this stage the only coherent organisation in Paris. Clemenceau pulled no punches at this meeting and made it quite clear that 'Paris has no right to revolt against France and must recognise absolutely the authority of the Assembly'. The only passage to normality was to allow the mayors the chance to negotiate on behalf of the *Comité*. Varlin was the spokesman for them and in response he laid out some surprisingly mild demands. He enumerated them as follows:

- An elected municipal council with genuine municipal liberties
- The suppression of the Prefecture of Police
- The right of the *Garde Nationale* to appoint its leaders
- The *Garde Nationale* to arrange its own organisation
- The proclamation of the Republic as the legitimate government
- The postponement of payment of rent arrears
- A fair law on maturities.

The negotiations dragged on but eventually a measure of agreement was reached. The mayors would try to get the Assembly to accept the demand as listed above and the *Comité* would delay the municipal elections it was planning for 22 March. It agreed to hand over the Hôtel de Ville to the mayors. That all seemed to constitute a reasonable first step. However, it did not satisfy the hard-left Vigilance Committees of the arrondissements. They had no faith in the good will of the Assembly and they completely mistrusted the bourgeois establishment – with good cause, it must be said, based on historical precedence. For the first time the revolutionaries were better armed and more numerous than their anticipated foe. There was a strong case for attacking Versailles as soon as possible.

In Versailles, the French Army was in poor order but, among many, there was deep anger and a desire for retribution against the insurrectionists. Time was needed to rebuild the Army and there was the fear that if Brunel had his way, several hundred thousand armed men could march on Versailles and take it. The entire future of France depended on what the *Comité* decided to do. In Paris, 'Friends of Order' held a demonstration on 21 March, when 3,000 individuals opposed to the Commune marched through the city. The next day, Admiral Jean Marie Saisset replaced d'Aurelle and was appointed to command the *Garde Nationale* of Paris. He organised a second demonstration; he baited the bear in his lair when he chose the location for the meeting – it was in front of the headquarters of the *Garde Nationale*. Henri de Pène, a journalist and director of *Paris Journal*, was in the crowd and although not leading, he was prominent. There was the usual shouting and shoving as there often is in political demonstration but nothing untoward.

Then everything changed, shots were fired, and twelve people died, one of whom was Henri de Pène. The dead and wounded were recovered from the street by people like Gaston Rafinesque, a medical student. He had no doubt that the fire was initiated by the *Garde Nationale*. The first corpse to be recovered was that of an elderly gentleman wearing the *Légion d'honneur*. This incident became known as 'The Massacre in the rue de la Paix' and the responsibility for the opening shots was never established, despite Rafinesque's conviction.[25] A byproduct of the incident was that anti-commune feeling was enhanced among the conservatives remaining in Paris.[26]

It was against that background that the next day the Assembly met with the aim of selecting a policy to deal with the insurrection of 17 March. Now it had to contend with this latest outbreak of violence and its results. The monarchist right demanded that there be a nationwide call for volunteers to defend 'order and society'. There was a consensus in the Assembly that the insurrectionists were criminals and as such they should be offered no concessions.

It was tacitly acknowledged that, in effect, a state of civil war existed. Édouard Lockroy observed, 'Only days after the people of Paris had taken control of their city, Thiers and the National Assembly were readying for a war they understood as a class war between the Bourgeoisie and Parisian workers.'[27] Despite this perfectly valid interpretation, it could reasonably be argued that a democratically elected government was under threat by a non-representative, violent organisation. In that case, 'class' was not the issue – but law and order were.

Alphonse Daudet, the novelist, was witness to the bloodletting and after the latest incident he wrote, 'The farce was turning towards the tragic, and in the boulevards, people no longer laughed.' The product of the 'massacre' was to make the possibility of conciliation based on compromise between Paris and Versailles even more unlikely.[28]

The *GN* reorganised and, as part of that process, Paul-Antoine Brunel, Émile Eudes and Émile Duval were all elevated to the rank of general. In the case of Lieutenant Brunel this was mind-spinning advancement of six or seven ranks. The *GN* set about identifying and removing from office any-one perceived to be an opponent of the Commune. Clemenceau was briefly detained on the orders of his deputy, Théophile Ferré, the latter now revealed as being a dedicated revolutionary. Although to many it was apparent that the mayors of Paris no longer had a productive role to play, nevertheless prominent Parisian republicans Édouard Lockroy and Jean-Baptiste Millière with Georges Clemenceau called on Adolphe Thiers, but he rejected their approach.

Admiral Saisset's position in Paris was untenable – he commanded nothing, and he made his exit from the city, ignominiously, on foot and in disguise. He voiced the view that it would take a force of 300,000 to capture Paris. The ever-stoic Ambassador Washburne of the USA thought it prudent to move to Versailles and he was highly unimpressed at what he found there. He visited the Assembly and found it to be chaotic and disorganised. 'In the over-crowded conditions about sixty Deputies were sleeping in the Council Chamber, sometimes appearing in their night shirts in the midst of a debate.' He added that he found 'that august body fiddling while Paris burned'.[29]

Spring had arrived in Paris, but the atmosphere was subdued and there was 'a terrible silence', according to British resident Edwin Child. He said that shops were open for business, but the shopkeepers kept their shutters close to hand, 'ready to close in an instant'.[30] Washburne, from Versailles, sent one of his routine despatches back to Washington on 25 March: he commented that, in his opinion, 'the appearance of things today is more discouraging than ever. The insurrectionists in Paris are gaining power and strength every hour.'[31]

The following day, further elections were held in Paris for the benefit of the 485,569 registered voters (only 24.27 per cent of the estimated original population). Less than half voted and Adolphe Thiers, who had encouraged abstention, saw this as a political victory, but he was deluding himself. The conservative middle class, the bourgeoisie, had abandoned Paris in great numbers and the 220,176 who did vote returned a Red municipal government with a 4:1 advantage. It was an overwhelming victory for the hard left, which lost no time in claiming the appellation 'Commune de Paris'. It was a firm indicator of the degree to which Adolphe Thiers and his acolytes had lost the hearts and minds of current Parisians.

The Commune exploited its win on 28 March in the grand manner. Red banners, flags, cockades and scarves were everywhere. The police chief, Raoul Rigault, paraded, clearly very proud of his new status. Jules Vallès described the proclamation of the Commune as 'making up for twenty years of Empire, six months of defeat and betrayals'. There was no doubt that, in late March 1871, the Commune enjoyed massive support.[32] The *Garde Nationale* was on parade and what it lacked in martial skills and courage it made up for in parade ground swagger as 200 battalions marched past the saluting dais. The captured guns roared out a salute, men and women cheered and waved. This was the high-water mark of the Commune.

The *Comité Central* of the *Garde Nationale* announced that it was prepared to transfer its powers and responsibilities to the Commune. Notwithstanding, the *Comité* started an internal reorganisation, as sixteen of its members were now elected to the Commune Government. The *Comité* was the self-appointed 'Guardian of the Revolution'. The result was an untidy form of dual government with the demarcation line between the *Comité* and the Commune somewhat blurred.

To put all of these French events into a wider context, in London, on 28 March 1871, Queen Victoria opened the new Albert Hall. In Berlin, the public waited for the payment of the war reparations and the return of its soldiers. Those soldiers, camped outside Paris, watched events inside the city with increasing incredulity.

There was a calm both in Paris and Versailles, but black storm clouds had gathered, and the military thunder and lightning was close to hand – very close.

Notes

1. Horne, p. 262.
2. Ibid., p. 263.
3. Vuillaume, M., *Mes Cahiers rouges au temps de la Commune* [1909] (Paris, 1971), p. 158.
4. Merriman, p. 36.
5. Tombs, R., *The Paris Commune* (London, Longmans, 1999), p. 66.
6. Lord Lyon to Foreign Secretary, Lord Granville, 12 March 1871.
7. Merriman, p. 39.
8. Washburne, E.B., *Franco-German War and the Insurrection of the Commune* (Washington, 1878), quoted by Merriman, p. 39.
9. Horne, p. 270.
10. Gullickson, G., *Unruly Women* (New York, Ithaca, 1996), pp. 35–6.
11. Merriman, p. 43.
12. Edwards, S., *The Communards of Paris 1871* (London, 1973), pp. 62–3.
13. Horne, p. 272.
14. Milza, P., *L'année terrible: La Commune – Mars–Juin 1871* (Paris, Perrin, 2009), p. 19.
15. Horne, p. 273.
16. *ILN*, 21 March 1870.

17. *MMK*, p. 404.
18. Ibid., p. 275.
19. Merriman, p. 51.
20. Milza, pp. 173–76.
21. Vignon, P., *Rien que ce que j'ai vu! Le Siège de Paris – la Commune* (Paris, 1913).
22. Gibson, p. 119.
23. Ranc, A., 'Small Memories', *Le Matin*, 12 October 1897.
24. Horne, p. 280.
25. Ibid., p. 286.
26. Merriman, p. 51.
27. Lockroy, E., *La Commune et l'Assemblée* (1871), pp. 26–9, 38.
28. Horne, p. 286.
29. Washburne, E.B., *Recollections of a Minister to France 1869–77*, Horne, p. 287.
30. Childs, E., Diary, March 1871, Horne, p. 287.
31. Washburne to Secretary of State, 25 March 1871.
32. Edwards, S., *The Paris Commune* (Newton Abbot, 1971), p. 186.

Chapter Nineteen

March: Thirteen Important Days

In the spring of 1871, and despite the recent election result, the hopes of the citizens of Paris were not all cast in blood red and, most probably, the majority merely wanted a quiet, productive life embellished with social justice. One such individual, a former corporal in the *Garde Nationale*, wrote:

> Now our Commune is elected, we shall await with impatience the acts by which it will make itself known to us. May God wish that this energetic medium will prove beneficial and will secure us genuinely honest and durable institutions. That's what everybody wishes and desires for we have been dissatisfied for a long time. That's why I believe everybody accords it his good wishes.[1]

There was then, and still is today, difficulty in defining precisely what the Commune was and determining its long-term political and strategic aims – if any. Many of the leaders of the Commune were either killed in the later street fighting or executed soon after their capture. Their demise denied us the political philosophy of the instigators of a world-famous rebellion. France had a history of rebellion and so this was by no means the first. The insurrections of 1789 and 1848 should have provided a road map of sorts indicating what to do, but, perhaps equally importantly, what not to do, like 'the unambitious, semi-legitimate, Commune of 1789 which turned into an omnipotent, insatiably devouring monster'.[2]

To fill the philosophical gap historians have sought to interpret the actions of the Commune and some accord it a cerebral dignity that, perhaps, it does not justify. Nevertheless, it is much studied and has been the focus of animated debate for 150 years. The bibliography of the Commune is vast, but much of it is partisan. John Merriman's book *Massacre* is a good example of an academic presenting the facts in a manner to accord with his views. Gopnik judged that *Massacre* 'is pro-Communard, emphatically so, and this gives his book both its great virtues and its real faults'.[3]

It would be a mistake to equate the Commune with communism, and communists the world over, such as Marx and Engels, had no part to play in its rise. However, after the event the communists embraced the Commune as being a prime example of 'the fight of the masses against capitalism'. They have been riding the Commune horse ever since. International communism has polished and enhanced the brief history of the Commune assiduously and cloaked it in false heroism and success. Who can blame them for that? It may be opportunistic but nevertheless, that is politics.

Karl Marx was taking his ease in London when the Commune erupted. He was the master tactician, manipulating the strings of the International, as its creed slowly spread across the globe. There was a branch of the International in France, but it was small, badly run and held in contempt by Marx, who described its adherents as 'these ragamuffins are half or two thirds of them bullies and similar rabble'.[4] Not a ringing endorsement. Anxious not to miss an opportunity, on 23 March Marx made contact with all his International cells in French provincial cities and urged them 'to create diversions to relieve pressure on Paris'. Auguste Serraillier, one of his lieutenants in Paris, acted as his liaison with the Commune.[5]

The public face of the Commune in 1871 was epitomised by Raoul Rigault. If rebellion requires fanatics, then Rigault fitted the role. He was an aggressive atheist who relished his role as Chief of Police and used the power it gave him ruthlessly. He did not seek to win friends, which was probably as well because he was, in British terms, 'not a very nice chap'. He failed to impress the *Association des Amies et Amis de la Commune de Paris 1871* (Association of Friends and Friends of the 1871 Paris Commune). They said of Rigault that he was hated for being a 'swagger of perversity', a 'scoundrel', an 'aristocrat of the thuggery' for making jokes about how he had improved the guillotine, for his 'militant atheism', and for creating a police system of 'informants and snitches'. *The New Yorker*, in a recent appraisal, described Rigault as 'the backward-looking aspect … A socialist polemicist of appetite and charm'.[6]

Raoul Rigault (1846–71).

Fellow Communards objected to Rigault's excesses and to his arbitrary arrests and imprisonment. Rigault's abiding and recorded aim was to engineer the release of Auguste Blanqui from prison in Versailles, where he languished, having been condemned to death on 11 March.

The principal opposition to the Commune was 'The Friends of Order'. Many of these were National Guardsmen who did not espouse the hard-left position of the majority. The Friends made it clear that they would use force if confronted. The governance of Paris was fragmented and uncoordinated, the *Comité* of the *GN* overlapped the function of the Commune's Central Committee. In effect, there was also an informal federation of arrondissement mayors that had somehow to be placated and kept in the governance loop. The Friends were at odds with all. Notwithstanding the administrative difficulties, the Commune had managed to secure significant cash loans with which to run Paris. The Bank of France provided 700,000 francs, together with a line of credit for 16 million francs. The Rothschilds banking organisation, which epitomised absolutely everything the Commune was apparently opposed to, also made a substantial loan. The Communards were nothing if not pragmatic.[7] It eventually dawned on the Central Committee of the Commune that some form of structured government was required, and new titles were needed to reflect the political realities. On this basis there could be no ministers but instead, 'Citizen Delegate' was the preferred appellation, as in Citizen Delegate to the Ministry of Finance, Education or War. A rose by any other name …

With ample funds now available the Commune was able to demonstrate its economic priorities. It forbade the expulsion of tenants with unpaid rent; it devised a reduction in the interest payments of debtors; and it ceased the sale of items previously pawned. It did not, however, dispense cash, food or clothing to the needy.

The Central Committee elected Charles Beslay as chairman on 28 March and then fell to discussing the legality of the Commune. This against a political background of the previous fifty years, a period in which France had been governed by four different regimes – Bourbons, Orleanists, Republicans and Bonapartists. None of these were democratically elected but, nevertheless, all had been recognised internationally. The difference was that the Commune appeared to be establishing a city state – if that involved secession from France, it had not been declared. The Committee debated the death penalty and considered whether or not it should march on Versailles. It abolished conscription and determined that, in future, no military force other than the *Garde Nationale* would have access to Paris. It ruled that all male citizens were *ipso facto* members of the *GN*. The likely response of the Germans to any measures taken by the Commune was the great unknown factor and was considered at length.

One productive measure in the right direction was to select the inner circle to manage Commune affairs. However, the thirty men selected comprised a group far too large to be efficient. Successful organisations are never run by committees and there was an urgent need for a single leader to emerge. The thirty had disparate backgrounds with a sprinkling of journalists and other professionals. They are listed below:

Charles Amouroux	hatter
Armand Arnaud	journalist for *La Marseillaise*
Adolphe Assi	colonel, *GN*
Charles Beslay	engineer
Louis Chalain	glass worker
Jean Chardon	factory worker
Georges Darboy	Archbishop of Paris
Charles Delescluze	newspaper proprietor
Louis Dereure	shoemaker
Émile Duval	foundry worker
Théophile Ferré	accountant
Gustave Flouren	failed academic
Léo Frankel	jeweller
Charles Gérardin	commander of a *GN* battalion
Paschal Grousset	writer and politician
Fortuné Henry	poet and journalist
Henri Mortier	wood turner
François Parisel	doctor and pharmacist
Eugène Pottier	poet
Eugène Protot	lawyer
Ernest Puget	painter and accountant
Paul Rastoul	physician
Raoul Rigault	anti-clerical, atheist
Albert Theisz	bronze worker
Gustave Tridon	anti-Semitic
Raoul Urbain	teacher
Èduoard Vaillant	politician and teacher
Jules Vallès	journalist
Eugène Varlin	bookbinder
Auguste Vermorel	journalist[8]

Who were these people? A British journalist wrote that:

the insurgents are simply the people of Paris, mainly and at first working men, but now largely recruited from the trading and professional classes. The Commune has been organised with extraordinary skill, the public services are efficiently carried out, and order has been for the most part preserved.[9]

That was a contemporaneous view of Commune efficiency that today seems to be a little rose-tinted. What was not mentioned was the motivation of the Communards. Some of those named above were to play a part in various commissions, but the reality was that they were merely puppets. They had no executive power, no decision-making authority and the decision on any issue had to be referred back to the Central Committee.

The measure of the Commune was the inadequate manner in which its leadership went about the assumption of authority. Albert Theisz was appointed Postmaster General and when he approached the incumbent and suggested that he hand over his duties he was nonplussed when M. Rampont declined. Theisz beat a hasty retreat for further direction. Charles Beslay, who had formed a bank and seen it fail, was deputed to take over the Bank of France. He was confronted by the Marquis de Ploeuc standing at the head of about 400 bank staff, armed with staves; all were determined to preserve the bank in its current form and under the same management. The Marquis delivered a homily on banking, successful banking, to Beslay, who, like Theisz, retired to consult the Committee. The lecture by the Marquis had actually convinced Beslay that the financial health of the Commune was dependent upon the bank. He had made it clear that if there was any interference with the banking system there would be 'no more industry, no more commerce'. The individuals above supplemented by selected others (note: one woman in Education) formed the various commissions and their composition was:

Organisation of the Commissions on 31 March 1871

Executive Commission:
Émile Eudes, Édouard Vaillant, Gustave Lefrançais, Émile Duval, Félix Pyat, Jules Bergeret, Gustave Tridon.

Commission of Finance:
Victor Clément, Louis-Eugène Varlin, François Jourde, Charles Beslay, Dominique Régère.

Military Commission:
Generals Émile Duval, Jules Bergeret, Émile Eudes, Colonels Jean-Baptiste Chardon, Gustave Flourens, Commandant Gabriel Ranvier.

Commission of Public Justice:
Arthur Ranc, Eugène Protot, Léo Meillet, Auguste Vermorel, Louis Le droit, Jules Babick.

Commission of Public Safety:
Raoul Rigault, Théophile Ferré, Adolph Assi, Frédéric Cournet, Émile Oudet, Louis Chalain, Charles Gérardin.

Victualling Commission:
Louis Dereure, Henry Champy, François Ostyn, Jacques Clément,
François Parisel, Émile Clément, Fortuné Henry.

Commission of Industry and Trade:
Benoît Malon, Leo Frankel, Albert Theiz, Clovis Dupont,
Charles Loiseau-Pinson, Eugène Gérardin, Ernest Puget.

Commission of Foreign Affairs:
Louis Delescluze, Arthur Ranc, Paschal Grousset, Ulysse Parent,
Arthur Arnould, Antoine Arnauld, Charles Gérardin.

Commission of Public Service:
Sicard Ostyn, Alfred-Édouard Billioray, Jacques Clément,
Henri Mortier, Paul Rastoul.

Commission of Education:
Jules Vallès, Dr Edmond Goupil, Blanche Lefèvre, Raoul Urbain,
Albert Leroy, Augustine Verdure, Antoine Demay,
Dr Jean-François Robinet.

* * *

While the Commune talked, Adolphe Thiers was engaged in building an army. The cream of the former French Army were prisoners of war and their release from captivity was progressing very slowly, and Bourbaki's Army of the East was interned in Switzerland – although the majority of those troops were *Mobiles* and of limited ability. Thiers believed that he was going to need 100,000 trained soldiers to retake Paris and in early April he had only about 55,000.[10]

From the Commune emerged a long chain of edicts; some, such as the repeal of the Rent Act, were welcomed, but others less so. Gambling was forbidden, and the Church was disestablished (to the delight of Rigault), urinating was proscribed other than in a public urinal, and displaying any document emanating from Versailles was likely to attract a death penalty. The defence of Paris was a low priority and apart from occupying the southern forts there was no military activity. The Commune had wasted thirteen valuable days talking when it should have been attacking Versailles.

Frederick Engels, who was no soldier, did know something about revolution and understood the need to maintain the impetus in a revolutionary situation. He wrote:

> The defensive is the death of every armed rising; it is lost before it measures itself with its enemies. Surprise your antagonists while their forces are scattering, prepare new successes, however small, but daily;

keep up the moral ascendancy which the first successful rising has given to you.[11]

The lethargic approach to matters military was a mistake and as Horne remarked, 'Marx's pupil, Lenin – about to celebrate his first birthday far away at Simbirsk on the Volga – would not repeat the error when his turn came.'

Notes

1. Louis Péguret in a letter to his sister, 28 March 1871.
2. Horne, p. 294.
3. Gopnik, A., 'The Fires of Paris: Why do people still fight about the Paris Commune?', *The New Yorker*, 22 December 2014.
4. Horne, p. 291.
5. Ibid, p. 292.
6. Gopnik, A., *The New Yorker*, 22 December 2014.
7. Varlin, E., *Pratique militant et écrits d'un ouvrier communard* (ed. Lejeune, P., 1977), p. 164.
8. Kaiser, K., Stanford Univ., Paris Commune of 1871, Crisis Committee, 17–19 October 2014.
9. Harrison, F., 'The Revolution and the Commune' (*Fortnightly Review*, 53:9, May 1871), pp. 559, 573.
10. Godineau, L., *Les Barricades de Mai 1871, chez Jules Vallès* (La Commune de Paris, L'Insurgé), p. 178.
11. Engels, F., 'Revolution and Counter Revolution in Germany' (*New York Tribune*, September 1852), Chapter XVII. Published as a book in 1896.

Chapter Twenty

April: Civil War

Raoul Rigault was emerging as the strong man of the Commune – first because of his aggressive manner and extrovert personality and second because of his very liberal interpretation of his power as Chief of Police. He was a fine example of power corrupting; he was a man to fear. In the period 18–28 March, he caused 400 people to be arrested – including Georges Clemenceau. Clemenceau was released, but many were not. Rigault had eighty local police posts/stations and 200 agents employed solely in seeking out 'spies'.

Although the two conservative newspapers *Le Figero* and *Le Gaulois* had been closed down, there had been no concerted attack on civil liberties, but Ambassador Washburne reported to Washington on the application of law and order. He drew attention to a routine report compiled by 'General' Garnier, the *GN* commander in Montmartre. Washburne wrote:

> He says in the first place that there is, 'nothing new; night calm and without incident'. He then goes on to say that 'at five minutes after ten o'clock, two *sergeants de ville* were brought in by the *franc-tireurs* and immediately shot'. He continues, 'at twenty minutes after midnight, a guardian of the peace, accused of having fired a revolver, is shot'. He closes his report of that 'calm night without incident' by saying that 'a gendarme, brought in by the guards of the twenty-eighth battalion at seven o'clock, is shot'.[1]

This single brief report gives a chilling insight into the mindset of Garnier and his ilk. This man was formerly a dealer in cooking utensils and, presumably, a civilised citizen of a civilised city. Now, like Rigault, the acquisition of the power of life and death had reset his values and priorities. Despite the Garniers and Rigaults, most citizens of Paris were still able to sleep in peace. Crime was much reduced; the citizens went about their business although postal services had ceased as M. Rampont and all his staff had abandoned ship.

The first confrontation, albeit very minor, between the Commune and Versailles took place on 30 March. Two squadrons of cavalry, under the command of Brigadier General Gaston Galliffet, Marquis de Galliffet, made a reconnaissance of the Courbevoie area, about 5 miles (8km) to the north-west of the centre of Paris. Galliffet was a law unto himself, with a reputation for personal courage and ferocity. It was he who had commanded the abortive cavalry charges at Sédan, just before that city surrendered on 2 September. This, unordered, very modest sortie had the effect of prising a small party of *Garde Nationale* from an unimportant outpost. Adolphe Thiers viewed Galliffet's modest success as sufficiently significant that, when he addressed the Assembly later that day, he assured the members that they had to hand 'one of the finest armies possessed by France'. He was overstating the case but, by his tone, indicated that he would put that army to use. 'This was nothing less than a declaration of war: painful the struggle would certainly be, but not short.'[2]

The Commune recognised that, perhaps, it should cease debating the disestablishment of the Church and apply itself to matters of defence. It was agreed that it would send a column in the direction of Versailles on 5 April.

Thiers beat the Commune to the punch and, on 2 April, his forces shelled Courbevoie and then followed up with an assault by infantry. The battle was close enough to be viewed from the city and, among the interested spectators was Elihu Washburne. He commented that he found it 'a singular sight to my family on that Palm Sunday morning to watch from the upper windows of my residence the progress of a regular battle under the walls of Paris, and to hear the roar of artillery, the rattling of musketry, and the peculiar sound of the *mitrailleuses*'.

At first it was difficult to determine who was winning, and one Versailles battalion was bloodily repulsed, just outside Courbevoie. However, a counterattack mounted by Zouaves turned the tables and the *Garde Nationale*, as it had done so many times before, panicked, broke, and abandoned its line. Reduced to a disorganised mob it fled across the Seine bridge at Neuilly and back into the city. Galliffet secured the bridge and, by so doing, had gained a ready access to Paris. This encounter, significant though it was, caused relatively few casualties. There was one fatality, that of Surgeon Major Pasquier, and that was no more than a tragic mistake. The doctor, in uniform and under a flag of truce, advanced towards the bridge. The Communards saw what they perceived to be an enemy general and shot him dead. The death of this one man was fully exploited by Adolphe Thiers and his Assembly, who termed it an atrocity and equated it to the recent murders of Generals Lecomte and Thomas.

This first significant armed clash caused a rethink among some Parisians, who could see that the Commune was not just a metropolitan administration set on good works for the masses. The Commune's 'generals' conferred, and it was decided that an immediate response was called for. On 3 April, Jules Bergeret and Gustave Flourens on the right would each lead columns that

The bridge at Neuilly captured, on 2 April 1871, by troops of the Versailles
Government but retaken by the Commune two days later.
(Photo by Auguste Bruno Braquehais, 1823–75)

would advance either side of Mont-Valérien, towards Rueil. In the centre,
Émile Eudes was to take Meudon and Chaville. On the left, Émile Duval was
to capture and hold the Châtillon high ground. (See map on page 90.
Châtillon, very small type, is just north of Sceaux.) As plans go this was all
feasible – other than that Mont-Valérien and its guns were held by government troops. On 3 April, as the Commune force set out, it was without any
artillery. The guns that had been so important just two weeks before, and had
triggered an insurrection, were left out of battle – an incredible and avoidable
deficiency. What the *Garde Nationale* lacked in military know-how it made
up for in brimming self-confidence and the posturing of its leaders. Both
Bergeret and Flourens were beautifully dressed in flamboyant, individualistic
raiment that would have shamed a flock of peacocks.

   The advance to contact was a relaxed and casual affair. No scouts were
employed ahead of the main bodies and there was a festive mood in the ranks.
Edmond Lepelletier, the journalist and novelist, commented that the armed
forces of the Commune reminded him 'of a horde of turbulent picnickers
setting out gaily and uncertainly for the country, rather than an attacking
column directing itself towards a formidable position'.[3]

As two columns of *Garde Nationale* marched in serried ranks past Mont-Valérien, one of the fort's guns cleared its throat and a single shell fell upon the ranks of Bergeret's column. A second shell followed and disembowelled an officer. The effect was out of all proportion. Mass panic caused an immediate breakdown in what very fragile discipline the *GN* had. The rear halves of both columns turned about and fled back to Paris. Bergeret and Flourens pressed on but with only 3,000 men between them.

A war correspondent observed that among those who had opted out of the fight were 'two officers hiding in a house and their men begging the villagers to lend them clothes in order that they might not be caught, in uniform, by the troops'.[4] The conduct of some of the *GN* had been as craven as it had ever been.

The depleted columns were spread out across a plain – ideal cavalry country – and all too soon, mounted soldiers swept down and inflicted stern punishment. The untrained *GN* infantry had no defence against experienced, determined horse soldiers who were ruthlessly efficient. The defeat of Flourens and Bergeret was complete. Flourens, with only a handful of soldiers, took cover at an inn, in Rueil, about 8 miles (13km) from central Paris and close to the bridge pictured above. Flourens was captured and when he was brought into the courtyard of the inn, he was recognised by cavalry officer Captain Jean-Marc Démaret as a fugitive, a man wanted since he was freed from prison on the night of 21/22 January. Démaret, from the back of his horse, smote Flourens with a swift, downward stoke of his sabre and cleft his head. Flourens was the first of the Commune's leadership to be killed – others would follow. His body was moved to Versailles in a dung cart, an object of curiosity to the inhabitants.

Galliffet's men had taken as prisoner a number of Communards and, on his instructions, at least five of these were immediately put to death – this was murder. The doubtful justification was that these men were treasonous rebels and did not merit the respect habitually given to a captured enemy soldier. Retribution for the killing of Surgeon Major Pasquier was also suggested as a further justification. These murders established a precedent. Galliffet took a strange line when he said that his soldiers killed in the engagement had been 'assassinated'. It was on that basis that he issued a statement that 'proclaimed a war without truce or mercy upon these assassins'.[5]

The Times had a correspondent on the spot and, having interviewed local people, he reported that many prisoners 'had been treated with the grossest cruelty by the Gendarmes and then shot'. *The Times* also repeated the rumour that General Vinoy had ordered the immediate execution of all surrendering *Garde Nationale*.

The Communard assault on Versailles had started to peter out, although the column led by Émile Eudes in the centre enjoyed a modicum of success, but he had to fall back to Clamart because of his dearth of artillery support.[6] By nightfall, Émile Duval was in occupation of the Châtillon heights with 1,500 men, having achieved his aim. The next morning, the Versailles force launched a vigorous assault and overran Duval's position. He was obliged to surrender. Any of Duval's men who wore any item of regular army uniform were singled out and summarily shot. The Commune lost about 3,000 men either killed or captured in this ill-judged sortie; it was a sound defeat. The previous self-confidence that had been a feature of the 'advance to contact' was now seriously deflated.

Survivors were marched along the road en route to Versailles. General Vinoy came across the crocodile of prisoners and asked if there were any Communard leaders present. Duval stepped forward and two others stepped up to his side. 'If you had taken me,' asked General Vinoy, 'would you not have shot me?' 'Without hesitation,' replied Duval. Vinoy gave the word of command and all three men died on the spot. Then, an unnamed captain removed Duval's boots as a trophy.[7]

The assault on Versailles had failed and the only product was the retaking of the bridge at Neuilly, a doubtful asset that was the path only to further military defeat. The Reverend William Gibson, uninformed as to the progress of the fighting, took note of the 'guardsmen wandering about in twos and threes, looking extremely dejected' – an indicator that things were not going well.[8]

On 6 April, the Commune staged the funerals of the 'heroes' who had died over the previous three days. Flourens was absent; his body was in Versailles and Duval's was never recovered. There was an element of theatre about the event. Hearses suitably adorned with red flags processed through the city, led by Louis Charles Delescluze. There was a large military contingent of several thousand. Drums were beaten, women wept, and the cadavers were interred in a common grave at Père Lachaise Cemetery. This sombre occasion brought home to Parisians that, although the Germans were long gone, the city was once more effectively under siege. Gibson commented, 'So we are shut up as in a cage.' He also noted that there had been a considerable exodus from Paris and suggested that '100,000 had left in the previous week'.

In true revolutionary manner heads were going to have to roll after the recent military debacle. 'Colonel' Adolph Assi, perhaps one of the most corrupt and limited of the Communards, was charged with communicating with Versailles and was arrested. This accusation was based on the submission of reports alleging that he had contact with a reactionary newspaper, the *Paris Journal*.[9] No evidence was produced, and he was later released.

The alcoholic Charles Lullier, the inadequate former commander of the *Garde Nationale* who had held office for just five days, was also arrested on suspicion of treachery. These two men were too far down the command chain to have any influence on events and were too limited to be treacherous. The suggestion that the failure to occupy Mont-Valérien was their sole responsibility and part of a plot was absurd. 'General' Jules Bergeret was arrested for 'insubordination', probably arising from his inept contribution to the defeat. He was released three weeks later.

At this point, Raoul Urbain, sometime mayor of the 7th arrondissement and a member of the Education Commission, came to the fore by proposing the adoption of the Law of Hostages. There had been similarly entitled legislation in 1799 that was long since abandoned. Urbain's proposal was that:

> Every person accused of complicity with Versailles shall be imprisoned; juries to be instituted to try these parties within forty-eight hours; those convicted to be held as 'hostages of the people of Paris' and the execution of any Commune prisoner of war to be followed immediately by way of execution of three hostages, 'drawn by lot'.

This civil war had started with atrocities, the rate of killings had accelerated, and the murder of prisoners was now routine and commonplace. This was a step in the wrong direction but, on 5 April, with only modest opposition, the Law of Hostages came into being – in Paris.

Adolphe Thiers did not overreact to the abysmal performance of Commune forces, recognising that he had time on his side when confronted by such low-grade opposition. Revolutionary movements in other French cities had been quelled, the last in Marseilles on 8 April, and the Commune was only drawing moral support from Marx and his International.

Thiers probably gave thought to the fact that Moltke, with his vast, well-trained resources, had nevertheless drawn the line at fighting in Parisian streets. Thiers knew that when he moved on Paris he would need to have overwhelming force, well led. On that basis, on 6 April, he replaced the uninspired and uninspiring General Joseph Vinoy with Marshal Patrice de MacMahon. Vinoy was decorated with the *Légion d'honneur* and sent to command the Reserve Army – a military backwater. de MacMahon had just returned from Germany, where he had been held as prisoner of war since September. de MacMahon could claim to be the only French general not to have been defeated in the recent war, although only a serious wound had saved him from defeat at Sédan. At the same time, Paul de Ladmirault, Ernest de Cissey, Francoise de Barail, Justine Clinchant and Félix Douay were all named for senior corps level command appointments.[10] All of these men were regular officers and, as such, were politically conservative, with no sympathy for the revolutionary cause.

Jules Favre, who had been treated with such scant respect by Bismarck, returned to the fray in order to obtain German permission to increase the size of the French Army beyond that prescribed by the terms of the armistice. Predictably, the Germans were watching events in and around Paris and, initially, the spectacle of Frenchmen killing other Frenchmen had been mildly entertaining. However, there were revolutionary elements in Germany and Bismarck did not want to feed their ambitions. The suppression of the Paris Commune would be in his, and Germany's, interest. He agreed to the expansion of the French Army in stages to 80,000, then 110,000, and finally to 170,000. He accelerated the release of French prisoners of war and as these men streamed home, so Thiers started on his expansion of the Army.

In Paris, after the fall from grace of Brunel, Lullier, Bergeret, Eudes, and with the deaths of Duval and Flourens, there were vacancies in the upper echelons of the Commune's army. Those searching for a new military leader quickly settled on Gustave Paul Cluseret. His claim to fame was that he was a real soldier. He was, or had been, but with a record that did not bear scrutiny. It is an indicator of the quality of the talent pool that Cluseret was even considered for the appointment.

Cluseret graduated from Saint-Cyr in 1843 but had a turbulent early career, and his participation in anti-Bonapartist activities led to his demotion, resignation and flight to London in 1849. He was reinstated in 1853 and thereafter served during the Crimean War, where he won promotion to captain, was present at the Siege of Sebastopol, was wounded and awarded the *Légion d'honneur*. In 1858, he was court-martialled for theft and dismissed in disgrace.[11]

Cluseret became a soldier of fortune and served briefly in the Union Army of the United States. The Americans welcomed 'a gallant Frenchman' to their cause and, despite the antipathy of President Lincoln, he was accorded the elevated rank of Brigadier General. However, he was out of his depth and very soon relegated to a mundane staff job, well away from the front line. Elihu Washburne knew Cluseret and commented that 'he only stayed in the USA long enough to be naturalised'.[12] Cluseret had strong revolutionary feelings and, while in the USA, engaged with the violently anti-British Fenian movement.[13] On moving to England he continued to be an adherent to the Fenian cause and participated in the attack on Chester jail in 1867. He returned to France and only avoided a prison sentence, for sedition, by resting on his American citizenship – he was deported. After the fall of the Empire and the declaration of a French Republic, Cluseret returned to his homeland and led the declaration of a Commune in Marseilles; he went so far as to proclaim himself as 'Commander of the Armies of the South'. Gambetta was discommoded and not impressed.

Cluseret was a fluent, dishonest braggart. He spun elaborate tales about his past and, in effect, was an unemployed confidence trickster until the very naïve Central Committee of the Commune gave him command of its forces. His disagreeable persona and his lack of interpersonal skills did not endear him to his new subordinates. It did not help that he allowed his contempt for the *Garde Nationale*, his soldiers, to show – indeed, he advertised it. The Commune needed a charismatic, energetic and innovative leader. Cluseret was none of those things and, despite his limitations, he had taken on the very taxing job of defending Paris, 'with undisciplined National Guard forces, vulnerable to the indecision and arguments of their commanders'.[14]

Gustave Paul Cluseret (1823–1900), photographed in US Union Army uniform.

It could be argued that the structure of the *GN*, which was organised into companies made up of residents from the same arrondissement, was its strength. However, there is a case that this ingrained, literally parochial, structure was also incestuous and its weakness. To further confuse a chaotic situation, each company elected a delegate who had wide-ranging, quasi-political responsibility. He was not bound by the chain of command, was free to call meetings, and to examine the political loyalty of individual members. The function had first appeared as *commissaire politique* or *representant en mission* (representative on mission) in the French Revolutionary Army 1789–99.[15]

The plethora of delegates, en masse, added another layer of 'management' to the Commune structure and made Cluseret's task all the more difficult. He found it necessary to remind the membership of the *GN* that he was the commander. However, he was obstructed by the *Comité*, which habitually concerned itself with affairs at unit level and worked against the Commune's appointee and his efforts to centralise.

Cluseret worked in a bizarre world of order and counter-order. He called for 1,500 men to assemble at Gare Saint-Lazare but only 200 attended the parade and they 'did not want to march'. It was thought that, at best, only about 80,000 men were ready and prepared to fight by mid-May.[16] The principle by which officers of the *GN* were elected on the basis of their popularity alone was the root of the problem. Their military aptitude or a capacity for leadership were irrelevant. The consequence was that there was a complete absence of discipline in the *GN*. An officer who issued an unpopular order was subject to immediate re-election and deposed. It was an absurd situation that produced a mob of armed, undisciplined, disorganised political zealots.

This mob lacked all the accoutrements of a modern army: it was devoid of any form of staff system; there was no supply or transport organisation; it had a wholly inadequate medical service; and no cavalry arm or engineers. The final straw that broke the military camel's back was the dearth of competent commanders – a product of the election system.

A phenomenon that became apparent in early April was the appearance of 'private armies', in reality, groupings of *GN* battalions. This included such as the *Vengeurs de Flourens*, the *Lascars*, the *Enfant Perdus* (lost children), the *Éclaireurs* (pathfinders) *de Bergeret*. There were many others, all with exotic names, and even more exotic uniforms. Cluseret would have none of this and on 7 April he announced that there were to be no more 'generals', nor would there be any 'lanyards, no more glitter, and no more gold braid rings'. Then he sensibly decided to split the *GN* into two components. These would be 'sedentary' and 'active' battalions. He recognised that those listed as sedentary were militarily worthless and including them in any operational plan gave a false sense of security. Unfortunately, in some sedentary battalions there were individuals who were of value and the hope was that they would transfer to an active unit.

Cluseret had selected as his chief of staff, Louis-Nathaniel Rossel, to carry out this reorganisation. Rossel, a 27-year-old former lieutenant colonel, had a middle-class background, but he had thrown in his lot with the Communards having seen the conditions under which many lived. He said, 'These people have good reason for fighting; they fight that their child may be less puny, less scrofulous and less full of failings than themselves.' Rossel was a capable man, perhaps too capable for Cluseret's liking, who saw him as a possible rival. Cluseret made a wise choice when he installed a Pole, Jaroslaw Dombrowski, as the Commandant of Paris.[17] Bergeret, the previous incumbent, was still languishing, at Rigault's pleasure, in jail.

Dombrowski was of noble but impoverished birth and had been an officer in the Imperial Russian Army. He was jailed in 1862 and sent to Siberia for his involvement in a plot against Tsar Alexander II. He escaped in 1865 and made his way to France. Allegedly, he offered his services to Trochu but was

Jaroslav Dombrowski (1836–71).   Louis-Nathaniel Rossel (1844–71).

roundly rejected. This was, of course, some weeks before the rise of the Commune.

On 7 April, in Place Voltaire, a crowd supplemented by a large group of *GN* from the 11th arrondissement assembled. This was the site where in the past miscreants had faced death on the guillotine. It was all very symbolic and to great applause a guillotine was ceremonially burnt. Leighton, who had been a spectator, commented, 'I fully approved of what had just been done as well as the approbation of the spectators.'[18]

The combination of Rossel and Dombrowski proved to be brief but productive as, between them, they injected a sense of purpose and urgency into the *GN*. They identified the probable axis of approach that the Versailles would use and moved guns to cover these avenues. On 9 April, two active battalions from Montmartre made a surprise attack on Asnières, to the northeast of Paris and about 5 miles (8km) from the city centre. The Communards inflicted casualties and captured two guns. There was an evident upturn in the spirit of the insurgents and Cluseret can take some of the credit for that. This change in attitude was noted by the anti-communard Goncourt who wondered why such courage and resolve had not been inflicted on the Germans. He concluded that it was 'because in this war, the common people are waging their own war and are not under the Army's orders'.[19]

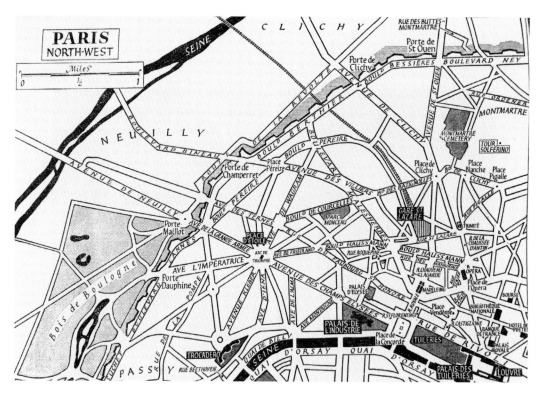

Dombrowski redistributed his assets and identified other likely Versailles targets such as the bridge at Neuilly, the scene of constant conflict. That beautiful and tranquil small town was the unhappy interface between the two sides. Colonel John Stanley, Grenadier Guards, visited during a lull in the fighting and reported that:

> Every single tree is cut to pieces and the ground is covered with grape, canister, shot and broken shells and flattened bullets. I entered what had been beautiful houses with floors wobbling and held up only on one side, utterly wrecked, billiard tables, looking glasses, sofas and costly furniture all smashed to pieces ... in many houses we found the dead laid out, where they had been placed some days ago ... and the people had lived as they could in the cellars all this long time on bread and nothing else.[20]

This civil war was affecting thousands of uninvolved civilians who lived in and around Paris but were caught up in the fighting. At Neuilly, the bridge that had once been an asset to the town was now the focus of hate and brutality. It was destroyed by Versailles guns, which, as more ammunition became available, switched to other targets on the western approaches to Paris.

It was ironic that the areas that now fell under the bombardment were the anti-communard suburbs. Neutral observers were nonplussed at the Versailles artillery pounding the areas of the city in which their supporters lived; it was inexplicable, self-defeating and barbaric. Dombrowski, conscious of the need to neutralise the power of Mont-Valérien, had installed a battery of guns at Trocadéro (bottom left of street plan), near the up-market, pro-Versailles, bourgeois area of Passy. Counter-battery fire on those guns from Mont-Valérien was devastating for the local inhabitants, and far worse than any German bombardment. Support for Adolphe Thiers in this neck of the woods waned as a result. The Communards who occupied Passy did nothing to charm the residents and the local doctor did not sit on any fences when he described them as 'a veritable army of unpaid mercenaries, a dirty, lewd, sordid, vicious and undisciplined rabble, but well-armed and well able to resist behind walls'.[21]

On 12 April, the Commune held the forts at Issy, Montrouge, Bicêtre and Ivry. The Versailles controlled Sevres, Châtillon, Meudon, Saint Cloud and the strategically important Mont-Valérien. It was from Mont-Valérien that the guns could reach into the centre of Paris and they were just as haphazard, arbitrary and destructive as the Germans had been. The shelling was constant, ill-directed and morale sapping.

Adolphe Thiers was particularly well equipped to assess the defensive strengths and weakness of the city defences – not least because he had been the minister responsible for their construction, forty years earlier. Thiers decided that the most vulnerable point in the defences was at Point-du-Jour, at the south-west and where the Seine left Paris (in 1871), just a few miles upstream of Neuilly. (See map on page 266, bottom centre of street plan.)

The Point-du-Jour was, by chance, the closest point to Versailles. However, for any assault here to succeed, the attackers would first have to silence Fort Issy, which dominated the area. On 25 April, the Commune asked for a ceasefire to allow succour for the surviving inhabitants of Neuilly – the town was now a total ruin and the survivors lived in cellars. These people were French, too, like Thiers, but it was not humanity that triggered Thiers's positive response. It suited Thiers's book to agree a truce because it gave him the chance to relocate his artillery in front of Fort Issy. He assembled fifty-three batteries of guns, say 200 or more tubes.

Edmond Mégy had been placed in command of Fort Issy. Although described as 'Colonel', he was in fact a militant railway engineer who related very well to his workforce and was a valued Communard, especially by Blanquists.[22] However, Mégy was a violent man and in 1870 he shot dead a policeman who sought to arrest him on a charge of conspiracy. He escaped the death sentence and the guillotine on a technicality – he was sentenced to fifteen years' hard labour. Freed from prison when the Commune took control, he busied himself fermenting civil unrest in both Marseilles and Bordeaux, with a degree of success.

On 18 April he was appointed to command Fort Issy and found himself confronting those fifty-three batteries supplemented by sixty naval guns, seventy battalions of infantry, a large cavalry force, ten engineer companies and an unreported host of gendarmes and chasseurs.[23] General Ernest Courtot de Cissey, commanding the Versailles force, offered Mégy the chance to surrender, an offer he declined.[24]

The Versailles attack commenced on 26 April, preceded by a massive bombardment to which Mégy could make no effective reply. The artillery assault on Fort Issy added to the damage inflicted by Moltke's guns only three months earlier. Once the fort's walls were breached the defences lost their cohesive integrity and were quickly reduced to rubble.

Edmond Mégy (1841–84).

Mégy held out until the morning of 29 April, when he telegraphed to Cluseret saying that only immediate and massive reinforcement would allow him to hold on. Cluseret could not meet the demand and Mégy spiked his guns and withdrew into Paris – with only seventeen surviving soldiers. One man was left behind to blow up the remains of the fort – and himself! Later that day, Generals Cluseret and Napoleon La Cecilia reached the village of Issy, where they found 200 men. They led these men back to the fort, the guns were unspiked, the demolition charge made safe and defence of the fort, badly damaged thought it was, organised. The remains of Fort Issy were defended, successfully, for ten harrowing days, during which over 500 casualties were inflicted on the defenders.

The destruction of Fort Issy was a major setback for the commune and the implications were not lost on Cluseret, but he was a man under great pressure despite the merits of his reorganisation that were beginning to reap rewards. He really was, by all accounts, his own worst enemy. His ill-concealed contempt for his troops won him no friends and he was often at odds with the Commune leadership. His forthright, strongly expressed views constantly ruffled Committee feathers. He found himself in the middle of the constant conflict between the *Comité* and the Central Committee of the Commune and was not above playing one off against the other. It was a risky strategy and one bound to end in tears.

The denouement came on 31 April, when he made his way to the Hôtel de Ville to report on his modest success in retaining Fort Issy. He was met by a discomforted Colonel Pindy, who was accompanied by several armed soldiers. The Colonel said, '*Mon cher ami*, I have a very melancholy mission to perform, I am forced to arrest you.'[25]

Notes

1. Washburne, March 1871, quoted by Horne, p. 305.
2. Horne, p. 307.
3. Lepelletier, E., *Histoire de la Commune de 1871* (Paris, Mercure de France).
4. *The Times*, 4 April 1871.
5. Horne, p. 311.
6. Rials, S., *Nouvelle Histoire de Paris de Trochu à Thiers 1870–73* (1985), pp. 262–3.
7. Leighton, J., *Paris under the Commune* (London, 1871), Chap. XXVIII.
8. Gibson, p. 157.
9. Prevost, M., 'Assi', *Dictionary of French Biography, Tome III* (Paris, 1939), Letouzey and Ané.
10. Merriman, p. 58.
11. Bargain-Villeger, A., 'Captain Tin Can. Gustave Cluseret and the Socialist Lefts, 1848–1900' (*Socialist History*, 2014).
12. Horne, p. 316.
13. Cluseret, G., *Memoires du general Cluseret: Tome III* (Paris, 1887), p. 155.
14. Merriman, p. 60.
15. The role was developed by the Russians and employed, in the Red Army from 1918 to 1942. The German army from 1943 to 1945 had Nationalsozialistischer Führungsoffiziere (National Socialist leadership officers). Today, the Chinese army employs political officers at all levels.
16. Vizetelly, E., *My Adventures in the Commune* [1914] (Wentworth Press, 2019), pp. 117, 132.
17. His real name was Jarosław Żądło-Dąbrowski, but Dombrowski was his *nom de guerre*.
18. Leighton, p. 128.
19. Goncourt, E. & J., de, Journal 1851–95.
20. Stanley, Col. J., April 1871, quoted by Horne, p. 321.
21. Dr Jules Rafinesque, writing from Passy, April 1871. Mercenaries are always paid – that is the only reason why they fight for any cause.
22. Hutton, P.H., *The Cult of Revolutionary Tradition; The Blanquists in French Politics 1864–1893* (University of California Press, 1981), p. 29.
23. Cordillot, M., *La Sociale en Amerique: dictionnaire biographique du movement social francophone aux Etats -Unis 1848–1922* (Editions de l'Atelir, 2002), p. 305.
24. Milza, P., *L'année terrible: La Commune, Mars-Juin 1871* (Revue Historique des Armées Perin, 2009).
25. Horne, p. 326.

Chapter Twenty-One

May: Rossel and the Fall of Fort Issy

The arrest of Cluseret was a clumsy, contrived affair. He had lost the confidence of the Central Committee because of his 'incapacity', in only a month, to transform the rabble of the *Garde Nationale* into a first-class fighting machine, all in the face of interference and administrative chaos not of his making. It was absurd, and without any supporting evidence, he was accused of 'treason'. It was the recently formed Committee of Public Safety that ordered his incarceration in the daunting gothic prison on Île de la Cité.

Louis-Nathaniel Rossel, the chief of staff, had been selected, prior to Cluseret's arrest, to replace Cluseret. The probability is that Rossel should have been appointed instead of Cluseret in the first place; he was a better man for the job. However, whoever was the military commander, that individual had to fight not only the Versailles but also contend with the labyrinthine machinations of the host of amateur politicians who sought to micro-manage all the affairs of Paris. An example was that, on 4 May, 'The Central Committee of the Commune challenged the Committee of Public Safety and demanded that it replace the War Delegation with new members.'[1] The destructive squabbling among the Commune's leadership was the backcloth to all of Rossel's plans for the defence of Paris.

Rossel was a military engineer and particularly well qualified to design and site barricades as a second defence line within the outer walls of Paris. He specified that barricades were to be constructed of cobblestones 4–5 feet high and 3–4½ feet thick. Rossel appointed Napoleon Gaillard, a shoemaker by trade, to oversee the work. Gaillard set to work with a will and, at Place de la Concorde, he built an enormous barricade supplemented with sandbags and barrels and fronted by a ditch 'about sixteen feet deep'. The barricade stretched right across the very wide *place* and had only one narrow passage that allowed one person to pass at a time. It was christened 'Château Gaillard'.[2]

Rossel well knew that a passive defence could only have one result and so, to take the initiative, he formed combat groups, each of five battalions (brigades, in British terms) with forty supporting guns. Unfortunately, the previously massive *Garde Nationale* had shrunk as each guardsman considered his future. There were no longer 200 battalions and those Rossel did have were reluctant to serve anywhere other than in their own arrondissement. Rossel insisted that his army should be disciplined, but he was a former regular soldier and he was dealing with untrained but armed civilians. He wanted those who failed in the face of the enemy to face trial by court martial. This was too much for the recently formed Executive Committee, who judged it to be unreasonable. One elected battalion commander had refused to march towards the enemy and, having been found guilty, was sentenced to death. However, when that sentence was rapidly reduced to imprisonment for the duration of the war, Rossel was beside himself with anger.

The Central Committee, when not supervising Rossel, got on with the business of creating the perfect society and issued multiple items of legislation – some of which were well considered. An example of that was the limit it placed on the salaries of government officials; other measures were less appropriate at a time of great danger.

Not all senior members of the Commune conducted themselves with dignity and decorum, and certainly not Rigault, who made the very best of his chances to pursue every woman who crossed his path. 'I want sexual promiscuity, concubinage is a social dogma,' he pronounced. Rigault personified evil and corruption; it was a pity that he was able defile the honest, if ill-judged, aspirations of the Commune.

One of those aspirations, however, suited Rigault, and he worked on measures to achieve it – that was anticlericalism. The Catholic Church was

'Château Gaillard' in Place de la Concorde, May 1871.

unpopular with left-wing Parisians and so the Church was an easy target. On 4 April, Rigault arrested the Archbishop of Paris, Mgr Georges Darboy, and two of his subordinates, Abbé Deguerry and Abbé Lagarde. They were all deemed to fall into the category 'enemies of the Republic'. Rigault intended to swap Darboy for his hero Louis Auguste Blanqui (see page 234), the revolutionary's revolutionary. Blanqui was a very serious player but he was imprisoned in Versailles and Thiers was determined that was where he would stay. Rigault did not stop at the three clerics and, by 23 May, he had arrested a total of about 3,000 individuals, very few of whom had any sort of hearing.

The three clergymen were to be used as hostages and their lives were seriously at risk. Rigault's action pro-

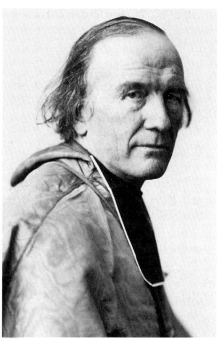

Archbishop of Paris Georges Darboy (1813–71).

voked a very strong reaction and not all members of the Commune were supportive. He was increasingly perceived as being a loose cannon and out of control.

On 2 May, Versailles forces captured the railway station and a large chateau in Clamart, and immediately after, summarily murdered all the former soldiers they had captured. They also killed two young women who were acting as nurses and were assisting a doctor with the wounded.[3]

Rossel was fighting an uphill battle. He was surrounded by individuals more interested in debating political issues and promoting their own views. The craven Félix Pyat was always at the centre of any debate but even he was moved to silence when an emissary came to report that the redoubt at Moulin-Saquet (between Bicêtre and Villejuif and not shown on the map on page 195) had fallen. The strongpoint was held by about 800 *Garde Nationale* but apparently, they were surprised while sleeping. Fifty were killed and 200 captured. The Versailles force suffered only thirty-six casualties – perhaps only twelve of those were killed. The loss of the position was a setback, but the manner of its loss was more worrying, and all the while Versailles soldiers were getting closer to the western ramparts of Paris.

Fort Issy was still holding out and rejecting calls from Colonel Leperche to surrender. Rossel responded to the latest message from Leperche in a letter. In it he wrote:

My Dear Comrade,
The next time you send a summons so insolent as that contained in your yesterday's letter, I shall have the man who brings it shot, according to the usages of war.
    Your devoted comrade.
    Rossel

Alistair Horne speculated that the tone of Rossel's letter was a factor that hastened his appearance in front of a firing squad when Versailles prevailed in just a few days' time. Fort Issy was putting up a very spirited and courageous defence, the fort was under continuous shellfire and its defenders faced overwhelming odds. It was reported that inside there were 300 dead, piled 6 feet high, there was no medical support, and only horse flesh to eat. The defence of Fort Issy was of a quality that should be a much-treasured incident in French military history – it is not, because the enemy were also French.

An officer inside the fort kept a journal, and on 5 May he recorded that Rossel had visited and studied the Versailles siegeworks: 'The embrasures no longer exist ... all our trenches smashed by artillery have been evacuated ... the Versailles parallel is within sixty metres.' He concluded, 'We are on the point of being surrounded.'

Émile Eudes, who had been sentenced to death for his revolutionary activities before the Commune, was appointed to command Fort Issy and replace Mégy. Eudes described himself as 'General', but he was no soldier, and finding Fort Issy to be a little dangerous, he decamped. Not to put too fine a point on it, he deserted in the face of the enemy. He should have been shot.

On the evening of 7 May, the situation at Fort Issy was critical and Rossel decided that only by taking the offensive could he redress the balance. He anticipated mustering a force of 12,000. Despite his orders, the troops required did not arrive at the assembly area. Rossel had only 7,000. He wreaked punishment on *GN* who had deserted their posts by cutting off the right sleeve of their uniforms. The effect of this cosmetic tailoring exercise was huge, and out of all proportion. It reduced Rossel's authority as battalion commanders publicly withdrew their support. Enough was enough and, after only eight days in post, Rossel sent his resignation to the Delegate for War. Rossel wrote angrily:

I feel myself incapable of continuing to bear the responsibility of a command which everyone discusses, and no one obeys ... The Commune

discusses and has resolved nothing … the *Comité Central* discusses and
has not yet been able to act. During this delay the enemy was surrounding Fort Issy by adventurous and imprudent attacks for which
I should punish him had I the least military force at my disposal … My
predecessor made the mistake of striving against this absurd situation …
I am withdrawing and have the honour to request from you a cell in
the Mazas.

What Rossel did not know was that the Committee for Public Safety had
already decided that he should be sacked and that Dombrowski should
replace him. The remains of Fort Issy were evacuated, and de MacMahon
had accomplished something that Moltke never could: he had captured one of
the defensive forts of Paris. This was the thin end of an increasingly powerful
military wedge.

The Commune had realised that Rigault needed to be reined in and he was
being interrogated as to the scale of his arrests when Delescluze interrupted,
imploring those present to stop the talking. He emphasised the importance of
the loss of Fort Issy and commented: 'While the National Guard does not
want to fight you discuss matters of procedure. We shall still save the country,
although now only from behind barricades. But, put away your mutual
hatreds.'[4] It was a passionate and moving speech.

There was dissension at every level with members of the Central Committee pursuing their own aims; of cohesion, there was none. Rossel was at
the Ministry of War when five members of the *Comité Central* called to tell
him that it was their intention that he should be appointed to be the Military
Dictator of Paris. It was not in the gift of the *Comité* to make such offers and
Rossel rejected it. He knew that de MacMahon would be breaking into the
city in the near future and the rhetoric of the Pyats and Delescluzes of this
world would not be any defence against a determined, increasingly confident
foe. He was confronted by Louis-Charles Delescluze and Augustin Avrial,
who announced that they had a warrant for his arrest. The offence was that he
had posted news of the fall of Fort Issy before consulting the Central Committee. Like so many Commune actions, this one went off at half-cock too.
Delescluze had second thoughts and said that he really could not arrest Rossel
without him first being interrogated by a plenary session of the Committee.
An appointment was made for 10 May – the next day.

Pyat and his acolytes did not want a confrontation with such a commanding
personality as Rossel and they opted instead for trial by court martial, the
president of which would be Jean Collet, a National Guard officer, who was
held in singular contempt by Rossel and wrote later, 'I could not bear the idea
of appearing as an accused before Collet whom I had seen cowering before

the shells at Issy and it was then that I determined to evade the justice of the Commune.'

Rossel had been an asset to the Commune had they but realised it. He decided not to face any interrogation and disappeared and left the Commune to its own chaotic devices.

Notes

1. Merriman, p. 124.
2. Ibid, p. 125.
3. Ibid.
4. Ibid., p. 342.

Chapter Twenty-Two

May: Bloody Week

Louis-Nathaniel Rossel may have lost the confidence of the Central Committee, but he was not without supporters. The Reverend Gibson noted that 'he was regarded by all as a man of talent and capacity, and his retirement a great loss to the Commune'. Gibson also noted on that same day that 'the Column Vendome is still standing; its fall has been put off until Friday'.[1]

Gibson was an astute, neutral observer of Parisian life. On 10 May, he observed:

> in walking through *some* [Gibson's italics] streets of the city, usually full of bustle and business, it seemed to me that I was walking through a city of the dead – no carriages on the roadway, no foot passengers … all silent and deserted.

If it was silent in the streets, it was not in the debating chambers of the Commune. On 15 May, a minority published a vigorous attack on the management of the Commune, which it accused of leading the way to dictatorship, and away from meaningful social and political reform. It provoked a furious response and four members of the Central Committee, including Louis-Eugène Varlin, were suspended. Twenty-two others were denounced as 'deserters in the face of the enemy who merited nothing more than the execution squad'.[2]

Thiers's refusal to agree an exchange of prisoners raised the temperature in Paris and put the lives of the three hostage clergymen at greater risk. There was now a lobby calling for their murder, described as 'execution'. Louise Michel was among the most vociferous. She had been at the forefront of Commune activity from the beginning and now she led the calls for the killing of the clerics and of other

Louise Michel, 'The Red Virgin' (1830–1905).

hostages every twenty-four hours, until Blanqui was released. She was a formidable woman.

The Vendôme Column, and its destruction, attracted rather more attention than it was worth, considering that Marshal de MacMahon and his army were at the gates. Place Vendôme is a square in the 1st arrondissement, dominated by a stone column erected to commemorate the victory of Napoleon I at the Battle of Austerlitz in 1805. A statue of Napoleon was placed at the head of the column.

The column, and Napoleon in particular, symbolised all that the Commune opposed, and its destruction was demanded. The proponent of the measure was the painter Gustave Courbet, a leading Communard and an elected member of the Central Committee who had previously expressed his irritation that this monument to war was located on the rue de la Paix. Courbet argued that:

> In as much as the Vendôme column is a monument devoid of all artistic value, tending to perpetuate by its expression the ideas of war and conquest of the past imperial dynasty, which are reproved by a republican nation's sentiment, citizen Courbet expresses the wish that the National Defense government will authorise him to disassemble this column.[3]

On 16 May, Courbet had his wish and the column was toppled to riotous applause and celebration. The Place Vendôme was located in one of the smart areas of the city and, in earlier times, Parisians would not be seen there unless they lived in the immediate area or worked there. The audience that greeted the well-advertised fall of the column were by no means all dyed-in-the-wool Communards. For many it was no more than a sight-seeing excursion. For Communards, however, it was a serious advance in their cause and all the Commune leaders were present.

The following day, as the Versailles Army moved closer to the walls, there was a violent explosion in a munitions factory on Avenue Rapp.

> The whole east of Paris was shaken. A pyramid of flame, of molten lead, human remains, burning timber and bullets burst forth from the Champ-de-Mars to an enormous height, and showered down upon the environs. Four houses fell in; more than forty persons were wounded.[4]

The immediate presumption was that of sabotage, and a knee-jerk response saw four entirely innocent people arrested. Lissagaray wrote later, 'Who was the culprit? Nobody knows.' Chances are it was just an industrial accident.

Henri de Rochefort, a left-wing journalist and sometime politician, drew the attention of the mob to Louis Thiers's grand house in Place Saint-Georges. Rochefort was not a Communard but sympathised with the cause.

The destruiction of the Vendôme Column, 16 May 1871.

Helpfully he pointed out that the house was full of works of art and he encouraged the sacking and destruction of the building, although he did not sully his hands with the mechanics. He must have taken satisfaction from the wanton vandalism he had initiated. This vandalism was fully endorsed by the Committee of Public Safety, which provided carts to remove the treasures and distributed them among libraries and museums. A young British man, Edwin Child, remarked, 'It was as striking an instance of futile spite as perhaps any revolution can or has to furnish.'[5]

The destruction of the guillotine, the Vendôme Column and Thiers's house were only three examples of a vengeful, irrational society. The two arms of the cross on the Panthéon had been removed and replaced by a red flag, and there was a stated desire to destroy Notre-Dame.

Raoul Urbain, by all accounts an unpleasant man, took the explosion as sufficient reason for him to insist on the execution of ten hostages at once. Rigault, never one to miss an opportunity to cause pain, misery or death, was in full support. The Commune was at a critical moment in its short life; to date, it had only executed three men for military offences but, in addition, it had murdered the two generals. Notwithstanding the ruthless, homicidal conduct of the Versailles troops, any further murders would surely bring the most savage retribution. Eugène Protot, the Minister of Justice, challenged the legality of the proposed measures, a rare voice of reason in a world in which sweet reason was in short supply. Urbain's proposal was rejected. Nevertheless, the lives of the clerics were on a knife-edge. Ambassador Washburne made an approach to Rigault, not the sort of person he usually met in diplomatic circles, and was able to obtain permission to visit the Archbishop in Mazas Prison. Here the Archbishop was housed in 'a gloomy and naked little cell, about six feet by ten'. Washburne wrote later:

> I was deeply touched by the appearance of this venerable man ... his slender person, his form somewhat bent, his long beard, for he has not been shaved apparently since his confinement, his face haggard with ill-health. ... He had no word of bitterness or reproach for his persecutors, but on the other hand remarked that the world judged them to be worse than they really were.[6]

Washburne had seen enough and he called on Thiers and urged him to exchange the Archbishop for Blanqui on the basis that Blanqui was no threat to the French Government and an exchange would save the Archbishop's life. Unfortunately, Adolphe Thiers did not respond well to the diplomat's interference in matters not of his concern and rejected the approach out of hand.

Lord Lyon, writing to Lord Granville, commented waspishly:

> They are very angry here with Mr Washburne for interfering about the Archbishop, and they are still more displeased with him for being so much in Paris. In fact, although he has a room here, he is much more in Paris than in Versailles. M. Thiers observed to me last night that my American colleague had a *conduit très singulière*. They would not stand this in a European representative.[7]

Lyon, who was a patronising apology for an ambassador, had none of the energy, compassion or people skills with which Washburne was gifted.

Washburne made another visit to the Archbishop on 19 May to tell him that Thiers would not negotiate his release. Darboy had pleurisy, was very feeble but apparently resigned to his fate. The two men shook hands, not knowing that this was a final goodbye.[8]

Rigault meanwhile busied himself sorting his hostages into two categories. The first included those perceived to be the most important and included the three clerics, Gustave Chaudey and Jean-Baptiste Jecker, a banker. The second category consisted of police agents, gendarmes and shopkeepers, and this group of fourteen was 'tried' first. The trial with Rigault as prosecutor and judge was a farce. Twelve of the group were sent back to prison to await their fate. The trial of the Archbishop and his group was set for the following week. Rigault's absurd trial alienated Henri de Rochefort, and he burst into print attacking the whole principle of hostage-taking. Warned that Rigault's agents were coming for him, de Rochefort then fled, with his secretary, only to be arrested by Versailles agents. Rigault's assiduous search for 'spies' was ill-directed and entirely arbitrary – he was detaining the wrong people and declaring them to be hostages. Colonel Stanley and the artist Auguste Renoir were both arrested but later released.

The Commune did not exploit its most valuable hostage, which was the Bank of France. Ostensibly now controlled by Beslay, in practice the Marquis de Ploeuc came and went at will and in that process passed funds to Thiers to pay for his rapidly expanding forces. Thiers attempted to suborn leading Communards and by doing so fostered an atmosphere of conspiracy. There were modest successes although the attempt to assassinate Dombrowski failed and the would-be assassin was bayoneted for his trouble. This incident led to the Commune deciding to issue identity cards.

In Versailles, Marshal de MacMahon was now poised to assault the city and he had briefed his commanders of the heavy fighting that lay ahead. In Paris the mayors were united in their aspiration to resolve the conflict between the Commune and the Government and at the end of April had sent a deputation to Versailles. Adolphe Thiers's response was uncompromising. He asked:

> Do you come in the name of the Commune? If so, I shall not listen to you, I do not recognise belligerents ... the supremacy of the law will be re-established ... Paris will be submitted to the authority of the State just as any hamlet of a hundred inhabitants.[9]

Paris was not a closed city and its investment was incomplete. It was not difficult for some people to come and go via Saint-Denis or any other part of the line held by the Germans. They were, supposedly, neutral in what was, now, an all-French affair. The Marquis de Ploeuc came and went at will but, in reality, the neutrality was loaded in favour of the Versailles. A blockade on food getting into Paris depended on the Germans' cooperation to make it a most useful weapon and by mid-May, this was having the desired effect. Inside the city every attempt was made to foster normality and public entertainments were well attended, with a commensurate effect on morale. On the evening of Sunday, 21 May, the Commune held a large open-air concert in the Tuileries Gardens; 1,500 musicians took part, although quite how they were coordinated and grouped is not recorded.

The evening had been a great success but, during the night between 0200 and 0300 hrs, Versailles troops entered the city in large numbers. Marshal de MacMahon had pondered at length the means by which he could break through the great walls of Paris but, in the event, and as one of the great anti-climaxes of military history, his soldiers walked through an open and undefended gate.

Jules-Auguste Ducatel (1830–95).
(Etienne-Gabriel Bocourt, 1871)

It transpired that a man called Jules Ducatel, a tax collector and previously a member of the *Garde Nationale*, was disillusioned with the Commune and all its works. He carried out several reconnaissances on behalf of Versailles whilst still being a member of the Passy Barricades sub-committee. This was dangerous work and, had he been unmasked, his death was assured.

During the night of 21/22 May, Ducatel discovered that the Porte de Saint-Cloud and its surroundings were undefended (see map overleaf, middle, left edge). Ducatel improvised a white flag and waved to draw the attention of the Versailles soldiers manning trenches below bastion 65 on the side of Parc des Princes. For the Commune it was inexplicable, incompetent and unforgivable but, for de MacMahon, it was to be a heaven-sent gift. General Félix Douay commanding IV Corps was alerted, and he referred the matter to Thiers because it was thought, not unreasonably, that it might be a trick.

Douay was given the go-ahead and his men poured through the open gate. Ducatel guided the leading division of IV Corps to the Trocadero. On the way, and at a barricade blocking access to the Quai de Passy, Ducatel was captured. He escaped, survived the ensuing battle and was appointed a Knight of the Legion of Honour by a grateful government.

Marshal de MacMahon had at his command overwhelming force. His army consisted of five corps of ten divisions and he had General Vinoy's Reserve Army in support. The Army, huge as it was, was nevertheless unproved and its reliability was in question. The generals at every level proceeded with caution and were aware that they had to spend the lives of their men very frugally.

Fortuitously for de MacMahon, the Commune were expecting a frontal attack, which they were confident they could repulse, clearly unaware of the size and power of their foe. Initially and fatally, the Commune was completely wrong-footed, and subsequently never recovered. Delescluze was briefed on the situation just before dawn and 'incredibly enough refused to allow the ringing of the tocsin [an alarm signal on a bell] and simply denied that the Versailles had penetrated the walls of Paris'.[10] Adolphe Assi was despatched

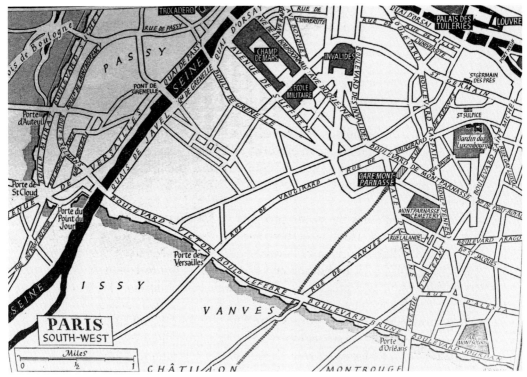

South-West Paris. The assaulting French troops made their entrance through
Porte de St Cloud, middle left of the map and Trocaderno is centre top. (*Horne*)

to reconnoitre the situation and later that day was the first Communard
leader to be captured.

By dawn, on 22 May, over 70,000 Versailles soldiers were inside the walls of
Paris and had seized the heights of Trocadero. With the cooperation of the
Germans, de MacMahon swiftly opened other gates, those at Auteuil, Passy,
Sevres, Porte du Point-du-Jour and Versailles. The city was now wide open,
and the Commune was in disarray. It hastily built more barricades, often with
labour conscripted at bayonet point. This spontaneous defence of the city was
haphazard and uncoordinated. 'The massed Commune guns at Montmartre,
for example, remained silent for many precious hours. Large numbers of
mitrailleuses, which could have killed many government troops, remained
quietly at Montmartre.'[11]

It was in the area of Passy and Auteuil where there had been little fighting
that the first evidence of unlawful killing occurred. A reporter from *Le Gaulois*
found the bodies of about thirty Communards. Local residents averred to the
reporter that the men had been lined up along a ditch and a *mitrailleuses* had
been turned on them.[12]

The French Army held the initiative and by executing a series of turning
movements, it negated many of the barricades by merely circumventing them.
The barricades could then be taken from the flank or rear. By dusk on 22 May,

the eventual outcome of this conflict was clear, just as it became increasingly clear to the National Guard that surrender was not an option.

Adolphe Thiers was an implacable and vengeful adversary. He had said that 'expiation will be complete. It will take place in the name of the law, by the law, and within the law'. Jacobsen remarked: 'Apart from the first sentence, he could not have been more misleading. The bloodbath that now began exceeded the toll of the Great Terror of 1793 and the Russian Revolution of 1917.'

The Army was making steady progress and taking and consolidating its hold on the ground. Much of western Paris was taken and, in the process, the uninhibited killing of prisoners flourished. The high ground of Montmartre was taken, along with its unused and ill-kept guns and forty-nine Communards. This group comprised men, women and a few children. The Army was merciless and took them to the site of the murder of the two generals just over two months before. The prisoners were made to kneel, and then they were summarily shot. This was wanton murder by any civilised measurement.

Wednesday, 24 May was a very black day. The Commune relinquished any residual external support it had when fifty hostages were transferred from Mazas Prison to La Roquette, under the direction of Gaston da Costa, the

Six dead *Garde Nationale* Communards. They are so closely grouped in death that it suggests that they might have been killed with a *mitrailleuse*.

21-year-old deputy Procureur to Raoul Rigault. The priests, trusting souls, thought that they were being released. In fact, they were now in the hands of the deeply unpleasant Théophile Ferré, an inadequate man who had previously eked out a living as a clerk but was now intoxicated by the power he had, having replaced Rigault as Chief of Police. The atmosphere around the prison at La Roquette was incendiary and there was a strident demand from the mob for the immediate execution of Darboy and his fellow priests. Ferré, to his eternal shame, commented: 'If they want the Archbishop, they can have him.' He retrieved his original order to the prison governor ordering the execution of six unspecified hostages and he wrote across it, 'and particularly the Archbishop'.[13]

Georges Darboy, Abbé Duguerry, Abbé Allard, Jesuit fathers Ducoudray and Clercs, and a magistrate, Senator Bonjean, were on the same list. The killing of these six men was as squalid and botched as any Communard enterprise. The firing squad failed and had to fire a second round to bring the victims down. The *coup de grâce* was administered by *GN* bayonets.

Raoul Rigault had reverted to major in the *GN* and had taken his place with his unit in the Latin Quarter. However, he did not stay long and repaired to a hotel on rue Gay-Lussac, where, by happy chance, he maintained a room and an actress. His presence was passed to the Army and Rigault's hotelier was seized and threated with death if he did not reveal Rigault's location. The hotelier's wife appealed to Rigault to save her husband. In a most uncharacteristic act of bravery, Rigault intervened, and by so doing revealed his identity. A sergeant promptly shot Rigault three times in the head. It was deserved, but it was not justice. His body lay in the gutter for two days being spat on by passers-by.

The Communards were being thrashed but they still held parts of eastern Paris and throughout the city they fought with the great courage of men with no hope. Residents everywhere kept a very low profile, but curiosity drove some onto the street to spectate war on their doorsteps – a hazardous pastime. Goncourt was one such and he wrote in his journal that he 'had to see and know'.

All across the city and despite tenacious resistance, the Army was gaining control; along the way, the Commune was losing its leadership. Felix Pyat had delivered a rousing call to arms with an encouragement for all to man the barricades, and then he disappeared, not to be seen again until he emerged in London. Charles Delescluze was made of sterner stuff, but he recognised that the cause was lost. He lamented the failure of the Commune and was seen to take his head in his hands and mutter, 'What a war, what a war ... everything is finished for me.' Wearing, as always, a frock coat, patent leather boots, a red sash around his waist and a silk hat, he strode with François Jourde

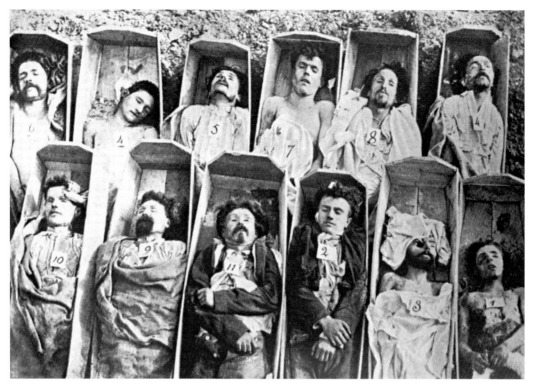

Communard dead, possibly laid out for press photographers.

towards a barricade in Place du Château d'Eau. Delescluze shook several hands and then mounted the barricade. He stood for only a moment before he was shot down. Four men ran to retrieve his body; three of them were shot. Delescluze lay in the street for several days.[14]

The Army did not have all its own way and although IV Corps took the Place d'Étoile and the Arc de Triomphe, it became complacent. Douay's men were marching down the Champs-Élysée heading for Place de la Concorde when they ran into sustained, accurate small arms fire from the Tuileries Gardens. The Commune soldiers were commanded by Brunel, who had been reinstated (see map on page 250). The Army withdrew to lick its wounds. This Commune success did nothing to halt the remorseless advance of de MacMahon across the remainder of the city. General Cissey swept up the rue de Vaugirard and took Montparnasse station.

The Communards were cornered, there was no way out. It was at this stage, on 24 May, that Brunel initiated the burning of Paris. He was holding out at the barricades in the rue Royale and Place de la Concorde. IV Corps had sited sixty guns and they were firing over open sights, wreaking frightful punishment on the defenders. Brunel ordered the torching of several buildings that hindered his defence; the flames spread quickly. 'A good-looking, young woman stood astride the barricade, with the flames as a backdrop. She was instantly shot dead.'[15]

The bodies of fifty or so Communards were gathered and thrown into
the ditch that had provided material for
the adjacent barricade. The bodies were
covered in quicklime, the ditch was
filled in and Douay's guns could trundle
over the mass grave to their next
mission. Dombrowski had resigned his
command position to fight as a rifleman
and, in that guise, he had been killed.
He now lay in state on a blue satin bed
in the Hôtel de Ville.

The flames started to engulf Paris
and any number of buildings had been
gutted, including the Tuileries, a large
section of the Palais-Royal, the Palais
de Justice, the Prefecture of Police, the
Cour des Comptes, the *Legion d'Honneur* and the Conseil d'État. These
flames were so spaced that they were,
clearly, the work of arsonists. Jules
Bergeret, who had been released from
prison, was responsible for the destruction of the Louvre. This was not some
shrewd tactical move but vindictive
vandalism. He moved several barrels of

THE PARIS CARNAGE.

Fifty Thousand Dead Bodies in the Houses and Cellars.

One-Fourth of the City Destroyed by the Flames.

Conflagrations Still Raging in Various Quarters.

The Captive Priests Supposed to Have Been Shot.

The Insurgents Surrounded Within Narrow Limits.

All Survivors to be Dealt With as Criminals.

PROGRESS OF THE STRUGGLE.

New York Times headlines.

gunpowder into the building, spread tar and petroleum liberally, and then lit
the fuse. The explosion blew the central dome to pieces. Bergeret was well
pleased with his work, and reported to the Committee of Public Safety that
'the last relic of Royalty just vanished'. Bergeret escaped the firing squad and
died in penury, in London, in 1905.

By 26 May, de MacMahon had persuaded the Germans to move 10,000
troops to the eastern perimeter of the city, from where their ring barred the
last possible line of escape for the Communards and, in addition, neutralised
the last fortress of Vincennes.

The fires still burned, corpses littered the streets, and Communards had
abandoned their barricades and were seeking hiding places. If they found
one, then here they divested themselves of any item of equipment or clothing
that would identify them. However, slowly and methodically they were all
rounded up. Some escaped the net but for others, retribution was on the
menu.

The Hôtel de Ville, the seat of the governance of Paris, in flames.

The senior army officers on the spot ignored the laws of war and routinely caused prisoners to be shot from their first entrance into Paris. They did not conduct any sort of enquiry, heard no evidence and did not entertain any plea of mitigation. Medical care was denied to wounded Communards and it was administratively much easier to kill them. Some prisoners were sent, under guard, to Versailles, but very few completed the journey and the majority were shot while, allegedly, attempting to escape.

The Marquis de Galliffet established his headquarters in the Bois de Boulogne, where he sorted prisoners, telling them as they arrived, 'I am Galliffet. You people of Montmartre may think me cruel, but I am even crueller than you can imagine.' He lined up prisoners and inspected them, tapping individuals on the shoulder. The person thus selected was marched out to the centre of the Paris-Versailles road, where a special firing squad dealt with him or her.

His basic method of triage was to select men with grey hair on the grounds that they must have fought in 1848, and therefore had erred twice. Men with watches were taken as probable 'officials' of the Commune. Any Communard who was found to have served in the regular army was, of course, shot. A correspondent witnessed Galliffet at work and wrote:

The French are filling up the darkest page in the book of their own or the world's history. The charge of ruthless cruelty is no longer limited to one party or to one class of persons. The Versailles troops seem inclined to outdo the Communists in their lavishness of human blood. The Marquis de Galliffet is escorting a column of prisoners to Versailles or Satory. He picks out eighty-two of them and shoots them at the Arc de Triomphe. Next came a lot of 20 firemen, then a dozen women, one aged 70.

The Revolution is crushed; but at what a cost, and amid what horrors! ... the Communists seem not very much worse than their antagonists. It sounds like trifling for M. Thiers to be denouncing the Insurgents for having shot a captive officer 'without respect for the laws of war'. The laws of war! They are mild and Christian compared with the inhuman laws of revenge under which the Versailles troops have been shooting, bayoneting, ripping up prisoners, women and children, during the last six days.[16]

Galliffet was a monster; he was one of very many.[17] Seventy years or so later, it was people like him who made the 'selections' at Auschwitz and Dachau. Galliffet went on to enjoy a full life, much bemedalled and decorated, and he died in his bed.

**Major General Gaston Alexandre Auguste, Marquis de Galliffet,
Prince de Martigues (1830–1909).**

Notes

1. Gibson, 10 May 1871, p. 231.
2. Godineau, L., *La Commune de Paris* (Parigramme Edition, 2010), pp. 74–7.
3. Nochlin, L., 'Courbet, The Commune and the Visual Arts', in *Courbet* (New York, Thames & Hudson, 2007), pp. 84–94.
4. Lissagaray, P., *History of the Commune* (London, T. Fisher Unwin, 1902), p. 290.
5. Horne, p. 349.
6. Washburne, 17 May 1870.
7. PRO, Lyon to Granville, 18 May 1871.
8. Washburn, E., *Franco-German War* (Washington, 1878), p. 29. Letter of 19 May 1871.
9. Horne, p. 362.
10. Lissagaray, pp. 164–5.
11. Jacobsen, M., *The War of the Paris Commune, 1871* (USMC Command and Staff College).
12. Merriman, p. 138.
13. Horne, p. 396.
14. Tombs, R., *The War against Paris* (Cambridge University Press, 1991), p. 157.
15. Horne, p. 386.
16. *The Times*, reports of 29 and 31 May 1871.
17. Jacobsen.

Chapter Twenty-Three

Retribution

The Franco-Prussian/German War has given rise to thousands of books, pamphlets and academic papers. It could be argued that all that endeavour is all about the facts – would that it were so simple. The presentation of the 'facts' to become 'history' is usually heavily influenced by the victor.

In every war retribution is in the hands of the victor. In Paris, in May 1871, when the shooting stopped in the war between the French Government and the Commune, the killing went on as justice, of a sort, was meted out to the vanquished. There is a healthy consensus among historians that 17,000 to 25,000 people were killed during the Commune and its suppression.

Lissagaray favours 17,000 to 20,000. Pellatan opts for 30,000 and estimated that, of these, 10,000 to 14,000 were incinerated and buried outside the walls of Paris.[1] Horne settled on 20,000 to 25,000, and in defending that span, avers that the Municipality of Paris paid for the disposal of 17,000 corpses.[2] These suspiciously neat and rounded-up figures were sometimes tweaked for political purposes. For example, when Louise Michel spoke at Louis-Auguste Blanqui's funeral in 1881, she favoured the Pellatan figure of 30,000. On occasions, even 40,000 is a figure that has been conjured with.

It is argued that these figures are vastly inflated and, although the suppression of the Commune was brutal and merciless, the numbers are not supported by the evidence. Professor Robert Tombs analysed public records and, in his erudite paper, concluded that the death toll was 5,700 to 7,400.[3] He quoted his evidence to support those figures.

No mass graves were recorded, and none have been found on the alleged sites of mass incineration and burial. This author is persuaded by Robert Tombs. His paper is recommended reading for other historians who might address the subject. This reappraisal of the death toll does not ameliorate the horror of the suppression, but it does provide a realistic platform from which to consider the bloodletting, which includes about 750 Versailles soldiers.

As passions cooled, so the summary shooting of prisoners slowed and then ceased. However, Adolphe Thiers and his government had a thirst for retribution and courts were established to try surviving Communards for a selection of crimes. There was a range of punishments open to the judges who sat in a city ravaged by fire: 36,309 people were confined and twenty-six courts martial were established to deal with them, and their work continued until 1875.

A number of the most high-profile Communards did not get the privilege of a trial but were summarily sentenced. Their number included Ferré and Lullier, who were both sentenced to death; however, Lullier's sentence was later commuted to life imprisonment. Rossel was tried twice, and there was a strong lobby for mercy on his behalf. He was sentenced to death, but the sentence was not carried out. He was then tried a second time when even his prosecutors evidently had some sympathy for him. Nevertheless, he was found guilty and re-sentenced. He and the odious Ferré were shot at the same time. Urbain was awarded 'hard labour for life'. A group including Alfred Billioray and Paschal Grousset were transported to New Caledonia, where they made the acquaintance of Antoni Berezowski, the man who failed to assassinate the Tsar (see page 8).

Justice was not rushed and eventually the three men judged to be prime movers for the murder of Generals Lecomte and Thomas and the individual responsible for the death of Chaudey all faced a firing squad. In April 1872, Gustave Genton, who had played a large part in the murders of the Archbishop and his fellow clerics, met a similar fate. It was bizarre that long after his death, Rigault was sentenced to be shot.

Rue de Rivoli after the fighting ceased and the fires were extinguished.

Many Communards escaped any sort of retribution and London proved to be a popular bolthole. By 1880, tempers had cooled and a general amnesty was declared. A number of Communards returned to play an honourable part in French public life.

Hippolyte-Prosper Lissagaray wrote a harrowing account of the privations suffered by Communards imprisoned or transported. He was a participant in Commune activities and a committed left-wing Republican. Unsurprisingly, his book makes no attempt at neutrality, although he made every effort to produce an accurate record. While producing his book he interviewed survivors in exile in London and Switzerland. Karl Marx collaborated in the writing of the book while Lissagaray was exiled in London until 1880. He starts his account by writing:

> From the first days of June the prisoners were filed off to the seaports and crowded into cattle-wagons, the awnings of which, hermetically closed, let in no breath of air. In a corner was a heap of biscuits; but themselves thrown upon this heap, the prisoners had soon reduced it to mere crumbs. For twenty-four hours, and sometimes thirty-two hours, they remained without anything to drink. They fought in this throng for a little air, a little room. Some, maddened, flung themselves upon their comrades.[4]

Lissagaray was a partisan reporter and the tone of his book reveals his sympathies and his residual anger. He held a strong view on the validity of the judicial system, commenting:

> Twenty-six courts-martial, twenty-six judicial machine-guns, were at work at Versailles, Mont-Valérien, Paris, Vincennes, St. Cloud, Sevres, St. Germain, Rambouillet, as far as Chartres. In the composition of these tribunals not only all semblance of justice, but even all military rules had been despised. The Assembly had not even troubled itself to define their prerogatives. These officers, hot from the struggle, and for whom every resistance, even the most legitimate, is a crime, had been let loose upon their overwhelmed enemies without any other jurisprudence than their fancy, without any other rein than their humanity, without any other instruction than their commission.

A year after the fall of the Commune the majority of the 36,309 of those incarcerated had been dealt with: 1,179 had died in prison and 22,326 had been released, albeit after almost a year in prison in appalling conditions. Of the 10,488 who faced a court martial, 8,526 were found to be culpable and awarded some degree of punishment; of these, 7,000 were transported.[5] In total, 250 Communards were executed – a surprisingly small number considering the number of insurgents fighting the Government.

Adolphe Thiers, having destroyed the Commune, could have anticipated a lengthy period in office but by the time he had put France on the successful road to economic recovery and paid in full the war indemnity to Germany, he resigned and was replaced by Marshal Patrice de MacMahon. de MacMahon was not content with the results of the courts martial and on 1 January 1875, caused the matter to be revisited. As a result, a further 10,137 were convicted and punished to some degree, and of these, fifteen people were sentenced to death.

By the mid-1870s the Republican Government realised that it could not realistically regain Alsace-Lorraine by military action. France's best chance to reclaim at least part of its former glory was to present a united, peaceful front to the rest of Europe. It was politically advantageous both within France and internationally to distance the Third Republic from the wars of the French Revolution, from the imperial pursuits of the first Napoleon, and from the revolutionary fervour of the Commune.[6]

Thereafter the economic and social recovery of France was remarkably swift. An amnesty, granted in 1880, went a long way, if not to healing old wounds, at least to ameliorating their effects. 'Though many former Communards remained bitter opponents of what they saw as a bourgeois republic, others accepted it as the best thing on offer, and some served it as elected politicians.'[7]

Notes

1. Pellatan, C., *La Semaine de Mai* (Paris, 1880), pp. 393–4, 396.
2. Horne, p. 418.
3. Tombs, R., 'How Bloody was La Semaine Sanglante of 1871?' (Cambridge University Press, *The History Journal*, Vol. 55, No. 3, September 2012), pp. 619–704.
4. Lissagaray, H.P., *History of the Paris Commune of 1871* (London, 1876).
5. Ibid.
6. Chrastil, R., 'Who Lost the Franco-Prussian War? Blame, Politics, and Citizenship in the 1870s', (*Journal of Western Society for French History*, Vol. 32, 2004).
7. Prof. Robert Tombs in an email to the author, 22 September 2020.

Chapter Twenty-Four

Did the Siege of Paris Change the World?

The Siege of Paris was the catalyst for social, political and military change, to some degree, in all Western countries. The change process started with the Paris city planning activities of Baron Georges-Eugène Haussmann from 1853 to 1870. He razed the poorer, medieval areas of the city, which were overcrowded and unhealthy. In their place he built the wide boulevards for which Paris is famous today, which although desirable architecturally were, at the time, socially disastrous. Although his schemes were challenged, they went ahead despite having only limited provision for the rehousing of those people evicted from their homes.

Although the installation of a sewage system, new parks and squares were sensible measures, they did little for those deposed families at the bottom of the social scale. They were correct when they believed themselves to have been abandoned by the remainder of French society. The siege, imposed by the Germans, added to their deprivation and frustration. Boredom and poverty combined with contempt for the politicians and generals led eventually to spontaneous anger and violence. Haussmann, although well-meaning, had initiated a domestic timebomb with a long fuse.

Parisian society was unequal. The social, educational and economic gap between the three classes – proletariat, bourgeoisie and nobility – was vast and apparently unbridgeable. The working conditions for those at the bottom of the social order were appalling, child labour was commonplace, there was no security of employment, no sickness benefit, no pension system – it was a social jungle and only the strongest or well-paid skilled workers survived. It is generally accepted that the Siege of Paris inadvertently provided the seedbed for a revolution as conditions led, inexorably, to the rise of the Commune when the majority rose in protest. Not all of those protesting sought violence and not all were members of the Commune, but all were united in seeking some more equable form of government, a Republic 'démocratique et sociale'.

The Commune, although not a communist organisation, has, for 150 years, been viewed with favour by communists worldwide. Trotsky averred, 'Each time we study the history of the Commune we see something new in it, thanks to the experiences gained, in later revolutionary struggles ...'[1] However,

This is a scene prior to Haussmann's planning. It shows a section of the Bièvre River, which ran through an industrialised area of Paris and was little more than an open sewer. It was used to dump the waste from tanneries; it emptied into the Seine.

although the Commune was/is much admired in some political circles, its deficiencies are not ignored, and:

> it is scarcely surprising that Trotsky, brilliant military strategist and creator of the Red Army, should have been exasperated by the Commune's lack of military success, by its vacillations, by the 'inefficiency' of a number of its leaders and by its total lack of a clearly thought-out military policy, when confronted by a cynical bourgeoisie prepared ruthlessly to destroy it.[2]

The revolutionaries' naïve blundering two months in control of Paris exposed the inherent weakness of a spontaneous uprising, anywhere. Unless it can meet Trotsky's clearly stated criteria and has clear administrative and military aims.

> The Communists had to be able to explain the defeat of the Commune in a way that did not make it appear that all revolutions were doomed to failure. Hence, from Marx onwards, they came up with ideas about how the Commune could have succeeded.[3]

For success in any activity, be it civil, military or commercial, there has to be a leadership equipped with the skills, determination and sense of urgency to see the task through. Flawed though the Paris Commune was, and despite its failure, nevertheless, its influence is felt worldwide today and in this respect the Siege of Paris changed the world. One outcome was the long-term establishment of a democratic, republican form of government in France, now the norm throughout Europe, where monarchies have been in retreat since 1918.

One of the more extreme political postures arising from the siege was the perceived merit of defunding and disabling of the police. There are groups today, in the UK and the USA, who promote the merits of a society without rules, without any hierarchical structure and without a police function. It certainly did not work in 1871 for Rigault, who rapidly changed his position. Thereafter, Paris was well ordered.

Notwithstanding the deficiencies of the Commune, in 1964 a three-man team of Russian cosmonauts embarked on a mission into space in the spaceship *Voskhod*. They took with them three items of significance. These were photographs of Marx and Lenin, and a ribbon taken from a Communard flag – a measure of the importance to Communist Russia of the ill-fated Commune.

The military impact of the Franco-Prussian War and specifically the Siege of Paris was huge, not least on Germany. It was the first European 'Railway War' that showed that logistic superiority, in purely materiel terms, is irrelevant unless there are the means of transport and distribution. Winston Churchill famously averred that 'victory is a bright-coloured flower. Transport is the stem without which it could never have blossomed.'[4]

The Prussian superiority in transport was a lesson well learned in the 1870s and sixty years later, in the 1930s, the German government of the day constructed the autobahn system for ease of military movement. Those roads are still here today, a tool of the NATO alliance.

The abject failures of the French Army and the overwhelming superiority of the Prussian/German Army exposed the criticality of several issues and provided armies around the world with ample food for thought. The first of these issues was the basis of military recruitment, and the second, the training of those officers and men. Third was the need for a well-trained, multi-skilled General Staff to manage a campaign. Finally, the need to accept that logistic support is a function of command.

It was this final issue that was the nemesis of the French Army. Its *Intendance* (Supply Corps, in English) was not prepared nor equipped to fight a war, even on its own territory, and it paid the penalty in blood. French soldiers were constantly deficient in food, ammunition, warm clothing and medical supplies. Soldiers around the world learned from the egregious French mistakes, of which the dearth of maps was the first. The need for coordinated railway movement was noted, as was the power of the telegraph. The most effective deployment of machine guns was considered, and the supremacy of artillery accepted. Krupp changed the world and won the war with his breech-loading rifled guns. The bolt-action rifle, like the Chassepôt, was the future, and it provided an example of the French, albeit briefly, leading in military technology. The one lesson not learned was the obsolescence of cavalry. Forty-four years later, European armies were still expecting to use cavalry to exploit the 'breakthroughs' that never came. The horse was not entirely redundant and, as late as 1945, the Germans and Russians were using horsepower.

France had been the pre-eminent military power in Europe, but its defeat in 1871 consigned it to a much-reduced status. Its army, once admired, no longer set the standard. Germany assumed its role, built on its strength and, eventually, from this springboard challenged the British Empire. The German staff system was admired and adopted or adapted to fit by most armies. Three French Marshals of France were young men in 1871. Ferdinand Foch (1851–1929) was a private soldier in 4th Infantry Regiment; Joseph Joffre (1852–1931) was a junior artillery officer during the Siege of Paris. Both of them held the Germans in low regard and the high point of their careers was fighting to defeat Germany in 1918.

The third, Marshal Phillippe Pétain (1856–1951), was only a schoolboy during the siege, but thereafter an implacable adversary of the Germans. He epitomised French martial spirit in 1915–16 in his defence of Verdun. However, he shares with Marshal François Bazaine the doubtful distinction of facing a court martial charged with treason. For these men, the siege and its aftermath shaped their lives and those of all their peers.

After mid-1871 there was a realignment of the world's leading powers. France, previously a leader of this group, had ceded territory to Germany and was completely humiliated. This was not a position from which to exercise any degree of influence and certainly not the platform to strike any sort of military posture. Elsewhere in Europe in particular there was increasing militarism and an anxiety from which the newly formed German Empire was not exempt. 'It was too easy for a generation which had seen its nation founded by military strength after centuries of division and impotence to believe that military strength must be the chief factor in its preservation.'[5] German militarism was born in 1871, grew in maturity over the next forty years and eventually felt able to challenge the UK, then the world power.

Post 1871, the USA, recovering from the wounds suffered in its civil war, was intent upon economic revival through the fostering of Big Business. It was aloof from European affairs.[6] The UK was enjoying the summer of its Empire and relishing its unchallenged place in the world order. There were some who were alarmed at Germany's demonstrable military prowess. One of them was George Chesney, who wrote a pamphlet in 1871 entitled 'The Battle of Dorking', in which he postulated the idea that the Germans might now invade the UK. The Germans had no such aspirations in 1871 but, seventy years later …

However, for the most part there was no appreciation that a monster had been born in 1871 that would, ere long, rise up and involve the UK in a war of unparalleled horror. A German historian, eighty years after all these events, identified the full significance of the Franco-Prussian War, writing of 'that sinister problem of modern national war from which the great catastrophes of our epoch have developed and on which we have foundered twice in succession'.[7]

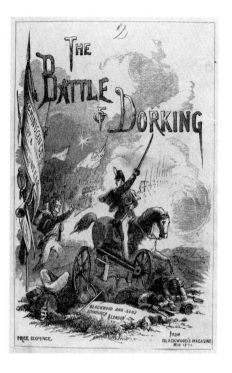

It is appropriate to give the last word on the subject to the doyen of military historians, Professor Michael Howard, in whose judgement:

> Germany's magnificent and well-deserved victory was, in a profound and unforeseeable sense, a disaster: for herself, and for the entire world.[8]

Notes

1. Talès, C., *La Commune de 1871* (Librairie du Travail, Paris, 1924).
2. Guillaume, P. & Grainger, M., 'The Commune: Paris 1871' (Solidarity pamphlet, No. 35).
3. Prof. Robert Tombs in an email to the author, 22 September 2020.
4. Churchill, W.S., *The River War: A Historical Account of the Reconquest of the Soudan* (London, Longmans & Green, 1899).
5. Howard, p. 455.
6. Horne, p. 428.
7. Ritter, G., *Staatskunst und Krirgshandwek: das Problemdes Militarismus in Deutschland*, Vol. I (Munich, 1954), p. 329.
8. Howard, p. 456.

Bibliography

Primary Sources

Andlau, Baron, d', *Metz: Campagne et Négociations* (Paris, 1871).

Bapst, C.G., *Le Marechal Canrobert* (Vol. IV, Paris, 1898–1913).

Bazaine, F.A., *Procès Bazaine* (Capitulation of Metz, Versailles, Paris, 1873).

Bismarck, O.E. von, *Bismarck, die gesammelten Werke*, 15 vols, (London, 1898).

Blumenthal, C.C.A., von Graf, *Journals of FM Count von Blumenthal for 1866 and 1870–71* (London, 1903).

Busch, M., *Bismarck: Some secret pages of his history*, 2 vols (New York, 1898).

Busch, M., *Graf Bismarck und seine Leute Wöhrend des Krieges mit Frankreich* (Leipzig, 1878).

Cluseret, G., *Memoires du General Cluseret: Tome III* (Paris, 1887).

d'Aurelle, de Paladines, *La Première Armée de la Loire* (2nd ed., Paris, 1872).

Daily News (London, 1870/71).

Defourny, P.G., *La bataille de Beaumont* (Brussels 1872).

Dresden, SKA, ZS, 158, 13 December 1870.

Ducrot, A.A., *Défense de Paris*, 2 vols (E. Dentu, 1876).

Ducrot, A.A., *La Journée de Sédan* (Paris, 1871).

Eichthal, L., *Le General Bourbaki* (Paris, 1885).

Engels, F., *Revolution and Counter Revolution in Germany* (*New York Tribune*, September 1852), Chapter XVII.

Evans, T.W., *History of the American Ambulance Established in Paris during the Siege of 1870–71* (London, 1872).

Favre, J., *Gouvernement de la Défense National* (Paris, 1871–75).

Forbes, A., *Daily News*, December 1870.

Frederick III, *The War Diary of the Emperor Frederick III, 1870–1871*, trans. & ed by A.R Allinson, 1927.

Freycinet, C. de, *Guerre en Province* (Paris, 1871).

GGS, The Franco-German War 1870–71: 1881, Part 1; Vols 1–3.

Gibson, W., *Paris during the Commune* [1895] (Trieste Publishing, 2017).

Godineau, L., *La Commune de Paris*, (Parigramme Edition, 2010).

Godineau, L., *Les Barricades de Mai 1871, chez Jules Vallès* (La Commune de Paris, L'Insurgé).

Goncourt, E. & J., de, *Journal 1851–95* (Paris, 1896).

Hansard, Vol. 206, 23 May 1871.

Harrison, F., 'The Revolution and the Commune', *Fortnightly Review*, 53:9, May 1871.

Herisson, M. D', *Journal of a Staff Officer* (London, 1885).

Heylli, G., d', *Journal du Siege de Paris*, Vol. 3, (Paris, 1871–74).

Illustrated London News, December 1870.

Jacqmin, F., *Les Chemins de fer pendant la Guerre de 1870–71* (Paris, 1872).

Kretschman, H. von, *Kriegsbriefe aus den jahren 1870–71* (ed. Lilly Braun) (Stuttgart, 1904).

Labouchère, H. *Diary of the Besieged Resident in Paris* (Project Gutenberg, 2006). Reprinted from *The Daily News*, with Several New Letters and Preface (London, Hurst and Blackett, 1871).

Larchey, L., *Mémorial illustré des deux sièges de Paris* (Paris, 1872).
Lehmann, G., *Die Mobilmachung von 1870–71* (Berlin, 1905).
Leighton, J., *Paris under the Commune*, Chap. XXVIII (London, 1871).
Lissagaray, P., *History of the Commune* (London, T. Fisher Unwin, 1902).
Lockroy, E., *La Commune et l'Assemblée* (1871).
London *Standard*, 13 July 1870.
Maistre, P.A., *Spicheren* (Paris, Berger-Levrault & cie, 1908).
Manchester Guardian, 18 January 1871.
Marx, K., & Engels, F., *The Communist Manifesto*, Chap IV (The Communist League, London, 1848).
Matthias, A., *Meine Kriegserinnerungen* (Munich, Verlagsbuchhandlung Beck, 1912).
Maurice, F., *The Franco-German War 1870–71* (London, S. Sonnenschein & Co., 1899).
Pall Mall Gazette, 1 August 1870.
Pelet-Narbonne, G. von, *Cavalry on Service* (London, 1906).
Pellatan, C., *La Semaine de Mai* (Paris, 1880).
Ranc, A., 'Small Memories' (*Le Matin*, 12 October 1897).
Reinach, J., *Dépêches, Circulaires, Décrets, Proclamations et Discours de Léon Gambetta*, 2 vols (Paris, 1886).
Roon, A.T.E., von, *Denkwurdigkeiten* (Breslsu, 1897).
Ryan, C.E., *With an Ambulance during the Franco-Prussian War 1870–71* (London, 1896).
Sarrepont, H. de, *Histoire de la Defense de Paris en 1870–71* (Paris,1872).
Simon, J., *The Government of M. Thiers* (New York, C. Scribner's Sons, 1879).
SKA ZGS, 158 Lt Hinuber 'Tagebuch'.
Stoffel, E.G., *Rapports militaires ècrits de Belin 1866–70* (Paris, 1871).
The Globe, 27 July 1870.
Thiers, L.A., *Notes et Souvenirs de M. Thiers 1870–73* (Paris, 1904).
Trochu, L.-J., *L'Armée française en 1867* (Paris, 1887).
Trochu, L.-J., *Oeuvres posthumes I: La Siege de Paris* (Tours, 1896).
Varlin, E., *Pratique militant et écrits d'un ouvrier communard* (ed. Lejeune, P.) (1977).
Verdy du Vernois, J., von, *With the Royal Headquarters in 1870–71* (London, K. Paul, Trench, Treubner & Co. Ltd., 1897).
Vignon, P., *Rien que ce que j'ai vu! Le Siège de Paris – la Commune* (Paris, 1913).
Vinoy, J., *Campagne Paris 1872 de 1870–71, Siège de Paris, Operations du 13e Corps et de la Troisième Armée* (Paris, 1872).
Vuillaume, M., *Mes Cahiers rouges au temps de la Commune* [1909] (Paris, 1971).
Wartensleben, H.L., von Graf, *Operations of the Southern Army in January and February 1871* (London, 1872).
Washburne, E. B., *Franco-German War and the insurrection of the Commune* (Washington, US Government Print Office, 1878).
Washburne, E.B., *Recollections of a Minister to France 1869–77* (New York, C. Scribner's Sons, 1887).
Whitehurst, F.M., *The Siege of Paris*, 2 vols (London, Tinsley Bros, 1875).
Wimpffen, E.F., *Sédan* (Paris, 1871).
World's Fair magazine, Vol. VI, No. 3.

Secondary Sources

Badsey, S., *The Franco-Prussian War 1870–71* (Oxon, Ospray, 2003).
Bargain-Villeger, A., 'Captain Tin Can. Gustave Cluseret and the Socialist Lefts, 1848–1900' (Lawrence Wishart, *Socialist History*, 2014).

Bismarck, O.E. von., *Erinnerung und Gedanke, die gesammelten Werke* (ed. Ritter, G. & Stadelmann R.) (Berlin, 1932).

BKA HS 856, *Landwehr* – Lt Josef Krumper.

Bronsart, S.P. von, *Geheimes Kriegstagebuch, 1870–71* (ed. Rassow, P.) (Bonn, 1954).

Bury, J.T.P., *Gambetta and National Defence* (Bath University).

Busch, W., *Das Deutsche Große Hauptquartier die Bekampfung von Paris im Feldzuge 1870–71* (Stuttgart, 1905).

Busch, W., *Das deutschegrosse 1492–2015* (4th ed.) (Jefferson, N. Carolina, McFarland, 2017).

Chalmin, P., *L'Officier française 1815–1870* (Paris, 1958).

Chrastil, R., *The Siege of Strasbourg* (Harvard University Press, 2014).

Churchill, W.S., *The River War: A Historical Account of the reconquest of the Soudan* (London, Longmans & Green, 1899).

Chrastil, R., 'Who Lost the Franco-Prussian War? Blame, Politics, and Citizenship in the 1870s', *Journal of Western Society for French History*, Vol. 32, 2004.

Clark, T.J., *The Painting of Modern Life: Paris in the Art of Monet and his Followers* (New Jersey, Princeton University Press, 1984).

Clearchus, 401 BC, 'Speech to the Ten Thousand'.

Clodfelter, M., *Warfare and Armed Conflicts: A Statistical Encyclopedia of Casualty and Other Figures* (Jefferson, N. Carolina, McFarland & Co., 2017).

Duveau, G., *La Siège de Paris* (Paris, Hachette, 1939).

Earle, E.M., *Makers of Modern Strategy* (New Jersey, Princeton University, 1941).

Edwards, H.S., *The Germans in France* (London, Stanford, reprinted 2019).

Edwards, S., *The Communards of Paris 1871* (London, Thames & Hudson, 1973).

Edwards, S., *The Paris Commune* (Newton Abbot, Eyre & Spottiswood, 1971).

Encyclopaedia Britannica, 1911.

Fermer, D., *Sédan, 1870: The Eclipse of France* (Barnsley, Pen & Sword, 2008).

Fitzmaurice, E.P., *Life of Lord Granville*, 2 vols (London, 1905).

Gopnik, A., 'The Fires of Paris: Why do people still fight about the Paris Commune?', *The New Yorker*, 22 December 2014.

Grosjean, E., *Belfort: la sentinelle de la liberté 1870–1871* (Colmar, 1970).

Guillaume, P. & Grainger, M., 'The Commune: Paris 1871', Solidarity pamphlet, No. 35.

Gullickson, G., *Unruly Women* (New York, Ithaca, 1996).

Horne, A., *The Fall of Paris: The Siege and Commune 1870–71* (London, Macmillan, 1965).

Horne, J. & Kramer, A., *German Atrocities 1914* (USA, New Haven, 2001).

Howard, M., *The Franco-Prussian War* [1961] (Oxon, Routledge, 2006).

Hutton, P.H., *The Cult of Revolutionary Tradition; The Blanquists in French Politics 1864–1893* (University of California Press, 1981).

Jacobsen, M., *The War of the Paris Commune, 1871* (USMC Command and Staff College).

Jellinek, F., *The Paris Commune of 1871* [1930] (reprinted by Hesperides Press, 2013).

Joubert de la Ferté, P., *The Third Service* (London, Thames & Hudson, 1955).

Kaiser, K., Paris Commune of 1871 (Stanford University, *Crisis Committee*, 17–19 October 2014).

Merriman, J., *Massacre* [2014] (Yale University Press, 2016).

Milza, P., *L'année terrible: La Commune Mars-Juin 1871* (Paris, Perrin, 2009).

Montaudon, J.-B., *Souvenirs Militaires*, 2 vols (Paris, 1898–1900).

Mumford, L., *The City in History: Its Origins, Its Transformations, Its Prospects* (Sidcup, Harcourt, 1961).

Nash, N.S., *Logistics of the Vietnam Wars 1945–75* (Barnsley, Pen & Sword, 2020).

Nochlin, L., 'Courbet, The Commune and the Visual Arts' in *Courbet* (New York, Thames & Hudson, 2007).

Pflanze, O., *The Rise and Fall of the Second Empire*, Vol. 1 (Princetown, 1990).

Prevost, M., 'Assi', *Dictionary of French Biography, Tome III* (Paris, Letouzey and Ané, 1939).

Rials, S., *Nouvelle Histoire de Paris de Trochu à Thiers 1870–73* (1985).

Ritter, G., *Staatskunst und Krirgshandwek: das Problemdes Militarismus in Deutschland*, Vol. I (Munich, 1954).

Roth, G., 'Field Marshal von Moltke the Elder, His importance Then and Now', *Army History*, No. 23, Summer 1992).

Rounding, V., *Les Grandes Horizontales* (London, Bloomsbury, 2003).

Seltzer, G., 'The American Ambulance in Paris, 1870–1871' (Univ. of Carolina, Wilmington, 2009).

Steinberg, J., *Bismarck: A Life* (Oxford University Press, 2011).

Talès, C., *La Commune de 1871* (Librairie du Travail, Paris, 1924).

Tombs, R., 'How Bloody was La Semaine Sanglante of 1871?', *The History Journal*, Vol. 55, No. 3, September 2012.

Tombs, R., *The Paris Commune* (London, Longmans, 1999).

Vizetelly, E., *My Adventures in the Commune* [1914] (Wentworth Press, 2019).

von Schellendorff, B., *Geheimes Kriegstagbuch, 1870–71* (Bonn, 1954).

Waldersee, Graf A, von, *Denkwurdigkeiten*, 3 vols (Berlin, 1922).

Wawro, G., *The Franco-Prussian War* (Cambridge University Press, 2003).

West, R., *War and Peace in Vietnam* (London, Sinclair Stevenson, 1995).

Index

10 Corps (P), 54

11 Corps (P), 54

1st Army (P), 33, 36–7, 39, 45, 51, 55, 59, 83, 91, 166–7, 189, 192

2nd Army (F), 147, 159, 167

2nd Army (P), 33, 36–7, 40, 45, 55, 59, 83, 120, 123–4, 183, 190–1

3rd Army (P), 33, 36–7, 42, 50, 62, 68–9, 73, 84, 98, 176, 224

II Bavarian Corps (P), 42–3, 117

I Corps (F), 30, 33, 44,

II Corps (F), 30, 34–6, 44–5, 49, 51, 53, 58, 152

II Corps (P), 117, 189

III Corps (F), 30, 35–6, 44, 46, 53, 151

III Corps (P), 53

IV Corps (F), 31, 39, 44, 265, 269

IV Corps (P), 59, 63–4

V Corps (F), 31, 36, 42, 44, 62–5

VI Corps (F), 31, 33, 35, 45, 53, 56

VI Corps (P), 105

VII Corps (F), 31, 44, 60, 62, 64

VII Corps (P), 46, 52

Army of Châlons (F), 30, 33–4, 49–50, 55, 59–60, 62, 65, 68, 120

Army of the East, (F), 171, 192, 207

Army of the Loire (F), 111, 116, 131, 143, 145, 152, 154, 159, 161, 168, 171, 176, 190–2

Army of the Marne (P), 84

Army of the North (F), 158, 167, 171–2, 174, 197, 204

Army of the Rhine (F), 33, 55, 101, 125–6, 129–30, 156

Army of the South, (P), 194

Abdication, 74

Adam, Edmond, 133, 137–8

Albert, Crown Prince of Saxony, 59, 149, 152

Alexander II, Tsar of Russia, 7–8, 10, 113, 192, 215, 248

Alsace, 33–4, 85–6, 98, 133, 139, 200, 210, 213, 277

Ambulance, 5, 145, 164, 169–70, 176–7, 283–4, 286

Amiens, 155, 157–9, 161, 163, 165–9

Ammunition, 16, 19, 26, 57, 59, 56, 83, 88, 92, 101, 109, 113, 118, 120–1, 130, 140, 142–3, 152, 161, 175, 179–80, 220, 250, 280

Amnesty, 276–7

Arago, Étienne, 8, 10, 74–5, 106, 135

Armistice, 71, 75, 109, 121–2, 128–9, 133–4, 138–9, 188, 191, 193, 197–206, 208, 212–13, 215, 246

Arrest, 76, 86, 95, 110, 135, 138–9, 234, 240, 244–5, 251, 253–4, 256, 258, 261, 264

Arsonists, 270

Assembly, 79, 139, 200, 210, 212–13, 216–17, 226–30, 241, 257, 276

Assi, Adolph, 236–7, 244, 265

Association des Amies et Amis de la Commune de Paris 1871, 234

Atrocities, 103, 107, 157, 169, 245

Avron, Mont, Fort, 149, 152, 169, 180–1

Balloon, 10, 102–103, 109–10, 140–2, 144–5, 152, 161

Ballot, 14, 17

Bank of France, 235, 237, 284

Bapaume, 174–5

Barricades, barriers, 86, 143, 254, 258, 265–6, 268–70, 283

Bavaria, Bavarians, 172

Bazaine, Marshal François Achille, 2, 8, 16, 30–3, 35, 44–6, 48, 50–1, 53–62, 65, 79, 106, 109, 117, 120–30, 132–3, 201, 281, 263

Bazeilles, 65–6, 70
Beaumont, 59, 62–5, 69, 71–2, 283
Belfort, 26, 49, 86, 155–9, 161, 163, 165, 167
Belleville, 134–5, 149, 198, 212, 217–18
Berezowski, Antoni, 8–9, 275
Bergeret, Jules, 237, 241–6, 248, 270
Besançon, 113, 201–202
Beslay, Charles, 235–7, 264
Bézier, Leonard, 143–4
Blanchard, Gen., 142, 158
Blankets, 16, 26, 113, 143, 152
Blanqui, Louis Auguste, 75, 104, 110, 134–6, 138, 199, 217, 234, 253, 256, 261, 263, 274
Bloodbath, 137, 267
Bois de Boulogne, 82, 95, 97, 271
Bombardment, 68, 101, 106, 119, 137, 143, 145, 171, 176, 178–81, 183–7, 250–2
Bonapartist, 75, 121, 213–14, 235, 246
Bordeaux, 157, 169, 197, 200, 204, 206, 210, 213, 216, 225, 251
Bourbaki, Maj. Gen. Charles-Denis, 31, 123–4, 142, 168–9, 171–2, 188–94, 197, 199, 201–202, 204–205, 207, 238
Bourgeoisie, 104, 229–30, 278–9
Bowles, Tommy Gibson, 143, 149–51, 154, 175, 177, 185
Boyer, Col. Napoléon, 58, 126–9
Bread, 97, 101, 128, 164, 167–8, 176, 194, 250
Break-out, break-through, break off, 2, 36, 44, 56–8, 60–1, 118, 120–6, 140, 142–3, 146, 192, 202, 264, 281
Brie, 145, 149, 151–2
Bronsart, Lieut. Col. Paul von Schellendorf, 106, 170, 173–4, 177–80, 187, 285
Brunel, Lieut. Paul-Antoine, 212, 224–5, 227, 229–30, 246, 269
Budget, 14, 26
Buzenval, 119, 192, 194–6

Capitulation, 2, 58, 79, 108, 110, 120, 124, 129, 180, 203, 283
Casus belli, 24, 29, 216
Châlons, 26, 30, 33–4, 44, 49, 55, 59, 61, 113
Chamber of Deputies, 74, 230
Champigny, 142–3, 145–6, 149, 152

Champs-Élysée, 269
Chanzy, Gen. Antoine, 152, 168–9, 171, 188, 190–3, 197, 199, 201, 205
Chassepôt rifle, 19, 35, 40–2, 46, 55, 108, 113, 115–16, 119, 130, 183, 222, 252, 281
Châtillon, 87–9, 92, 117, 182, 242, 244, 251
Chaudey, Gustave, 199, 263, 275
Chaville, 242
Chevilly, Battle of, 105–106, 108
Chief of Staff, 25, 32, 73, 117, 134, 173, 176, 240, 254, 281
Child, Edwin, 230, 262
Churchill, Sir Winston, 111, 280, 282, 285
Citizen Delegate, 235
Civil disobedience, disorder, 56, 58, 68, 86, 88–9, 108–109, 111, 161, 191, 199, 208, 216, 217, 218
Civil war (F), 2, 88, 137, 200, 229, 240, 245, 250
Civil War (USA), 5, 13, 20, 115, 281
Clamart, 89, 117, 183, 244, 256
Claretie, Jules, 139, 143
Clément-Thomas, Gen. Jacques, 213, 220–3
Clinchant, Justine, 245
Clubs, 97, 104, 139, 167, 190–1, 194, 199, 206
Cluseret, Gustave-Paul, 246–9, 252–4, 283–4
Coeuilly, 149–52
Coffinières de Nordeck, Gen. Grégoire, 57, 124
Cold, 40, 49, 130, 137, 139, 160–1, 172, 176, 188, 196–7, 209, 218
Colours, regimental, 17, 22, 73, 116, 129–30, 211
Comité Central de la Garde Nationale, 208, 213, 217, 226–9, 231, 235, 247, 252, 258
Commissariat, 115
Committee of Public Safety, 135–6, 237, 254, 258, 262, 270
Commune de Paris, Commune, Communards, 2, 12, 76, 79, 120, 134, 136–7, 139, 157, 190, 215, 217, 221, 225–7, 229–47, 249, 251–62, 264–9, 271, 273–4, 276–86
Communication, 1, 19, 26, 52, 63, 99, 118, 141, 157, 166, 190, 201, 206, 225

Communism, communist, 2, 76, 91, 233, 272, 278–80, 284
Complacency, 16, 42, 48
Conscription, 235
Convention, 98, 184, 203, 206
Coulmiers, 133, 141–2, 158, 190
Council of Regency and National Defence, CRND, 74–6, 79–87, 96–7, 99, 101, 103, 109, 122, 127–8, 133, 136, 138, 141–2, 164, 166–7, 180, 185, 198–200
Courbet, Gustave, 261, 273
Courbevoie, 240–1
Court martial, 110, 112, 124, 138, 173, 246, 255, 258, 275–7, 281
Covid-19, 95
Cremieux, Adolphe, 74
Cresson, Ernest, 138
Crimean War, 8, 12, 22, 30, 32, 113, 176, 179, 192, 246

d'Aurelle de Paladines, Gen. Claude, 112, 114, 116, 131, 141–2, 159–60, 169, 208, 213, 218, 229, 283
Daily News, 81, 96, 103, 131, 164, 168, 170, 177, 283
Darboy, Mgr. Georges, Archbishop, 236, 256, 263, 268
de Barail, Francoise, 245
de Bellemare, Maj. Gen. Carey, 118–19, 151, 194–5
de Canrobert, Marshall François, 30–1, 33, 35, 49, 123, 130, 283
de Cissey, Ernest Courtot, 245 252, 269
de Freycinet, Charles, 112, 114–15, 117, 145, 159–60, 168–9, 171, 191, 194, 197, 201–203, 205, 283
de Goncourt, Edmond, 7, 89, 91, 107, 137, 146, 154–5, 169, 185, 187, 198, 205, 207, 209–10, 214, 228, 249, 253, 268, 283
de Kératry, Émile, 110, 137
de Ladmirault, Lieut. Gen. Paul, 31, 39, 245
de MacMahon, Marshal Patrice, 2, 30–1, 33, 42, 44, 49–50, 55–66, 78, 120, 126, 133, 162, 245, 258, 261, 264–6, 269–70, 277
de Palikao, Gen. Charles, 49–50, 61–2, 65, 74
de Ploeuc, Marquis, 237, 264
de Rochefort, Henri, 74, 208, 213, 261, 263–4

de Wimpffen Gen. Felix, 65–6, 69–72, 284
Delescluze, Louis Charles, 75, 77, 104, 134–6, 138, 199, 208, 236, 238, 244, 258, 265, 268–9
Deprivation, 101, 188, 209, 278
Discipline, indiscipline, 46, 48, 55–6, 64, 87, 97, 99, 102, 108, 111–12, 114–15, 124–5, 160, 220, 243, 248, 251, 254
Disease, 7, 78, 101, 209
Dispossessed, 10
Dombrowski, Jaroslaw, 248–50, 253, 259, 264, 270
Dorian, Gustave, 74, 108, 135, 138
Douay, Maj. Gen. Abel, 39–42
Douay, Maj. Gen. Félix, 31, 49, 60, 64, 71, 245, 265, 260–70
Dreyse needle-gun, 3, 19, 36
Ducatel, Jules-Auguste, 265
Ducrot, Gen. Auguste-Alexandre, 39, 64, 66, 68–9, 71–2, 87–9, 106, 118, 131, 135, 137, 139–55, 167–8, 176, 180, 194–6, 198, 205, 283
Duval, Émile, 217, 222, 225–6, 230, 236–7, 242, 244, 246
Duvernois, Clément, 74, 82
Dysentery, 124, 128

Election, 16, 25, 83–4, 102, 104, 108–109, 128, 135, 200, 204, 207–209, 211, 213, 228, 230, 248, 272, 274
Electric telegraph, 19, 26, 45, 65, 159, 189, 212, 252, 281
Emperor, 5, 8, 13, 16–17, 30, 32–3, 35–6, 49, 51, 60, 62, 69–70, 74, 78–9, 101, 109, 121–2, 126–7, 159, 179, 283
Engels, Frederick, 76, 91, 233, 238–9, 283, 284
Eudes, Emile, 56, 226, 230, 237, 242, 244, 246, 257
Eugénie, Empress, 7, 48, 85, 128–9
Execution, 8, 44, 98, 181, 199, 222–4, 228, 243, 245, 260, 260, 262, 268, 276
Expertise, 5, 16, 111, 159
Exposition, 5–6, 8–11, 87, 186

Faidherbe, Col. A./Maj. Gen. Louis, 166–7, 169–72, 174–5, 188–9, 191, 193, 197, 199, 201, 205

Farre, Brig. Gen. Jean-Joseph, 158
Favre, Jules, 74–5, 79, 85–6, 91, 103, 107,
    122, 129, 132, 135, 139–40, 154, 167–8,
    170, 192, 197–8, 200–201, 204–205, 207,
    210, 214, 223, 228, 246, 283
Ferré, Théophile, 220–1, 230, 236, 268, 275
Ferry, Jules, 74–5, 164
Firewood, 78, 161
Flour, 80, 82, 110, 126, 164
Flourens, Gustave, 104–105, 108–10, 134,
    136, 138, 198, 217, 237, 240–4, 246, 248
Fontenoy-sur-Moselle, 157
Food, 26, 55, 57, 66, 81–6, 96–7, 101,
    115–16, 118, 120–1, 124–6, 128, 130–1,
    140, 152–3, 161–2, 164, 167–8, 185, 188,
    201, 204, 208, 235, 264, 280; rationing,
    81, 97, 162, 164, 194
Foraging, 60, 124, 167
Fortress, 2, 5, 20, 26–7, 51, 53, 55, 57,
    59–60, 64–8, 83, 85, 87, 93, 99, 120, 122,
    124–8, 130–1, 166, 171–2, 202, 227, 270
Fourichon, Adm. Léon, 74, 99
Francs tireurs, 81, 96–9, 102, 106, 156, 169
Frederick Charles, Prince, 33, 36–7, 41, 51,
    53, 58, 62, 85, 124, 128–30, 152, 159, 183,
    191
Fröschwiller, 39, 42, 44–5, 47, 49, 162, 215
Frossard, Maj. Gen. Charles, 30, 34–5,
    44–6, 49, 51
Frostbite, 167
Frozen, 153, 171, 181, 189

Galliffet, Maj. Gen. Gaston, 240–1, 243,
    271–2
Gallstones, 11
Gambetta, Léon, 74–5, 83–6, 91, 101, 106,
    109–18, 121, 126–7, 131, 139, 140–3,
    145, 152–3, 157, 159, 162, 168–9, 171,
    183, 189–92, 210, 204–205, 207–208, 213,
    246, 284, 285
Gangrene, 157, 175
Garde Mobile, 17, 19, 22, 50, 55, 83, 87–8,
    113, 166, 171
Garde Nationale, GN, 15, 17–18, 76, 80, 87,
    99, 104, 108–10, 113, 116, 118, 134, 136,
    138–40, 145, 149, 171, 175, 195–200, 204,
    208, 211–14, 216–18, 220, 222–30, 233,

235–6, 240–3, 245, 247, 249, 254, 256–7,
    260, 265, 267–8
Garibaldi, Giuseppe, 98, 108, 116
Gastric flu, 128
Gate, gates, 40, 68, 83, 92, 135, 145, 168,
    198, 261, 264–6
Gennevilliers peninsula, 118, 194, 196
Genton, Gustave, 275
German Empire, 4, 171–3, 176, 281
Gibson, Rev. William, 214, 225, 232, 244,
    253, 260, 273
Goncourt, Edmund, 7, 89, 91, 107, 137, 146,
    154–5, 169, 185, 187, 198, 105, 207,
    209–10, 214, 228, 249, 253, 268, 283
Government of National Defence, GND,
    74, 78, 80, 84, 99, 104, 110, 113, 122–3,
    127, 133, 136, 140, 168, 207
Governor of Paris, 78, 88, 106, 190, 198, 208
Grain, 82, 97, 125
Gravelotte-St Privat, 53, 55–6, 120
Graves, 1, 80, 274
Guerrilla war, 80, 98–9, 171
Guillotine, 55, 234, 249, 251, 282

Hastings, 122–3
Haussmann, Georges-Eugène, 10–11, 278–9
Howard, Prof. Sir Michael, 4, 23, 29, 38,
    46–7, 58, 72, 91, 106, 121, 131–2, 154,
    170, 177, 187, 205, 282
Hugo, Victor, 134, 208, 213

Iges, 65, 78, 101
Imperial Guard (F), 31
Indemnity, 133, 140, 277
Insurrection(s), insurrectionists, 79, 134,
    138, 217, 222–3, 225–6, 229–31, 242, 284
Intendent (Quarter Master), 201
Issy, Fort, 181–3, 186, 203, 251–9
Italy, 16, 20, 29, 30, 85, 98

Journal de Rouen, 97
Journel Officiel de la Commune, 226–7

L'plan Trochu, 106, 118, 143, 191
La Patrie en Danger, 75, 131
Labouchère, Henry Du Pré, 81, 95, 110,
    131, 170, 176, 186, 205, 251, 266, 275,
    278, 283

Landwehr, 17, 26–7, 33, 72, 285
Law of Hostages, 245, 264, 267
Le Bourget, 108, 119, 131, 151, 155, 167–8
Le Combat, 75, 199
Le Figaro, 240
Le Flô, Gen. Adolphe, 156, 207, 223
Le Gaulois, 240, 266
Le Rappel, 203, 208, 214, 227
Leadership, 16, 31, 58, 66, 80, 84, 99, 111,
    120, 124, 134, 137–8, 159, 168, 172, 191,
    197–9, 206, 213, 216, 224, 237, 243, 248,
    252–4, 268, 280
Leboeuf, Gen. Edmond, 22, 32–4, 39, 44,
    48, 51
Lebrun, Gen. Barthélémy, 32, 62, 64, 66,
    71–2
Lecomte, Brig. Gen. Claude, 219–23, 241,
    275
Lefrançais, Gustave, 237
Legion d'Honneur, 134, 229, 245–6
Legislature, 14, 17
Lenin, 280
Leningrad, 4, 76, 81
Leopold, Prince of Sigmaringen, 26–7
Lerouse, Lieut. Camille, 35–6, 38
Les grandes horizontales, 6, 80, 286
Leveson Gower, Granville, 2nd Earl
    Granville, 79
Liaud, Maj., 40, 47
Lisaine, river, 189, 192
Lissagaray, Hippolyte-Prosper, 136, 173,
    274, 276–7
Lockroy, Edouard, 229–3
Logistic, 1–2, 4, 20–2, 26, 32, 35–6, 39–40,
    42, 48, 50, 60, 92–3, 95, 97, 99, 105, 111,
    113, 119, 125, 128, 142–3, 145, 157, 167,
    169, 171, 173–4, 185, 191, 200–202, 206,
    280, 285
London, 10, 12, 27, 30, 38–9, 68, 72, 79, 91,
    106, 129, 131–2, 136, 154, 162, 178–9,
    186, 192, 216, 231, 227, 234, 246, 253,
    268, 270, 276
Lorraine, 32, 34, 57, 86, 98, 139–40, 155,
    200, 210, 213, 277
Louvre, the, 80, 134, 186, 270
Lullier, Charles, 226–7, 245–6, 275
Lyons, Richard, 1st Earl Lyons, Ambassador,
    81, 216

Malmaison, 118, 156, 194
Malnutrition, 126
Manpower, 17, 24, 55, 92–3, 96, 114
Manteuffel, Gen. Edwin, 158, 166, 189,
    193–4, 201–202
Marne, river, 84, 86, 140, 142–3, 145–6,
    149, 151–3, 155, 169
Mars-la-Tour, 53–4, 56
Marseilles, 84, 86, 225, 245–6, 251
Marx, Karl, 10, 76, 91, 233–4, 239, 245, 276,
    279–80, 284
Mazas prison, 139, 198, 258, 263, 267
Meat, 65, 97, 125, 128, 153, 163–4
Mégy, Edmond, 251–2, 257
Metz, 1–2, 16, 26, 30, 32–3, 35–9, 45,
    48–58, 61–2, 65–6, 78–9, 83, 85–6, 91,
    93, 95, 97, 101, 106, 108–109, 111, 113,
    115, 117, 120–33, 152, 155, 171, 201, 210,
    215, 283
Meudon, 91, 242, 252
Mexico, 8, 17, 30, 32
Mézières, 61, 171–2
Michel, Louise, 199, 219, 227, 260, 274
Military honours, 69, 129
Millière, Jean-Baptiste, 135, 138, 208, 230
Mitrailleuse, 19–20, 40–1, 46–7, 55, 68, 130,
    241, 266–7
Moat, 92–3
Mob, 55, 76, 78, 80
Monarchist, 84, 116, 180, 207–208, 229
Mont-Valérien, 92, 194, 227, 242–3, 245,
    250–1, 276
Montmartre, 80, 133, 212, 216–19, 240, 249,
    266–7, 271
Montmédy, 57, 60, 61, 62, 158, 171
Montparnasse, 89, 184, 269
Montrouge, Fort, 89, 117, 181, 183–4, 251
Moratorium, 216, 226
Moselle, river, 53, 57, 98, 124, 167, 171
Mouzon, 62–4
Mud, 78, 125, 128, 197
Murder, murderous, 102, 157, 211–12, 220,
    222–3, 227, 241, 243, 245, 256, 262, 267,
    276
Muzzle-loaders, 18–19, 92, 134

Napoleon III, Louis, 2, 4–5, 7–8, 10–13,
    16–17, 26, 29, 31–3, 35, 39, 45, 48, 55,

65, 68–71, 73, 78, 80, 84–5, 104, 109, 121–2, 225, 252, 254, 261, 277
Navy (F), 31, 74, 99
Negotiate, 109, 122, 218, 228, 263
Neuilly, 146, 151, 241–2, 244, 250–1
Neutral, neutrality, 83, 117, 179, 223, 250, 260, 264
New Caledonia, 275
Nice, 86
Niederwald, river, Niederwald, 44–6, 51
Niel, Marshal Adolphe, 14, 16–17, 19, 22, 34–5
Noisseville, 58, 65
North German Confederation, 3–4, 24, 26, 79

Obsidional fever, 209–11, 222
Obsolescent, 47, 113
Ollivier, Émile, 48–9
Orléans, 73, 84, 108, 111, 112, 116, 140–1, 142, 144–5, 157–61, 168, 176, 215
Oslo, 145

Paris-Journal, 229, 244
Pasquier, Surgeon Major, 141, 243
Passy, 251, 253, 265–6
Pawnshop, 216
Peace of Prague, 4, 8
Persévérance, 146
Pétain, Marshal Phillippe, 281
Picard, Ernest, 74–5, 103, 134, 137–8, 176, 207, 223
Pigeons, 109, 144–5
Pillage, 201, 217
Place de Concorde, 254–5, 269
Plebiscite, 138
Point-du-Jour, 184, 251, 266
Pontarlier, 202–203
Pontoons, 145–6, 151
President, 31, 60, 74, 78, 84, 88, 100–104, 106, 108, 116, 119, 133, 198, 246, 258
Punishment, 243, 257–8, 269, 274, 276, 277
Pyat, Félix, 75–7, 104, 134–6, 138, 199–200, 208, 213, 237, 256, 258, 268

Railway, 20–2, 26–7, 32–6, 49, 51, 55, 59–60, 84, 92, 95, 97, 99, 101, 111, 127,

144, 156–7, 171–2, 179–80, 191, 251, 256, 280–1
Rain, 51, 53, 57, 78, 110, 125–6, 128, 130, 137, 140, 218
Rations, 49, 60, 96, 124–5
Reconnaissance, 26, 105, 240
Reds, 76, 79, 110, 133, 136–8, 153, 190, 199, 206–208, 213, 216
Re-equipping, 65, 108, 110, 114
Refugees, 185
Régnier, Edmond, 122–4
Reparations, 86, 98, 139, 200, 210, 231
Reprisals, 98, 138–9, 157
Republic, republican, 2, 8, 55, 74–5, 79, 81, 84, 88, 95, 109–10, 117, 122, 126, 159, 168, 192, 198, 206–208, 211, 216, 225–6, 228, 230, 235, 246, 256, 261, 277–8, 280
Reserves, 14, 17, 21, 33, 44, 65, 118, 143, 149, 157–9, 196, 224, 245, 265
Resupply, 22, 118, 180
Rethel, 60
Retribution, 98, 229, 243, 262, 270, 274–7
Revolution, 2, 10, 14, 61, 70, 75–6, 80, 97–9, 104, 108, 110, 127, 134, 190, 194, 198–9, 208, 212, 222, 224–5, 228, 230–1, 238–9, 244–7, 256–7, 262, 267, 272, 277–8
Rheims, 59–61, 166, 171
Rigault, Raoul, 10, 137–8, 225–6, 231, 234, 236–8, 240, 248, 255–6, 258, 262–4, 268, 275, 280
Riot, 146
Rochefort, Henri de, 74, 208, 213, 261, 263–4
Rossel, Louis-Nathaniel, 248–9, 254–9, 260, 275
Rotherberg, the, 45, 46
Rouen, 118, 158, 225
Rouher, Eugène, 60
Russell, W.H., 68

Saarbrücken, 34–6, 39, 42, 44–7, 48, 157
Saarlouis, 27, 39
Saisset, Adm. Jean Marie, 229–30
Sapia, Théophile, 109–10, 199
Saumur, 16
Schmitz, Gen. Isadore, 134, 137, 192
Second Empire, 2, 7, 11, 16, 55, 68, 76, 87, 176, 208

Security, 73, 143, 167, 248, 278
Sédan, 2, 26, 58, 61–72, 73–4, 80, 83, 87–8, 98, 101, 104, 123, 137, 171, 215, 241, 245
Seine, river, 74, 80, 84, 92, 95, 99, 105, 118, 136, 140, 142–3, 146, 152, 161–2, 187, 211, 241, 251, 279
Self-confidence, 80, 104, 121, 201, 242, 244
Septicaemia, 175
Shelling, 178, 184–6, 188, 251
Siege park, 179–80
Simon, Jules, 74–5, 167–8, 207, 223
Smallpox, 126, 188, 209
Smooth bore, 92, 101
Snow, 127, 144, 159–61, 179, 181, 191
Sortie, 85, 101, 105, 108, 118, 124, 133, 135, 140–2, 145, 150, 168, 158, 168, 180, 190–1, 194–7, 241, 244
Sortie torrentielle, 142, 145–6, 190, 191
Southern German States, 24, 33, 36
Sovereign, 3, 34, 69, 78
Spicheren, 44–6, 53, 215
St Avold, 48–9
St Cyr, 16, 246
St Maur, 142, 149, 152
Staff College, 16, 62
Starvation, 1–2, 78, 97, 125, 128, 137, 153, 161–2, 185–6, 188, 216
Stenay, 51, 62
Stoffel, Baron Eugène, 25, 30, 181
Strasbourg, 26, 30, 35, 42, 85, 91, 95, 99, 101, 105, 122, 155–7, 215
Summarily, 27, 137, 244, 256, 267, 275
Surrender, 55, 59, 69, 73, 85–6, 93, 99, 101, 119, 120, 123, 128–30, 133, 139, 171, 176, 178, 186, 189, 194, 198, 200, 204, 207, 241, 243–4, 252, 257, 267
Survival rates, 22, 98, 210
Swinburne, Dr John, 176
Swiss, Switzerland, 124, 201–204, 207, 238, 276
Syphilis, 7

Temperature, 29, 143, 159, 167, 217, 260
Tents, 16, 49, 78, 128, 176
The New Yorker, 234, 239
Thiers, Adolph, 75, 79, 120, 133, 139–40, 154, 188, 206–208, 210, 212–20, 223,

226–30, 238, 241, 246, 251, 253, 256, 260–7, 272, 277
Threat, 14, 16–17, 42, 58, 75–6, 80, 92, 190, 194, 213, 216, 220, 229, 263
Tombs, Prof Robert, 274
Toul, 59, 86, 93, 99, 113, 155, 157
Tours, 99, 101, 106–11, 116, 131–2, 139, 141, 157
Training, 13, 17, 24–5, 45, 48, 50, 87, 112–14, 160, 174, 191, 196–7, 280
Treason, treasonous, 79, 120, 124, 129, 133, 212, 243, 254
Trenches, 62
Tridon, Gustave, 237
Trochu, Maj. Gen. Louis-Jules, 22, 48–9, 51, 56, 78–9, 83–5, 87–8, 92, 95–7, 104–10, 115–19, 122, 133–8, 140–3, 145–6, 151, 158–9, 162, 164, 166–8, 176, 180–1, 185, 190–1, 194, 196–8, 248
Trotsky, Leon, 179
Truce, 152, 241, 243, 252
Tuileries, 264, 269–70
Typhus, 126, 128

Urbain, Raoul, 236, 238, 245, 262–3, 275

V Corps (F), 31, 36, 42, 62–5
V Corps (P), 43–4, 196
Vaillant, Édouard, 76, 236–7
Valérien, Fort, 92, 181, 194, 227, 242–3, 245, 251, 276
Vallès, Jules, 231, 236, 238
Vandalism, 137, 262, 270
Varlin, Eugène, 109, 222, 228, 236–7, 260
Vendôme, 190
Vendôme, Place, Column, the, 222, 260–2
Verdun, 53–4, 59, 156, 158, 171, 281
Versailles, 93, 126, 172, 179, 196, 206, 216–17, 223–4, 226–7, 229–31
Victoria, Queen, 81, 162, 178, 231
Villersexel, 172, 189, 192
Villiers, 142–3, 149–52
Vincennes, 270, 276
Vincenzoni, 211
Vinoy, Maj. Gen. Joseph, 49, 50, 87–8, 105, 117, 140, 146, 149, 168, 180, 194, 198–200, 208, 217–18, 220, 243–5
Vionville, 53

von Alvensleben, Gen. Constantin, 53–4
von Bismarck, Graf Otto, 3–4, 7–8, 21, 24,
  26–7, 29, 48, 60, 68–70, 73, 76, 78, 85–6,
  88, 96, 106, 109, 113, 121–2, 124–8, 139,
  157, 159, 162–3, 169, 172–6, 178–9, 186,
  198, 200–206, 210, 214, 246
von Blumenthal, Gen. Karl Graf, 73, 176,
  183
von der Tann, Gen. Ludwig, 111, 141
von Goeben, Gen. August, 158, 175
von Kameke, Gen. Georg, 46
von Moltke, Gen. Helmuth, 4, 20–1, 24–7,
  33, 36, 38, 40, 44–5, 48, 51–2, 55, 59, 62,
  68–9, 73, 78–9, 84–5, 89, 91–2, 95–6,
  111, 115–17, 120–1, 123–4, 127–8, 146,
  158–9, 166–9, 172–4, 176, 178–81,
  183–4, 186, 188–90, 200, 204, 206, 224,
  246, 258
von Roon, Gen. Albrecht Graf, 21, 24, 26,
  68, 73, 173–4, 180, 186
von Steinmetz, *Generalfeldmarschall* Karl, 33,
  36–8, 45, 51, 55, 59
von Werder, Gen. August, 156, 189
Vosges, 99, 156, 189
Voters, 139, 207, 230

Wagons, supply, 32, 36, 53, 63, 71, 78, 125,
  127, 143, 145, 196, 220, 276
Washburne, Elithu, US Ambassador, 82,
  103–104, 115, 145, 164, 186, 198, 230
Wilhelm I, King, 4–5, 7–8, 27, 36, 38, 66,
  70, 124, 128, 172–3, 179–80, 195, 198,
  203, 215
Wind, 109, 138, 144, 160, 167
Wissembourg, 39–42, 215
Withdraw, 47, 58, 61, 63, 66, 89, 105, 111,
  126, 143, 151, 153, 158–9, 166, 189, 191,
  196, 203–204, 223, 258
Wœrth, 42, 46
Wounded, 1, 3, 22, 40–1, 44, 52, 54–5,
  65–6, 68, 71, 78, 83, 101, 118, 125,
  127–8, 131, 149, 151–2, 160–1, 175–6,
  184, 185, 189, 191, 194, 196, 199, 204,
  218–19, 229, 246, 256, 261, 271
Württemberg division, Prussian, 149

XI Corps (P), 43–4, 54

Zouaves, 88–9, 194, 241–9